D1526312

In the Pride of the Moment

In the Pride of the Moment

ENCOUNTERS IN JANE AUSTEN'S WORLD

JOHN A. DUSSINGER

The Ohio State University Press, Columbus

Engraving from Thomas Wilson's *Panorama*, reproduced by permission of
the Houghton Library, Harvard University.

Library of Congress Cataloging-in-Publication Data
Dussinger, John A.
    In the pride of the moment : encounters in Jane Austen's world /
John A. Dussinger.
        p.   cm.
    Bibliography: p.
    Includes index.
    ISBN 0-8142-0491-0 (alk. paper)
    1. Austen, Jane, 1775–1817—Criticism and interpretation.   2. Social
interaction in literature.   3. Conversation in literature.   I. Title.
PR4037.D87 1989
832'.7—dc20   89-31597
⊚   CIP

The paper in this book meets the guidelines for permanence and durability
of the Committee on Production Guidelines for Book Longevity of the
Council on Library Resources.

Printed in the U.S.A.
9 8 7 6 5 4 3 2 1

For Astrid, Karin, and Camilla

I do not write for such dull elves

As have not a great deal of ingenuity themselves.

—*Chawton, 29 January 1813*

Contents

Acknowledgments

Many of the ideas for this book originated while I was teaching the novels of Jane Austen in the late 1970s at the University of Illinois, when her comic subversity suddenly quickened in the minds of the students and prompted considerable rereading to find some answers. Northrop Frye's brilliant ordering of comic fiction in *Anatomy of Criticism* immeasurably eased my task in the classroom and also emboldened me to undertake this study.

For the early stages of research and contemplation, I owe special thanks to James Sambrook for making possible my teaching exchange at the University of Southampton in early 1979, where I enjoyed spending the precious time retracing Jane Austen's footsteps in southern England as well as meeting astute British readers of her novels, who were always generous in imparting insights to an American visitor.

I am especially grateful to the Department of English and the Center for Advanced Studies at the University of Illinois for a sabbatical research fellowship during 1980–81. My colleague Jack Stillinger was encouraging from the start and gave helpful advice on the rough draft. Frederick Keener and Charles Knight wrote painstaking and constructive criticisms of the whole argument in its earliest stages. An enormous debt goes to Alistair Duckworth, who devoted many hours of his time trying to make sense out of confusion. Besides the anonymous readers of the later drafts of this book, I should thank Ronald Rosbottom and James Thompson for comments invaluable for the final revision, and Barbara Folsom for the meticulous copyediting. If darkness still lingers in the corners of this phenomenological reading of Austen's novels, the responsibility is entirely mine.

Finally, without the conversations at home with a wife and two daughters, all keen and perennial readers of Jane Austen, writing this book would have been a much more lonely endeavor.

Champaign, Illinois   J.A.D.
February 1989

Abbreviations

All references to Jane Austen's novels and fragments are taken from the edition of R. W. Chapman, 6 vols. (London: Oxford University Press, 1933–34, 1954); page numbers are included in parentheses within the text. All references to her correspondence are from Chapman's edition, *Jane Austen's Letters to Her Sister Cassandra and Others*, 2d ed. (Oxford: Oxford University Press, 1952 [reprint 1979]), cited hereafter as *Letters*. Wherever necessary, the following abbreviations are also used:

NA	*Northanger Abbey*
SS	*Sense and Sensibility*
PP	*Pride and Prejudice*
MP	*Mansfield Park*
E	*Emma*
P	*Persuasion*
MW	*Minor Works*

Introduction

"Writing, when properly managed . . . is but a different name for conversation."

—*Tristram Shandy*, II, xi

Jane Austen's narrative art excels in rendering the texture of actual speech, and almost any scene in her novels alludes to the precarious circumstances of conversation: "The meeting was generally felt to be a pleasant one, being composed in a good proportion of those who would talk and those who would listen" (*MP*, 238–39). Even when the participants in the social event *seem* to be interacting, the narrator hints, there is usually a residue of mistrust about the gestures of the moment, something that remains open to interpretation.

The dual card games in chapter 25 of *Mansfield Park*, for instance, are activities symbolic of the "real-life" roles played by the characters in the room, reflecting not only the Crawfords' competitive energy, expressed in their conversation on improving Thornton Lacey, but also the heroine's quiescent spirit. In response to Edmund's cautious rejection of Henry's expensive plans for the parsonage, Mary insinuates her libertine indifference by playing a card recklessly:

> Miss Crawford, a little suspicious and resentful of a certain tone of voice and a certain half-look attending the last expression of his hope, made a hasty finish of her dealings with William Price, and securing his knave at an exorbitant rate, exclaimed, "There, I will stake my last like a woman of spirit. No cold prudence for me. I am not born to sit still and do nothing. If I lose the game, it shall not be from not striving for it." (*MP*, 242–43)

Mary wins the hand, we are told, but at too high a cost. In contrast to this selfish motive, Fanny, who resorts to the game mainly to conceal her interest in the conversation about Thornton, almost squanders her queen on William, much to Henry's dismay, causing Edmund to observe that she would rather have her brother win the game: "Poor Fanny! not allowed to cheat herself as she wishes!" (*MP*, 244).

In the other part of the room, at the whist table, there is "steady sobriety and orderly silence" during concentrated play until Mrs. Norris, "in high good-humour" after taking a trick with her partner, Sir Thomas, against the Grants, enters into the conversation in a predictably self-seeking way. While the older members of the group engage conventionally in winning and losing without any thought of the future, the younger ones express their "real-life" attitudes through the metonym of the game of speculation; and just as the activity defines a sphere of interest, so it also marks off the nonplayers and strengthens their ties as outsiders: "William and Fanny were the most detached. They remained together at the otherwise deserted card-table, talking very comfortably and not thinking of the rest, till some of the rest began to think of them" (*MP*, 249). The card games in this scene thus rehearse the parts that are played elsewhere on more "serious," less categorical occasions.

This scene illustrates Austen's general narrative strategy of bringing her characters together in an *encounter*,[1] a radically focused interaction, to reveal nuances of behavior; and we have seen that it serves at least four important functions: (1) it divides the group into playing two ideologically different games—the young at speculation (Lady Bertram is encouraged to participate here mainly because her husband does not want her for a partner in *his* game) and the old at whist; (2) it divides them according to the rules of the game as "winners" and "losers" without any connection to their status in the everyday world (both Mary Crawford and Mrs. Norris "lose" by the end of the novel despite their momentary triumphs here); (3) it divides them according to their competitive or noncompetitive motivation, thus isolating the heroine and her brother from the others; and (4) it subdivides them into various fields that restrict or prevent communication among certain persons in the room (at one extreme the whist players are wholly absorbed in the game, silent, without any ulterior purpose, while at the other extreme, the speculation players use their game to supplement conversation about life choices or to cover up their interest as listeners). As in other "play-within-the-play" situations in Austen's novels, this particular encounter symbolically conveys the participants' attitudes and intentions; and if the nominal activity in the scene is significant in forming political alignments, it also defines the alienation of the individuals outside the frame of reference.

Such deliberately choreographed performances add weight to the idea of writing as another name for conversation. Despite occasional emphasis on sprained ankles, putrid sore throats, colds, fevers, hoarse voices, concussions, and similar dire consequences of physical exertion, the principal action in Austen's world is talking; and hence the represented encounter fosters the illusion of spontaneous, if contingent, speech. It is Austen's art of coloring narrative and dialogue to render a character's point of view within carefully arranged encounters that is the subject of this book.

Although Austen, as we shall see, was astonishingly innovative in bringing into play a variety of competing discourses, her narrative art is generally indebted to the eighteenth-century novelist's relentless experiments in imitating actual speech within typographical space. Just as printed texts since Gutenberg's invention had usually retained traces of an oral culture, so the early novel parallels the first newspapers in exploiting facticity, including the means of representing living speech by certain contextual devices.[2] Of these devices the two most conspicuous are the temporal dividing up of the story through self-conscious narrators and the depiction of the reading process within the story as the primary conflict to be resolved.

In the epistolary novel the temporal separation between story time and narrative time is an inevitable part of the mise-en-scène; and thanks to Samuel Richardson's own extensive comments about the rhetorical effects of "writing-to-the-moment" in storytelling, until recently his achievement has been highlighted at the expense of other early eighteenth-century novelists equally concerned with voice and time in narrative. Daniel Defoe's first-person fictional accounts on the pattern of spiritual autobiography, for instance, imply a temporal as well as a moral split between a regenerate narrator and a culpable agent. Furthermore, as Paul Alkon has argued, Defoe's gratuitous anachronisms not only obviate any intention of giving the story historical authenticity but, more importantly, diminish the significance of past time to augment the narrator's present time. What matters to the reader finally is not an imaginative leap into the distant past of the story's action, as in Scott's novels, but rather the effect of hearing a story being told by a weathered observer: "He [Defoe] viewed writing as a more permanent kind of talking. . . . His readers are often encouraged to imagine themselves listening while someone talks to them."[3] This privileging of living speech over writing (as inert, dead language) is a predominant rhetorical strategy in the whole genre of the early novel and attains a remarkable technical sophistication in the novels of Jane Austen.

Perhaps to compensate for the age-old neglect of Defoe's conscious artistry, Alkon ignores Richardson: "His [Defoe's] fiction, more successfully than any later in the century except *Tristram Shandy*, adapts oral forms to typographical media by combining strategies from traditions of speaking and traditions of writing to work together, instead of concentrating mainly on one or another mode of appeal within the framework of printed pages."[4] Without denying Defoe's real interest in the material artifact of the printed page, we should not find it surprising that a major London printer like Richardson had a professional advantage over him and most of his contemporary authors, not only in being able to edit his own manuscript into a typographical analogue, but also in making full use of the technical resources of the press to simulate the conditions of oral discourse by using various prompter's marks, indentations and spacings, footnotes and afterwords, and the like, producing in the end a monument of fictional hermeneutics.[5]

As a result of the strategy of foregrounding "present" narrative time and emphasizing "spoken" over written language, the early eighteenth-century novel, doubtless influenced by the *Don Quixote* vogue, often thematizes the act of reading and thus mirrors our own struggles with the text. Because of its requisite context, the letter-novel draws attention to this narrative device most transparently: "As we read *Les Liaisons*," Janet Altman remarks, "we develop the illusion that we are reading a novel in the process of being written. Merteuil and Valmont speak self-consciously of themselves as creators of their own novel, as 'historiens,' playwrights, and directors. . . . we the external readers are not the only readers of this novel in the making, for the vicomte and the marquise themselves gradually become privy to almost as many letters as we."[6] Both in Richardson and Laclos, the power of reading is the ultimate intellectual act and the basis of any significant writing. Only good readers make good writers, and those characters who prevail to the end—Pamela, Clarissa, and Merteuil (despite her final punishment by the author)—are the ones in control at the "switchboard." Clarissa's posthumous letters, moreover, even give her a power beyond the grave, in contrast to Lovelace, whose last words, "LET THIS EXPIATE!" remain dubious.

Temporalizing narrative stances and thematizing the reading process are not the only means of contextualizing and privileging "speech" in the novel. The most immediate quality of oral communication is the sense of its circumstantial uniqueness, its ability to place a character both as a social class member and as an individual. Under the aegis of Mikhail Bakhtin, current linguistic criticism has stressed the dialogicity of the novel as a fictional genre; and despite the recent pioneering work of such scholars as Paul Alkon, Janet Altman, Walter Reed, and Michael McKeon, we have hardly begun to analyze the various kinds of discourse in eighteenth-century fiction.[7] Direct discourse, for example, is a principal means of creating present time *within* the story, wresting the story away from the narrator-observer and allowing the characters a moment of autonomy; and the merest hint of dialect or other speech peculiarities may prejudice our responses in any given scene. Yet we still lack a poetics for this phenomenon.

As McKeon points out, among the early English novelists, Bakhtin mentions Fielding, Sterne, and Smollett to illustrate his theory of polyvocal structure; because of the prevalence of certain foil characters in comic myth—the *alazons* and *eirons* that Frye has defined—these particular English novelists seem especially germane.[8] Thus Squire Western's wildly explosive speech in *Tom Jones* casts him as the premoral, libidinous Silenus, as Robert Alter ingeniously remarked, in contrast to the morally upright but sterile Allworthy, as well as to the sadistic and impotent young Blifil and the foppish Lord Fellamar.[9] On the other hand, despite their offensive entrances into the story as naked déclassé protagonists, both Tom Jones and Humphry Clinker speak like romantic heroes, at once betraying their real identity to the reader, if not to the other characters. Although Winifred Jenkins's observation of the hero's "skin as fair as alabaster" already signals his leisured-class origins, Jery Melford's account of Clinker's reply to Matt Bramble fails to note anything unusual about the speaker: "— My uncle, having surveyed him attentively, said with an ironical expression in his countenance, 'An't you ashamed, fellow, to ride postilion without a shirt to cover your backside from

5

the view of the ladies in the coach?' 'Yes, I am, an please your noble honour; (answered the man) but necessity has no law, as the saying is—And more than that, it was an accident—My breeches cracked behind, after I had got into the saddle—.'" [10] Besides his mock-deprecatory address, Clinker's articulate defense that he had been seriously ill and impoverished by doctors' fees rings true with Bramble's own criticism of the medical profession, and thus announces a character who will be discovered as worthy of membership in the family.

Notwithstanding Bakhtin's emphasis on the English comic novelists, Defoe (though to a lesser extent) and Richardson also employed the dialogical principle in their texts, as is seen most tellingly in the conversations between Crusoe and Friday, Roxana and Amy, Pamela and Mrs. Jewkes, Clarissa and Anna Howe, and of course between Clarissa and Lovelace. An annoyance to some of his first readers, Richardson's use of slang, as well as his continual underscoring to emphasize the delivery of speeches, testifies to his conscious imitation of spoken language. [11] Furthermore, his potential as a comic novelist is evident even in *Clarissa*, "a work of tragic species," when he fills out dramatic scenes with servants and other working-class people. For instance, the episode with the Widow Bevis playing Clarissa as if "bloated, and in a dropsy" offers a humorous contrast between the clown's idiom and the supposed heroine's relatively standard usage:

Widow.	Dost thou know my right name, friend?
Fellow.	I can give a shrewd guess. But that is none of my business.
Widow.	What *is* thy business? I hope Miss Howe is well?
Fellow.	Yes, madam; pure well, I thank God. I wish you were so too.
Widow.	I am too full of grief to be well.
Fellow.	So belike I have *hard* say.
Widow.	My head aches so dreadfully, I cannot hold it up. I must beg of you to let me know your business.
Fellow.	Nay, and that be all, my business is soon known. It is but to give this letter into your own *partiklar* hands—here it is. [12]

So much had been attempted, indeed, between Richardson's time and Scott's in representing regional and class differences of character through a quasi dialect, that in reaction Austen appears to have eschewed the more percussive effects of colloquial usage and instead sought the finer shades of mental difference traceable in polite conversation. Just as innuendo and incomplete sentences often carry the most weight in an Austen encounter, in contrast to the all too lucid meanings conveyed by the smooth talkers, so perhaps because of her recognition that deflating a character by colloquialisms reveals social disadvantages rather than evil intentions, Lucy Steele's poor grammar is a rare instance in Austen's presentation of a coarse intelligence.

Concomitant with experiments in direct discourse, the early eighteenth-century news/novel media recognized the subtle effects of reported speech in conveying information with an aura of authority. The mere recording in print of what has been said confers privilege upon the reporter as it did upon the old town crier in an oral culture.[13] Although the printing press had been in use for centuries before Defoe, it was not until the late seventeenth century that the improved political climate, enhanced printing technology, economic growth, and increased literacy combined to bring about the remarkable book and pamphlet industry surrounding the novel as a historical genre.[14] With this abrupt development of reportage came a more rigorous encoding by typographical conventions, though compared to nineteenth-century standards, Augustan writing basked in a semiotic playground. After years of groping for more and more exact methods of rendering speech in print, by the 1790s novelists had become adept at handling time and voice in various forms of indirect discourse. Jane Austen thus came along at a propitious moment to grasp the whole range of meanings possible in closing the traditional distance between narrator and character to effect the spontaneous, undiluted flow of speech and thought only a few steps removed from the Flaubertian technique of depicting a character's daydreaming.

More than other kinds of fiction, the novel centers on the whole complex problem of enabling an authoritative discourse within an ostensibly random vocal structure, to the extent that the principal action within the story concerns the intention and meaning of the other characters. *Pamela*, for instance, opens with the crux of the word *kind* in the heroine's description of her young master's attitude after his mother's death; and *Clarissa* begins with the basic question of whether the duel between James Harlowe and Lovelace really does portend a love story. Both Pamela and Clarissa are immediately hard put to interpret the meanings of what people are saying and to defend themselves against their readers' intentions of drawing them into the "mill of the conventional." Without trying to be a paragon of virtue, Moll Flanders nevertheless has a similar difficulty with what others are saying and exerts herself—or at least seems to do so—to be fair in her reporting. Although much of her narrative involves perfecting her own terms for describing events, the episode with the counterfeiters is notable for her efforts to distance herself from her underworld colleagues' euphemisms: "I durst see them no more, for if I had seen them, and not complied, tho' I had declin'd it with the greatest assurances of Secresy in the World, they would have gone near to have murther'd me to make sure Work, and make themselves easy, *as they call it;* what kind of easiness that is, they may best Judge that understand how easy Men are, that can Murther People to prevent Danger."[15] Like Polly in *The Beggar's Opera*, whose sentimental ideal of marriage conflicts with her parents' cutthroat "business," Moll is appalled at the professional criminal's cant, thus proving that she is not really incorrigible.

As the eighteenth-century novelists at least partly understood, imitating speech is a form of parody, a repeating of what was said *with a difference;*[16] and by this means narrative gains authority even while abandoning omniscience and assigning to characters the main burden of the storytelling. When Austen began writing fiction in the 1790s, she had ample models in Defoe, Richardson, Fielding, Sterne, Smollett, Fanny Burney, Maria Edgeworth, Charlotte Smith, Ann Radcliffe, and many other authors whose works were available in the Steventon parsonage; but what is most striking, from Austen's first juvenile spoofs to her last, incomplete novel, is her radically critical eye toward literary forms in general and toward novelistic discourse in particular. Indeed, Viktor Shklovsky's insight that "any work of art is created as a parallel and a contradiction to some kind of model" is germane to Austen's own theory of the novel.[17]

That Austen's narrative art is essentially parodic has been long recognized; just as she participated with family members in theatricals, charades, epigrams, and other forms of literary fun, so she delighted in ridiculing the popular cults of sensibility and Gothic horror. *Love and Freindship* capitalizes on the most obtrusive weaknesses of the eighteenth-century epistolary novel—the embarrassing need to refer to one's own virtues, as in *Pamela*, and the often annoying interruptions of a narrative thread to keep within the physical limits of the letter. In the process of debunking, however, Austen also raised serious questions for the novelist, like how to render emotion convincingly. In *Love and Freindship*, Laura's effusions are pointed clichés from sentimental novels rather than the feelings of the moment: "A sensibility too tremblingly alive to every affliction of my Freinds, my Acquaintance and particularly to every affliction of my own, was my only fault, if a fault it could be called. Alas! how altered now! Tho' indeed my own Misfortunes do not make less impression on me than they ever did, yet now I never feel for those of an other. My accomplishments too, begin to fade—I can neither sing so well nor Dance so gracefully as I once did—and I have entirely forgot the *Minuet Dela Cour*" (*MW*, 78).

Austen's intention in such parody has always been transparent, namely, to burlesque a literary fad as well as affected social behavior. Yet a similar irony directed against Marianne Dashwood's expression of feeling about the leaves at Norland in the autumn has a more complex effect: "How have I delighted, as I walked, to see them driven in showers about me by the wind! What feelings have they, the season, the air altogether inspired! Now there is no one to regard them" (*SS*, 87–88). Within the story's plot, of course, Marianne will have to pay the price for her "transports"; but, nevertheless, invoking the pathetic fallacy here deepens her character in contrast not only to Laura's sentimental plagiarisms in *Love and Freindship* but also to Elinor's and Edward's wooden attitude in the scene. Austen implies that *any* language of feeling has precedents in literary texts, which include the most cherished lyric poetry as well as the many forgettable sentimental novels of the day; and the fact that discourse has a doubling effect is not necessarily negative or proof of insincerity. Even though expressed in the fashionable romantic idiom, we are to believe that Marianne's emotions are nevertheless visceral.

Parody as a genre has a wider purpose than merely subverting another literary text the way a parasite feeds on its host; and recent theoretical discussions of this ironic form in contemporary metafiction suggest that it is only a special case of the intertextuality inhering in most autoreferential discourse, from Greek comedy and Augustan mock-heroic to James Joyce's and T. S. Eliot's retrospectively allusive texts. Biographical evidence that Jane Austen wrote *Northanger Abbey* with an awareness of a reader who did not believe in novels (James Austen as the source of the monitor-hero Henry Tilney) supports the thesis of this study concerning her primary interest in the literary illusion—that is, in representing spoken language and creating the "realistic" effect of the quixotic, multiple discourses of a text.[18] Aside from the satire on Gothic romance and sentimental mannerisms, Austen's first novel, Park Honan argues, focuses generally on education as a deciphering of spoken language: "Bath, then, becomes a place of social talk in which Catherine learns what a girl can never gather from Addison's essays or from James and Henry Austen's *Loiterer*, the very difficulty of intuiting human character in a society in which men and women shield themselves with words. Ironically her mother searches upstairs at Fullerton for a 'very clever essay' to help her—and one detects in that search a laughing reply to Austen family essayists."[19] That the novel is a polyvocal structure, a palimpsest of "living" and only partly erased "dead" writing, is fundamental to Austen's practice; and with her extraordinary ear for timbre in conversation, mere gossip is transformed into a vibrant parodic art, a critical refining of thought through aggressive emendment of defunct expression.

Considering the simultaneous upsurge in readership and book production during her youth, Austen's reflexive art was timely, as Honan emphasizes: "The English novel with few exceptions *was* degenerate in the 1790s because there was no coherent and deeply based theory of fiction to inspire new artistic developments of the genre or to defend it against its moralistic attackers. Jane Austen joined the debate over the moral value of novels not by theorizing, but by showing that what a novel imitates is far less important than its technical 'forms of expression.'"[20] Even as she perfected these forms, however, Austen never doubted the primacy of voice in reproducing character and quickly noted interpretive weaknesses in the oral delivery of family members trying to read her text: "Our second evening's reading [of *Pride and Prejudice*] . . . had not pleased me so well, but I believe something must be attributed to my mother's too rapid way of getting on:

and though she perfectly understands the characters herself, she cannot speak as they ought" (*Letters*, 299).

"*She cannot speak as they ought*"—this may be just another hint of Mrs. Cassandra Austen's wearying presence, but it also serves as a warning to future readers of the Austen novel to listen carefully to how words are spoken. An analytical approach is not enough for enacting the *lived* character within the suspended moment: ideally, reading is a performance, an imitating of the individual voices in the polyvocal text. But "speaking as they ought" also implies *listening* to how they speak: and though all the major Austen characters must exhibit prowess as listeners, from the beginning both Elizabeth Bennet and Emma Woodhouse misconstrue what others say and suffer as a consequence. To some extent all six completed novels focus on some problems in communication—several characters in each story have secrets to keep or to reveal and pose a challenge to the heroine's powers of interpretation. But *Emma* is most radically structured on a game theory, with the charade presented as the model of how people interact with each other in an encounter; and only those who can listen to the words of the moment turn out to be winners. Or to put it in another way, only those with a gift for parody can gain control over the babel of rival voices in the world represented.

With all her faults, Emma Woodhouse, then, is Austen's chief candidate for reflecting our own indulgence in the "pleasure of the text." Unlike the other central characters, including Elizabeth Bennet, Emma has an incurable ludic spirit and to the end confronts the fact that some things always lie hidden in the layers of narrative, that no matter how much can be revealed to the understanding, something remains unheard in the most sincere exchange of feeling. It is only in *Emma*, furthermore, that minor characters hold such a large share of the central mystery to be solved; of all the many talkers in Austen's repertory, none has the shamanistic insights into the language of the text that Miss Bates and Mr. Woodhouse reveal on important occasions.

Because of Austen's refusal in *Emma* to tidy up everything that has aroused our curiosity, perhaps directly resisting the Radcliffean commonsense ending, this novel will always be a stumbling block for readers insistent on eternal verities and smooth surfaces. Comic conventions do hold the larger units of the story together, to be sure; unlike *Tristram Shandy,* it does have a linear plot and reaches a conclusion of sorts. But it also compares with Sterne's anatomy of discourse and shows the ultimate solipsism involved in communication. The truth always lies hidden; even to the exemplary listener, words are ever fragmentary and deceitful.

Rather than follow past custom of devoting a chapter to each of the six novels and repeat efforts to find unities, I have chosen *Emma* as the centerpiece of Austen's parodic art and tried to fathom what its discourses reveal about reading a text and conjuring the intended illusion.

The first chapter centers on play as regulated activity that imitates certain behavior in the "serious" world but enables the performers to fulfill limited objectives without the worry of a "real-life" commitment. As desiring subjects, Austen's characters are usually hard put to find something to do; and if not directly involved in matchmaking, they are nevertheless engaged largely in "reading" the actions of others according to some predictable trajectory. Against the arbitrary and open-ended consciousness of mere daydreaming, her characters focus on the events of the moment as if they were participating in some activity whose rules might be discerned by an energetic mind. Except for Anne Elliot, who has felt the personal loss of eight years of solitude after rejecting an offer of marriage, the distant past has little apparent influence on the heroines' present consciousness; and the future is seldom more than a few months away. What counts above all is the moment at hand—a dinner party, a dance, a card game, a walk in the garden, a carriage ride, and other framed actions useful to promote conversation among the principals.

All play involves performance of some kind; but not all performances are play—many are "serious" encounters. Even the more narrowly self-disciplined minds are called upon to execute what the occasion requires: for example, Elinor Dashwood's mandatory conversations with Mrs. Jennings on the journey to London and afterward, Fanny Price's walk with Henry at Portsmouth, and Anne Elliot's first-aid assistance to Louisa at Lyme. Such performances demonstrate the heroine's exemplary will in discharging her social obligations and are surely important moments in the characterization. But to highlight the meaningful ritual action in Austen's most festive novels, I have concentrated for analysis on the playful scenes, especially those involving music and dancing, in *Pride and Prejudice* and *Emma*.

The second chapter looks at the narrative structures of desire that underlie the presentation of character as subjective consciousness and also at the cathectic objects described that give the consciousness its raison d'être. It has been usual to see Austen's characters as moving toward some kind of knowledge—of self and of others—before being assimilated to their world; but my stress is upon their states of being, their encounters in everyday situations, which may be discrete experiences and do not always contribute to the resolution of the plot. By selecting certain speech patterns to individualize a given point of view, Austen's narrative renders the character as perceiving subject, caught in the exigencies of the moment and absorbed in the implicit rules of an encounter. Because she is a more elaborate development of Catherine Morland and Elizabeth Bennet in a comedy of illusions, Emma Woodhouse is of primary interest here in the erotics of the text.

In the third chapter I examine the provenance of character itself in Austen's text, especially the means of interiority and temporality deriving from her fictional predecessors. Discontinuous narrative forms, as in Richardson's epistolary modes and in Sterne's similar use of fragmented texts, demonstrated the major illusional effect of splitting the self into past and present consciousness. Through a method of contrapuntally arranged voices within the storytelling, Austen's parodic novels present character both as an individual, thinking subject and as a stereotypical imitation, a composite of other texts borrowed for the moment.

Although previous scholarship has generally assumed a mimetic model to describe Austen's characterization, this approach has been at odds sometimes with a parodic art that calls attention to literary analogues and deliberately subverts trusting the text.[21] The aesthetic of representation, however, tends to be a contradictory mixture of the natural and the artificial: the Meissen porcelain figurine delights not only by its lifelike resemblance but also by its cold, fragile composition—the two opposite qualities being somehow interdependent. Similarly, even fictional characters most patently rooted in motivations of the plot and contrived for thematic purposes can strike us as psychologically reified beings. An assurance of the characters' artificial origins seems actually to enhance their mimetic value.[22]

In contrast to other performances represented, speech acts, as the fourth chapter will explore, can have a deceptive immediacy, especially when conventional markers of dialogue like inquits are reduced or omitted.[23] No matter what a character is said to be doing, all that the text can provide is written language; it is up to the reader to imagine the action referred to in the narrative. Rather than "fill in" a scene with static description, however, Austen notes only the barest essentials of the setting and relies instead on multiple discourse to create the impression of persons talking and thinking aloud "characteristically." Perhaps the first English novelist to grasp the full mimetic implications of imitating other language within the text, Austen renders not only humorous talkers who seem to live by words alone but also derisive interlocutors who parody the original comic discourse while addressing yet another stratum of the comic audience.

Conversation in Austen's scheme of things may appear to be spontaneous, an arbitrary act of individual wills; but it is usually represented as an encounter between "those who would talk and those who would listen," whose rules are best known once they are broken. A character may talk from a variety of motives—whether ejaculating to assert a presence for oneself while remaining schizoidally indifferent to any audience, sympathizing with another's happiness or distress, or asserting an opinion determinedly to hold sway over another. What matters most, however, is not the actual spoken words but their perceived intent within a given situation. If the encounter is competitively triangular, for instance, a mere token of address is sufficient to arouse desire or antagonism: Elizabeth's euphoric tête-à-tête with Colonel Fitzwilliam at Rosings arouses Darcy's jealousy and seems to bring on the marriage proposal (*PP*, II, 8), and Anne's gratuitous chat with Mr. Elliot during the concert at Bath has a similar effect upon Captain Wentworth (*P*, IV, 8). I shall emphasize the humorous talkers in Austen's repertory, whose performances in carefully staged moments may appear, to the inattentive within the story, to be empty gestures but may actually disclose important clues to the plot, articulate some otherwise unnoticed aspect of a character, and even give voice to the anxiety or boredom inherent to his or her consciousness.

The last chapter rounds off our opening inquiry into Austen's game theory of writing by examining her textual reflexivity. Despite the novelist's artful tactics, a character is finally no more than the reader's mirage; the agency of desiring, playing, and talking attributed to the cipher named Elizabeth, Fanny, or Emma, say, depends on our willing suspension of disbelief while engaged with the text. Just as the sonata that we *really* hear is an event—the interpreter's performance, not the abstract arrangement of symbols in the musical score—so the mimetic information encoded in the author's written language only comes to life in the temporal act of reading; a dramatic production of the Austen text would complete my musical performance analogy.

As if to overcome the inertia of the static medium itself, the novel represents not only "real life" but its own devices of illusion-making; and hence Austen's characters "listen" as well as "talk," even to the extent of eavesdropping on others behind hedgerows. Richardson's scribblers refer to their *cacoethes scribendi* to account for their obsession and comment nervously on their requirements of pen, ink, and paper to write the letters we read. Austen's characters also value the letter as proof of the writer's mind, but they are much more self-conscious about the role of the reader in constructing the story. Besides writing implements, reading materials of all sorts—Gothic romances, agricultural reports, poetry, charades, conundrums, and alphabet games—enter into the action of puzzling the text.

To highlight the truly perceptive mind, however, Austen subordinates the activity of reading books to the ongoing process of "reading" character. In emulation of the author's role, her principals occasionally step out of their fictional frame to discuss strategy toward an implied reader. Henry Tilney's first speech to Catherine about what they are expected to say in their situation at a Bath assembly automatically sets them apart from the stereotypes addressed ironically; and Admiral Croft's plans for Wentworth after an important turn in the plot mirror the author/reader at her work: "I think we must get him to Bath"(*P*, 173). By interrupting the narrative movement reflexively, Austen thus adopts the Cervantic principle of negating the conventions of reading to imply a more elusive reality beyond representation.

In view of the many studies over the past forty years that have seen Austen as the prototype of political, moral, and aesthetic order, my general emphasis here on her fragmentary representation of character in purposefully staged scenes may appear eccentric at the outset. Without denying the authoritative voice in her novels, familiar to even the most cursory reader and inspiring confidence in resolving any social obstacle, I argue that her artistic strength lies not so much in the larger design of the story as in its minute encounters, the ivory miniatures revelatory of the character's inner life.

In opposition to the familiar view that Austen's novels are stylistically polished but lacking in substance, I hope to show that they give unusual significance to the most ordinary events and, indeed, that in this respect they deserve comparison with the worldly metaphysics of such modern thinkers as Heidegger and Sartre.[24] But to glance back to her predecessors, it was the eighteenth-century novelists who depicted the intensity of personal being in the contingent moment; hence, one of Austen's great merits as a writer today is her adroit narrative craft in evoking the lived self implicit in the spoken word.

I.   Play

On the smaller scale of daily events as opposed to momentous questions of human destiny, there are forms of desire that reach completion and even become absorbed in the individual's future actions. The exigencies of time and place imposed on the Austen story give significance to the most minute circumstances and invite something like a game theory of behavior, as described in John Dewey's empirical model:

> We have *an* experience when the material experienced runs its course to fulfillment. Then and then only is it integrated within and demarcated in the general stream of experiences from other experiences. A piece of work is finished in a way that is satisfactory; a problem receives its solution; a game is played through; a situation, whether that of eating a meal, playing a game of chess, carrying on a conversation, writing a book, or taking part in a political campaign, is so rounded out that its close is a consummation and not a cessation. Such an experience is a whole and carries with it its own individualizing quality and self-sufficiency. It is *an* experience.[1]

Dewey's indefinite article before the noun emphasizes experience as a quantity, as something to be measured, evaluated, and stored up; and, like power, it may be recalled by the agent as a commodity to be compared, priced, and exchanged in the daily give-and-take. Dewey's examples of conversation and games are especially apropos to the main action in the Austen novel; but his idea of closure as fulfillment and consummation is bracketed in her world, where play, though usually an "educational experience," tends to be disruptive and fragmentary, even portentous, as in her elliptical endings that disarmingly remind us to finish the story in the conventional way.

But reducing the scale of the everyday uncertainty through play brings consciousness into temporary focus and permits control over desire; and at some point the miniature, whether it is Uncle Toby's bowling green or the game of speculation at Mansfield, throws into relief what is essential to the relations and objectives in question. If art imitates life, there must be a structure to everyday situations that can be imitated. For this reason it is misleading to set "culture against play"[2] in spite of Austen's tendentious narrators. A more accurate dichotomy would be the contrast she draws between good and bad forms of playing—between encounters that allow the individual participants to lose themselves, say, in the flow of conversation and encounters that end in boredom or despair. Rather than opposing the sentimentalist's sincere ideal to the ironist's role-playing, Austen's text implies that the language of "real feeling" comprises both these aspects within a given moment. Without emotion, nothing is expressed; without form, nothing is communicated. It is the experience of regulated activity brought to some sort of limited fulfillment that gives meaning to leisure; and Austen's comic world, like any cathartic fiction, resolves "real-life" conflicts under privileged circumstances.

Since characters themselves are verbal and behavioral imitations, to speak of them as playing games is yet another Cervantic trick of representation, denying their fictionality by having them mimic their own roles reflexively and implying at the same time that they have genuine, inner selves in abeyance. Characters so engaged also reflect, of course, the parodic author, who cleverly exposes the various masks, gestures, and props of her trade by slipping in a new illusion of reality. As mimetic ruse as well as symbolic action, therefore, play is important to Austen's metaphorical enterprise, being revelatory of character in specifically defined situations.

No matter what we imagine the characters to be doing in the story, all that is concretely before us is the printed text; and if play in Austen is not simply a thematic contrast to the morally "serious" actions represented, we need to ask exactly how it affects the novel's discourse. Apart from such allegorical analogies as those between the country dance and marital trust or between the Kotzebue drama and marital infidelity, the narrative uses play activities of various kinds for three main purposes: (1) to frame characters within a "text"—that is, within a controlled situation already known to us from other sources—not only to give them prescribed roles to perform but also to give them a specific vernacular for conversation; (2) to allow narrators/characters to perceive other characters in motion, when the slightest gesture may communicate something only hinted at in the dialogue; and (3) to render the character's emotions, whether excited, bored, or depressed, while engaged with another in some performance.

As in other areas of Austen's text, the description of any given activity is spare; and readers today require little knowledge of the particular recreation alluded to in order to understand its manner. What is at issue is how the characters move within a certain discourse and find their voice—or lose it—during moments of interaction. The following discussion turns on the experience of the encounter as conveyed by the narrator, the performer, and the spectator within the scene. Since dancing at a ball was no idle pastime to the unmarried author but the most opportune moment for knowing the other sex, it is perhaps not surprising that some of the most crucial encounters involve this activity; and our focus here is on this not-so-innocent diversion.

1. Performance

Not play in the abstract but the particular performance, the *experience* of the moment, is usually what matters in Austen.[3] Unless read in context, an action, whether performed well or not, may have quite contradictory values for the agent. For instance, John Thorpe's rude driving, dancing, and talking are a comic foil to Henry's grace in these same activities, which enhances his role as hero; but Willoughby is a far more sinister alazon[4] because of his smooth horsemanship and conversation. Whereas Mr. Collins's clumsy dancing reveals a flawed personality that the narrator even ascribes to a deprived childhood, Admiral Croft's reckless driving betrays only a lovable, childlike humor. Nonperformances themselves can be problematic: at given times Darcy, Elton, and Knightley all are reluctant to dance, and for very different reasons, even though all move like gentlemen. Likewise, Fanny's refusal to play a part in the theatricals may reflect a scrupulous sincerity; nevertheless, as a spectator she freely enjoys Henry's acting in the Kotzebue play and his reading of Shakespeare. Furthermore, her heartfelt indulgence in the country dances obviates any puritanical feeling against recreational activity in principle. More complex than this configuration of good and bad performers and nonperformers, Austen's stories tend to divide characters according to their inclination toward play or work (or rather being "serious"); a small third category includes those who are mainly bored or inactive. Of course, if the conditions are right, characters may move from one category to another. Again, as with the classification of performers, there is no fixed hierarchy: being serious is not always better than being playful; and being bored, if usually an anomaly, may even have merit. Austen's comic irony seems deliberately to thwart any complacent schematization. The Marianne/Willoughby (play) versus Elinor/Edward (work) contrast, for example, seems clear from the beginning; but Marianne's sufferings and nearly fatal illness, and Willoughby's honest confession elevate both to seasoned realists in the end. Although entering the novel as the bored husband of a garrulous, pregnant woman, Mr. Palmer later proves to be an attentive host and parent at Cleveland. Elizabeth and Mr. Bennet at first share a detached view of their world in contrast to the others, who either assume the "universal truth" of economic unions or simply have no theory at all; yet, even before Lydia's elopement disgraces the family and exposes her father's irresponsibility, the heroine has been touched by Darcy's seriousness. Nevertheless, in the end, though renouncing her father's cynicism, Elizabeth regains some of the liveliness that Darcy admires; and thus the dichotomy between play and seriousness (the unbridled energy of Lydia and Kitty versus the unimaginative pedantry of Mary) is subject to as many variations as a figure in music.

From the foregoing survey, we can see that characters gain an identity and form alliances by the quality of their movements. A performance separates at once not only two interest groups—the performer(s) and the spectator(s), but inevitably splinters these constituencies into rival factions and maybe even a few disinterested observers. An artificially concentrated acting out of desire, the performance is a kinetic situation rendered in the text by positioning contrary, often tenuously balanced, attitudes in discourse to imply an encounter, in Erving Goffman's sense.[5] Various kinds of focused activity (a dinner or tea, a card game, a dance, a polite conversation) bring persons together for a limited duration according to a set of rules; and such encounters tend toward euphoria or dysphoria to the extent that the self is assimilated in the performance. What is of primary interest to those involved is not the particulars of the ritual act itself (the dinner party may be a success despite the mediocre food served) but its power to create a field in which individual selves merge for the moment of the experience. It is the "we rationale," to quote Goffman, "a sense of the single thing that *we* are doing together at the time,"[6] that prompts the individual to join the dance and transcend for a while the insignificant motion of daily life.

This rationale creates a sense of intimacy between partners while presenting themselves in public, an idea implicit in Henry's analogy between the country dance and marriage: "Fidelity and complaisance are the principal duties of both; and those men who do not chuse to dance or marry themselves, have no business with the partners or wives of their neighbours" (*NA*, 76). As Catherine understands, his point about "duties" has less to do with a moral imperative than with the state of mind sought in the activity of the country dance itself: "'when once entered into, they belong exclusively to each other till the moment of its dissolution . . . it is their duty, each to endeavour to give the other no cause for wishing that he or she had bestowed themselves elsewhere'" (*NA*, 77). Clearly, the likelihood of rivalry with the other dancers in the set is an unavoidable risk worth taking; and John Thorpe's bogus claim on Catherine as a promised partner gives Henry an occasion to ask assurances of her "fidelity" in their present engagement, culminating in her emphatic, "I do not *want* to talk to any body [else]" (*NA*, 78). Later, on their way to Northanger, we learn how much emotion is compressed in her response here; and all their dialogue in the story confirms the partnership initiated in a physical activity that defined their mutual opposition to the others (the Thorpes, General Tilney, the Allens, Bath society). From this bonding experience, furthermore, Catherine gains insight for judging the alazons correctly: on seeing Isabella and Captain Tilney as partners in a dance after each had protested against joining the group, she is witness to the incipient betrayal of her brother; and her "pain of confusion" and good-natured alibi for their treachery have the advantage of raising Henry's esteem for her (*NA*, 133). Hence, the first triangle of desire (Catherine and Henry versus John Thorpe) gains all the more by opposing the second, illegitimate one (Isabella and Captain Tilney versus James).

Although the encounter is always regulated, aside from the more obvious rules of decorum, the most valued principles lie hidden in the actual performance, one reason why even a champion tennis player or professional opera singer must still depend on a coach's expert eye and ear. Furthermore, an irony that serves the parodic narrator's interest, the important rules of a performance are mostly to be observed when they are broken, as in the example of Isabella's "infidelity" with Captain Tilney and the consequent consternation registered by Catherine and Henry. It is only when an apparently inchoate happening is interrupted, the faithful dancers suddenly confronted by their unfaithful counterparts, that the rules of "irrelevance" can be comprehended. As Goffman states: "an encounter exhibits sanctioned orderliness arising from obligations fulfilled and expectations realized."[7]

Using the model of a game, Goffman illustrates how participants in an encounter focus their attention on a single objective for the duration of the gathering (the moving of the chessmen until the fulfillment of winning or losing) and tacitly banish any aesthetic, economic, or sentimental interest that would interrupt this attention. Ideally, if the encounter is going well the participants will experience the autotelic immersion of self in the activity, without any thought of time or place.[8] Breaking the rules, "irrelevance," however, will suddenly wrench one's attention away from the event as when, say, the self-indulgent piano recitalist lingers a trifle too long in a mellifluous passage and turns Beethoven into schmaltz. One of the pleasures of playing a game as opposed to engaging in "serious" activities is that specific rules are in effect to protect the performer from external causes of interference (the audience's mandatory silence, hence also irrepressible coughing); and perhaps for similar reasons, numerous other activities in everyday life, conversation above all, turn out to be structured events. At any rate, Austen's novels take a peculiar delight in both the ecstatic experience of a performance and the embarrassment caused by its interruption.

Without "flow" any performance is doomed to fail— the performer shrinking back into her solitary self and becoming an alien observer of the scene at hand. Despite their habitual reflectiveness, all of Austen's heroines experience such moments of ecstatic performing; but, in contrast to the less self-conscious characters, they do not usually sustain their euphoria very long. One obvious reason for this abridgment is that without a self-interested awareness of time and place, narrative in Austen's classical style would have little material to develop. In the stream-of-consciousness technique of later novelists, of course, the lyrical state of mind can last for many pages without flagging.

Failed performances, nevertheless, are useful to Austen's parodic characterization, as in the opening conflict of *Pride and Prejudice*, when the protagonists share dysphoria together toward the community-sponsored event. Thus Darcy's predicament at the Meryton ball is not unlike Elizabeth's own antagonism to that lackluster occasion:

> Bingley had never met with pleasanter people or prettier girls in his life; every body had been most kind and attentive to him, there had been no formality, no stiffness, he had soon felt acquainted with all the room; and as to Miss Bennet, he could not conceive an angel more beautiful. Darcy, on the contrary, had seen a collection of people in whom there was little beauty and no fashion, for none of whom he had felt the smallest interest, and from none received either attention or pleasure. (*PP*, 16)

By means of free indirect discourse, the narrator contrasts each character's attitudes without taking sides, though Bingley's angel worship, like Henry Crawford's, connotes a sinister obeisance to the female, which enhances Darcy's blunt honesty.

Failed performances may not only form unexpected intimacies but also cause tension and hence store up energy to be involuntarily released later in a "flow" experience. For instance, when Darcy and Elizabeth do at last dance together at the Netherfield ball, it is a portentous moment for the love/hate theme of the story, the entire performance uniting them in the same way experienced by Catherine and Henry vis-à-vis the Bath world. Again, as in the use of Thorpe, a clown mimics the rival's role in the triangular arrangement: "they were dances of mortification. Mr. Collins, awkward and solemn, apologising instead of attending, and often moving wrong without being aware of it, gave her all the shame and misery which a disagreeable partner for a couple of dances can give. The moment of her release from him was exstacy" (*PP*, 90). In a comic reversal of the norms for an encounter, Elizabeth is in ecstasy *after* the performance! Then, while in this dazed state, she feels no resistance to Darcy's request to dance with her ("without knowing what she did, she accepted him" [*PP*, 90]).

Once together in the performance, however, the protagonists use the dance as a pretext for verbal dueling, the only kind of exchange immediately available to us in direct discourse. But instead of giving expression to mutual hostility, the situation actually draws them together as ironic commentators on their assigned roles. Although these are presumably not mortifying dances, there is no description of the hero's movements; the fact that he is a gentleman bred implies the requisite grace. Rather than fuss with such details, the narrator remarks Elizabeth's indulgence in the attention they are drawing: "Elizabeth made no answer, and took her place in the set, amazed at the dignity to which she was arrived in being allowed to stand opposite to Mr. Darcy, and reading in her neighbours' looks their equal amazement in beholding it" (*PP*, 90). What happens next resembles the tit for tat between Catherine and Henry at Bath, undercutting the conventional chatter expected of first acquaintances engaged at a ball; but here it is the woman who is on the attack:

> They stood for some time without speaking a word; and she began to imagine that their silence was to last through the two dances, and at first was resolved not to break it; till suddenly fancying that it would be the greater punishment to her partner to oblige him to talk, she made some slight observation on the dance. He replied, and was again silent. After a pause of some minutes she addressed him a second time with
> "It is *your* turn to say something now, Mr. Darcy.—*I* talked about the dance, and *you* ought to make some kind of remark on the size of the room, or the number of couples."
> He smiled, and assured her that whatever she wished him to say should be said. (*PP*, 91)

After the initial triumph of exhibitionism, the dance itself is valuable mainly for occasioning their first tête-à-tête; yet the actual words said here are as unimportant as the particular figure of the dance in process. It is Elizabeth's power to command the situation, skillfully using the tension of silence as a preparative to aggressive speech, which is at stake. Apparently without being aware of it, she has scored a direct hit, not through the dance itself but the erotic freedom it has released. The two signs—the smile and the assurance—are enough to validate for us, if not for them, an intimacy bound toward eventual wedlock.

In this encounter, it may be observed, Elizabeth is at first aware of being publicly humiliated while dancing with Mr. Collins; then, after recovering self-esteem by her place with Mr. Darcy, she loses all sense of the others at the ball and concentrates exclusively on her partner. Neither one is at ease, not only because of their personal differences but more importantly because they are unable to lose themselves in their roles. Dancing is more a social obligation than a pleasure for Mr. Darcy, and Elizabeth knows it. The usual resort would be to create small talk to avoid the mounting tension caused by an all too self-conscious exercise of the body. However, by stepping out of her role, Elizabeth suddenly impresses upon her counterpart that she has a mind of her own; and the lively conversation that ensues is just the diversion that Mr. Darcy most enjoys.

The rationale here is the characters' equivalent to the author's parody, what sociologists call "making a situation." Goffman educes the above scene to illustrate how an individual can "tamper" with the "frame" (the implicit rules in a given encounter) deliberately to project the self.[9] After jumping course in the dance, Elizabeth keeps her partner off balance in the repartee and prophetically ventures to note a likeness between them: "I have always seen a great similarity in the turn of our minds.—We are each of an unsocial, taciturn disposition, unwilling to speak, unless we expect to say something that will amaze the whole room, and be handed down to posterity with all the eclat of a proverb" (*PP*, 91). When this admission of her own pride forces him to demur, she responds discreetly: "I must not decide on my own performance." Despite the initially overwhelming experience of being singled out to dance with the hero, Elizabeth not only reduces the tension between them by recasting their roles as outsiders to the event but also elicits both parodic and sincere conversation from him—a fine performance.

Because a performance, like conversation, is usually triadic in the narrative structure—the two principals and the storyteller or other witness—it is not only associated with desire but almost inevitably with "frame tampering" to project the self. At Rosings, Elizabeth's encounter with Colonel Fitzwilliam is another classical mediation of desire, no matter that it is unplanned:

> He [Colonel Fitzwilliam] now seated himself by her, and talked so agreeably of Kent and Hertfordshire, of travelling and staying at home, of new books and music, that Elizabeth had never been half so well entertained in that room before; and they conversed with so much spirit and flow, as to draw the attention of Lady Catherine herself, as well as of Mr. Darcy. *His* eyes had been soon and repeatedly turned towards them with a look of curiosity. (*PP*, 172)

Again the actual words are beside the point: it is the vertiginous phenomenon of immersing themselves "with so much spirit and flow" in conversation that depresses the spectators with a sense of being excluded from the euphoric "togetherness." The narrator does not analyze Darcy's motive beyond "curiosity," but there is little doubt that his cousin's ease with Elizabeth here is a cause for jealousy.

As if charged from the energy of her encounter with Colonel Fitzwilliam, Elizabeth feels the power to compensate for the weakness of her piano-playing by "making" the situation accommodate her superior wit: "You mean to frighten me, Mr. Darcy, by coming in all this state to hear me? But I will not be alarmed though your sister *does* play so well. There is a stubbornness about me that never can bear to be frightened at the will of others. My courage always rises with every attempt to intimidate me" (*PP*, 174). Her acknowledgment that her "fingers do not move over this instrument in the masterly manner which I see so many women's do" slyly reduces a piano performance to mechanical agility rather than allowing for the whole interaction of mind and body with the motion. As before, during their dance together at Netherfield, Elizabeth attacks Darcy's radical individualism as her own, but this time with the added advantage of a witness in Colonel Fitzwilliam. While presumably intent on reducing the tension of the encounter, Elizabeth again claims Darcy's shyness in public to be a zone of selfhood they have in common: "We neither of us perform to strangers" (*PP*, 176). The hero's and narrator's silence toward this remark is typical of the many indeterminacies in the reliance on dialogue to carry a scene; but in contrast to an egregiously bad performance like Mary Bennet's "long concerto," mere ego gratification that fails to communicate anything to her audience, Elizabeth's ironic undercutting of her situation (the piano-playing, after all, was obligatory at this moment) is exactly what answers to Darcy's refusal to play without purpose.[10]

Although "frame tampering" may have the positive effect of uniting characters as outsiders to their official roles (Catherine and Henry, Elizabeth and Darcy), the rules of "irrelevance" may apply to situations where the actor only pretends to be playing as a ruse to manipulate the other, sometimes with dangerous consequences. The much debated crisis over the theatricals in *Mansfield Park* illustrates this kind of encounter. Lionel Trilling's stress on Austen's link with Rousseau in distrusting histrionic art in principle not only ignores the biographical evidence to the contrary but also repeated scenes in the novels, like those between Elizabeth and Darcy, where the presentation of self requires artfulness in communicating with the other. Within the story, the chief objection to producing the Kotzebue play is the implicit rebellion against Sir Thomas in his absence.[11] Rather than condemning acting as immoral, Austen seems remarkably close to Diderot's insight in *Rameau's Nephew:* "There is only one man in the whole of a realm who walks, and that is the sovereign. Everybody else takes up positions."[12] Edmund, we recall, does not condemn the impropriety of *Lovers' Vows* but worries instead about the kind of performance likely to result: "True, to see real acting, good hardened real acting; but I would hardly walk from this room to the next to look at the raw efforts of those who have not been bred to the trade,—a set of gentlemen and ladies, who have all the disadvantages of education and decorum to struggle through" (*MP*, 124). If Mr. Yates bears out Edmund's worst fears on this account, it is the "good hardened real acting" of the Crawfords that disrupts the Bertram amateurs, who are incapable of disinterested playing and inject the irrelevance of their selfish pursuits into the rehearsals. The sinister Crawfords have it both ways, acting their roles persuasively while enjoying their power over the others; and serious trouble brews when the amateur comes "alive with acting" and still feels herself a pathetic heroine off-stage when her Frederick departs from Mansfield:

> —The hand which had so pressed her's to his heart!
> —The hand and the heart were alike motionless and passive now! Her spirit supported her, but the agony of her mind was severe. (*MP*, 193)

Free indirect discourse renders Maria's confusion of play and seriousness, where histrionic gesture becomes equivalent to feeling to the extent that sincerity can no longer be distinguished from role-playing. It is a confusion, however, that Fanny herself experiences momentarily later in the story, during Henry's reading of Shakespeare. One's autonomy depends on breaking the spell.

A performance is ideally the work of the moment, its agents transcending the normal self/other relationships to the environment. Just as agape in the religious sense occurs through divine grace, so loss of self-consciousness in the activity is a phenomenon of being in motion, with all one's feelings concentrated on the purpose at hand. Surrendering one's rational faculties to the current of involuntary forces obviously involves a certain risk; and whether one is walking, playing the piano, singing, or engaged in polite conversation, there is always some danger of falling, of a wrong note or a faux pas to damage the ego during the moment of exertion. But at some point it becomes more dangerous to resort to reason than to trust the instincts of the body. (One can imagine the consequences if a ski jumper began to reconsider his move once he was launched into the air.) The danger, furthermore, is a vital element of the tension that generates the energy to perform in the first place; and for this reason the spectator, real or imagined, is necessary to the actor's reaching his peak of performance. The spectator, at least vicariously, takes part in the action—ideally, to the extent of feeling himself in danger (Coleridge's "willing suspension of disbelief").

Always a risk for the spectator, no matter how otherwise secure, is the surrendering of critical judgment, of being seduced by the artist's deceptions; and for a repressed personality the experience does not come without guilt feelings. In her capacity to lose herself in a performance yet regain her personal freedom to judge, Fanny Price is a model spectator as well as reader of plays: she is responsive to Henry's skillful acting for the moment but afterward is detached enough to distinguish between art and life. A tendentious scene, which explicitly interrelates the topoi of histrionic art, pulpit eloquence, and the language of "true feeling," casts Edmund as pander, while Henry tries to win Fanny through the contagion of reading Shakespeare—presumably with all the voice, countenance, and gesture that authorities on eloquence recommended.[13] While Lady Bertram dozes as usual upon the sofa (a convenient defusing of the chaperone, as in the case of Mrs. Bates's poor eyesight and broken spectacles), Fanny's cousin indulges in voyeurism throughout the performance:

> Edmund watched the progress of her attention, and was amused and gratified by seeing how she gradually slackened in the needle-work, which, at the beginning, seemed to occupy her totally; how it fell from her hand while she sat motionless over it—and at last, how the eyes which had appeared so studiously to avoid him throughout the day, were turned and fixed on Crawford, fixed on him for minutes, fixed on him in short till the attraction drew Crawford's upon her, and the book was closed, and the charm was broken. Then, she was shrinking again into herself, and blushing and working as hard as ever. (*MP*, 337)

It is a strange moment for Edmund, almost sexual, and though at present he is interfering on Henry's behalf, it is not an inappropriate feeling toward the woman he will eventually wed. For her part, troubled by her lapse in self-control, Fanny refuses to give the expected compliments afterward: "Her praise had been given in her attention: *that* must content them" (*MP*, 338). To gauge the effect of the reading, Henry observes that even the indolent aunt is aroused: "Crawford was excessively pleased [free indirect discourse mimics his insincere hyperbole].—If Lady Bertram, with all her incompetency and languor, could feel this, the inference of what her niece, alive and enlightened as she was, must feel, was elevating" (*MP*, 338). He quickly dispels the charm, however, by his subsequent harangue on pulpit eloquence and then almost drives Fanny out of the room with his hackneyed gallantry ("it is 'Fanny' that I think of all day, and dream of all night.—You have given the name such reality of sweetness, that nothing else can now be descriptive of you" [*MP*, 344]). In contrast to his natural eloquence while reading Shakespeare, Henry's bad performance as a polemicist and a suitor is blatantly self-serving and wholly underestimates his audience.

Yet bad acting is morally useful. The failure of performance not only reveals grease paint, meaningless gesture, and borrowed speech; but, far worse, it also exposes the artist as a déclassé member of the community, an unscrupulous trickster rather than an inspired prophet. Without the benefit of illusion, the spectator is at liberty to go behind the scenes and contemplate manipulative behavior there in terms of real-life encounters; and the shame of having once been taken in adds to the moral condemnation of the impostor. All the while we are engaged with Fanny in this enterprise, however, we ourselves are caught in the illusion of her sincerity as a real presence.

2. The "Irresistible Waltz"

Performances recalled become significant in conversation at a later point in the story, and hence they give characters a certain depth of experience as well as a basis for alliances and rivalries. Because performances create a memory bank or field, sometimes only a word or phrase is enough to call forth associations in a character's mind. Moreover, since the narrator may choose to withdraw from the storytelling for a while, leaving the responsibility to the protagonists themselves, there are many encounters in Austen that rely heavily on innuendo in dialogue to suggest meaning. The scene where Jane Fairfax demonstrates the Broadwood piano for Emma, with Frank Churchill present, is an example of a performance rendered with very little narrative assistance; but it bears out what is said elsewhere concerning the politics of politeness.

Nonperformances, we have noted, may be a means of affirming selfhood against socially predetermined behavior. Both Darcy and Knightley demonstrate "good faith" by refusing to dance simply because it is expected of them, and their blunt manners are even made to reflect the national character. Mr. Knightley's warning to Emma about Frank Churchill's gratuitous amiability invokes an ancient distrust of Gallic politeness among the British upper classes: "he can have no English delicacy towards the feelings of other people: nothing really amiable about him" (*E*, 149). It also shows that Knightley can detect a ham actor when he sees one, and to the end he triumphs while others are taken in by the interloper. But, like Fanny, he avows the sincere ideal without knowing that what he really demands is good acting. Habitually in "bad faith," Churchill is merely "*aimable*"; and, long before the heroine, the reader is privileged to witness his infidelity through the action at the Coles's party in chapter 26 (*E*, II, 8), when Mr. Knightley becomes angry with *his* rival for exploiting Jane Fairfax's singing, and when subsequently Emma outshines *her* rival by leading the impromptu dance with the encroacher ("They were a couple worth looking at").

To render his amiability as underhanded, even treacherous, the narrative suppresses the information of Churchill's actual part in manipulating the event that night: "soon (within five minutes) the proposal of dancing—originating nobody exactly knew where—was so effectually promoted by Mr. and Mrs. Cole, that every thing was rapidly clearing away, to give proper space" (*E*, 229). As on other occasions, notably at the Crown Inn ball, Churchill is a shadowy presence, in fact, a double agent whose real motives go undetected; and the narrator captures in free indirect discourse a few superlatives associated with the text of the *aimable:* "Mrs. Weston, capital in her country-dances, was seated, and beginning an irresistible waltz; and Frank Churchill, coming up with most becoming gallantry to Emma, had secured her hand, and led her up to the top" (*E*, 229).

At first glance the phrase "irresistible waltz" seems harmless enough, eliciting no more than the idea that the participants, if not Mr. Knightley among the bystanders, were fond of dancing. But as in Isabella's "infidelity" with Captain Tilney at the Bath ball, the irresistible power of attraction once more stems from the triangular desire latent in the social occasion. In the second chapter after this scene, when Emma visits the Bateses' to hear the intriguing Broadwood piano, Frank Churchill's cryptic dialogue with Jane goes unheard except by the wary outside reader:

> "If you are very kind," said he, "it will be one of the waltzes we danced last night;—let me live them over again. You did not enjoy them as I did; you

appeared tired the whole time. I believe you were glad we danced no longer; but I would have given worlds—all the worlds one ever has to give—for another half hour."

She played.

"What felicity it is to hear a tune again which *has* made one happy!—If I mistake not that was danced at Weymouth."

She looked up at him for a moment, coloured deeply, and played something else. (*E*, 242)

Here two previous moments of an intimate encounter converge in a simultaneous lie and betrayal. The man who had danced with Emma the night before and had expressed his relief at escaping Jane's "languid dancing" continues at this point to tyrannize over his fiancée unbeknownst to the others. Because of the secret that gives him the power, Jane is reduced to a mere instrument again and made to play the same tunes from the previous night at the Coles's, apparently including the "irresistible waltz" rendered on the keyboard by the pregnant Mrs. Weston and danced with Emma as his partner. Churchill's innuendo, furthermore, about hearing this same tune previously at Weymouth suddenly brings out the horror of his infidelity: having danced with a rival the "irresistible waltz" that symbolizes his promise to the beloved.[14]

Apart from their situation of having to keep their intimacy secret, Frank Churchill, it would appear, enjoys the author's prerogative of manipulating character as well as plot; and his mischief in punishing Jane throughout various intrigues belongs to the trickster's role in comic fiction. One of his most sadistic moments occurs when he forces Jane to sing to the point of exhaustion at the Coles's, before the hero intervenes to rescue her:

Towards the end of Jane's second song, her voice grew thick.

"That will do," said he, when it was finished, thinking aloud—"You have sung quite enough for one evening—now, be quiet."

Another song, however, was soon begged for. "One more;—they would not fatigue Miss Fairfax on any account, and would only ask for one more." And Frank Churchill was heard to say, "I think you could manage this without effort; the first part is so very trifling. The strength of the song falls on the second."

Mr. Knightley grew angry.

"That fellow," said he, indignantly, "thinks of nothing but shewing off his own voice. This must not be." And touching Miss Bates, who at that moment passed near—"Miss Bates, are you mad, to let your niece sing herself hoarse in this manner? Go, and interfere. They have no mercy on her." (*E*, 229)

They have no mercy on her. Being victim is a large part of Jane's charm in this story, and this scene invokes reflexively the text of the Gothic heroine that Mr. Knightley is recalling in emotional terms.

This anxious performance is notable for what the narrator does not describe, especially the motive for Mr. Knightley's anger and the reason for Jane's exhaustion. As Patrick Piggott observes: "It is part of Mr. Knightley's personality to be frank and outspoken, but his manner of addressing Miss Bates on this occasion was as near to plain rudeness as makes no matter." Piggott also explains that Jane's condition after only two songs "does not speak very well for the soundness of the vocal training she had received in London."[15] Surely this is to miss the significance of the whole encounter. What is at issue is not Mr. Knightley's politeness or Jane's vocal training but the severe tension she is under while performing with her secret lover. Mr. Knightley not only resents Churchill's exhibitionism here; but, perhaps drawing on his Gothic imagination for the moment, as does Emma in other places, he also suspects him of abusing Jane almost perversely.

In contrast to her rival caught in yet another double bind, Emma sings blissfully, aided by the flattering attention that Churchill bestows on her in this encounter:

> She knew the limitations of her own powers too well to attempt more than she could perform with credit; she wanted neither taste nor spirit in the little things which are generally acceptable, and could accompany her own voice well. One accompaniment to her song took her agreeably by surprise—a second, slightly but correctly taken by Frank Churchill. Her pardon was duly begged at the close of the song, and every thing usual followed. (*E*, 227)

Although Emma's "little things" were probably simple folk songs as opposed to Jane's Italian arias, what matters is her ease of performance while being abetted by a male admirer. Unlike Mary Bennet in her "long concerto," Emma "knew the limitations of her own powers too well to attempt more than she could perform with credit"; and the narrator's approbation on this account, we may assume, is identical with Mr. Knightley's attitude toward the heroine.

Since play is activity that ideally involves a loss of self-consciousness within regulated encounters, Frank Churchill's behavior, on the contrary, is quite serious, capable of inflicting injury upon the betrothed and her family. On the mistaken assumption that Emma is in on the secret, he acts out duets with her in the manner of a Don Giovanni intriguing with a Leporello. If this behavior qualifies as play in the stageable sense, his covert intimacy with Jane, which he goes to great lengths to protect, may be serious enough to make his flirtation with Emma mere child's play, a game of pretended sexual innocence without the requisite euphoric loss of self in the performance. In fact, to grant him a measure of sympathy, his frequent discomfort while concealing his intimacy with Jane may help to account for his occasional petulance toward her. His situation disallows the true ludic spirit, an idea brought out when he tries to play the alphabet game with his cheerless partner at Hartfield as a pretext for communicating with her in front of the others. Having blundered about Mr. Perry's carriage, Churchill seems to be at a loss to carry on the performance and squirms like an amateur under Mr. Knightley's disapproving gaze: "Disingenuousness and double-dealing seemed to meet him at every turn. These letters were but the vehicle for gallantry and trick. It was a child's play, chosen to conceal a deeper game on Frank Churchill's part" (*E*, 348). But, as we know, the "deeper game" is not really a game at all; and Jane's blush at seeing herself observed signifies that playing is out of the question. She "pushed away the letters with even an angry spirit, and looked resolved to be engaged by no other word that could be offered" (*E*, 349). Despite her share of guilt in the deceit practiced against the others, Jane has no real inclination to play the roles thrust upon her; and the only moment of euphoria for her comes after the truth can be revealed, when at last she can stand with Emma in a triumphant duet against Mrs. Elton. Churchill does enter into the game for the fun of it, but his self-centered apartness while actively engaged with others, his moping and lack of spontaneity, hardly represent the "ludic" personality as fulfilled in Huizinga's sense.[16]

3.   *The Crown Inn Ball*

To judge from her biography, Austen had no qualms about playing games; and her letters to Cassandra abound with private jokes and witticisms, including some "black humor." As a novelist, from the beginning to the end her parody of fictional forms is central to her art. Yet the ideal of play as euphoric encounter is a rare moment in her stories, a respite from nervous conflicts proliferating on every page; at least among the young, recreation proves to be disruptive, a gratification at the expense of others, until some authority appears to repress the frolicking. Nevertheless, a too solemn moralization of the play element is precisely what Austen's comic irony militates against in retrospect; and, significantly, all her heroines are good performers in some kind of diversion. The Austen text, then, is simply ambivalent about the will to pleasure. There is an eerie foreboding at the margins of her comedy, as if at any moment something might happen to dispel the joy, a note of sadness resembling Don Quixote's moods when contemplating his textual fate. It is not easy, after all, to inhabit the world of parody, where at any moment a character may discover his illusions to be not even his own. Perhaps it is this contingency that haunts play in the most ludic novels, a persistent reminder of biological as well as literary mortality.

Less conspicuous than the repeated dichotomy between players and nonplayers in Austen's novels is the implied distrust rampant in the community as a whole; and it is in *Emma* that the hazards of village recreation loom darkly in the central action. Highbury's decline reflects the snobbism analyzed in the next chapter, and the Woodhouse humor to fidget behind the shrubbery is part of the general malaise. No wonder that in this stultifying atmosphere the heroine seems to await the arrival of Frank Churchill as if for her deliverance. To some readers, however, it seems that Churchill is at fault for initiating the Crown Inn ball and, in general, for introducing "movement and flexibility into a landscape of peace and stability," [17] a belief that would make Mr. Woodhouse's dread of the whole event the norm for the reader to accept. The terms "peace and stability" hardly fit the deep social changes attested throughout the novel and neurotically shunned by the nominal patriarch of Hartfield.

Frank Churchill is told, we recall, "the history of the large room visibly added" to the Crown: "it had been built many years ago for a ball-room, and while the neighbourhood had been in a particularly populous, dancing state, had been occasionally used as such;—but such brilliant days had long passed away, and now the highest purpose for which it was ever wanted was to accommodate a whist club established among the gentlemen and half-gentlemen [!] of the place" (*E*, 197). Despite Churchill's fickle language of the improver and his fascination with the building's "capabilities," the objection against reviving the "former good old days of the room" because of the "want of proper families in the place, and the conviction that none beyond the place and its immediate environs could be tempted to attend" (*E*, 198) is not satisfactory. The mocking narrator adopts the Woodhouse humor to set forth the current divisiveness in the community. Not only has Mr. Woodhouse never met Mrs. Stokes, the present occupant of the Crown, but his daughter "was rather surprized to see the constitution of the Weston prevail so decidedly against the habits of the Churchills" (*E*, 198) when Frank suggests a public entertainment at the inn. Free indirect discourse shades in Emma's consternation at the interloper's proposal: "Of pride, indeed, there was, perhaps, scarcely enough; his indifference to a confusion of rank, bordered too much on inelegance of mind. He could be no judge, however, of the evil he was holding cheap. It was but an effusion of lively spirits" (*E*, 198). Without endorsing either the extreme of democratic leveling or that of a rigid caste system, the narrative warns from the outset of the story that the old Woodhouse order is rigid and needs pumping with new energy to keep viable. Churchill may be a nuisance, but his intrusion is necessary to arouse desire and bring about the change in Emma's situation near the end of the novel.

Perhaps the overall success of the Crown Inn ball in bringing a rare moment of euphoria to the Highbury world is enough to justify Churchill's manipulative scheme. Far from being the subversive activity the theatricals at Mansfield Park were, this event brings together for the only time in the novel such diametrically opposed characters as Emma and Miss Bates in a surprisingly celebratory mood; and, of course, after forcing Mr. Knightley into action to rescue Harriet from the Eltons' vendetta, the ball climaxes in uniting him with Emma in the dance, their first consciously erotic moment together.

Highbury will never again meet under such relatively cohesive conditions; and just as the social contract depends on the subordination of the individual will to the common good, so the country dance once more proves its efficacy in animating the spirit, for the moment at least, needed to achieve this end. It is as if Austen were deliberately showing us the power of the dance by allowing its temporary revival at Highbury to put into motion the traditional steps of village life that summon a less fragmented culture than the present one now abandoned by the Hartfield squire; after the Crown event, the activities at Donwell and Box Hill will increasingly fail as group play, notwithstanding Mr. Knightley's hospitality and noblesse oblige. Although the Eltons try to sabotage the festivities at the Crown and the hero has to come into the dance to rescue Harriet (a serious rather than ludic motive), as far as is possible the community is temporarily in step.

The teleology of plot implies an aesthetic and moral rationale; but the sequence of events in Austen's story, like the experience of daily life, does not occur as a suspended part of a final cause awaiting fulfillment in the last chapter. Instead, characters undergo continually changing circumstances and register levels of energy on a scale from ennui and low self-esteem to euphoria and a sense of power. They usually have a short memory, or almost none at all, precisely because what matters happens to them in the course of a few days, weeks, or months. Not even Anne Elliot, the most retrospective of Austen characters, summons up any particular event from the distant years with Wentworth; it is their shared experience during the crisis at Lyme that works on their present consciousness.[18]

Play, we know, is inherent in religious ritual and provides a culture with a measure of control over the essential issues of life and death. With the perspicacity of a modern anthropologist, the "authorial narrator" in *Emma* declaims on the cathartic function of a ball:

> It may be possible to do without dancing entirely. Instances have been known of young people passing many, many months successively, without being at any ball of any description, and no material injury accrue either to body or mind;—but when a beginning is made—when the felicities of rapid motion have once been, though slightly, felt—it must be a very heavy set that does not ask for more. (*E*, 247)

The interesting point here is the difference between the initial motives toward the event and the actual euphoria of motion, when the I-thou relationship gets lost in the dance.

Regardless of his selfish motives in promoting the ball, therefore, Churchill, with Jane as sacrificial lamb, is needed to instill energy into the stagnant Highbury community just when the titular heroine is in danger of never marrying, as well as never dancing. Apart from his welcome injection of play into the community, furthermore, his sincere alliance with Emma against the presumptuous Eltons, supplemented later by Jane's equally sincere friendship with her former rival, demonstrates that he is *not*, in fact, indifferent to a "confusion of rank," after all. Churchill's arrival on the scene is threatening to the "peace and stability" of the town, but the event at the Crown proves well worth the risk, if only because it unites hero and heroine in the dance with a heightened consciousness of their fidelity toward one another. Of course, various complications still lie ahead before the novel reaches its ending: to modify Dewey's principle, this performance is neither a "consummation" nor a "cessation"; besides arousing false expectations in Harriet, it also stirs new feelings in Emma, which will not be clear to her until the discovery that her poor friend is no less than a serious rival.

The ball at the Crown Inn, above all, reveals Emma's capacity for agape, a loss of self-awareness in motion, social love, and other redeeming qualities that distinguish Mr. Knightley's values. Although from the earliest stage of planning she had flattered herself that the ball was intended for her personally, by the time of its happening not only has Mrs. Elton as bride taken precedence but also Churchill's mind seems oddly distant from her throughout the event. While preparing for the

ball she had desired the occasion "even for simple dancing itself, without any of the wicked aids of vanity" (*E*, 247), a motive she could fathom, if not Mr. Knightley, from her experience of being "well matched in a partner" (*E*, 230) at the
Coles's. What was "wicked" about that event was the egotism:
"They were a couple worth looking at," a thought that would
have caused some discomfort to Jane sitting in the shadows. At
the Crown affair it is Mrs. Elton who enjoys the advantage of a
"vanity completely gratified" (*E*, 325); but since the "felicities
of rapid motion" obliterate the heroine's concern with a "confusion of rank," nothing can disturb her: "—In spite of this
little rub, however, Emma was smiling with enjoyment, delighted to see the respectable length of the set as it was forming, and to feel that she had so many hours of unusual festivity
before her" (*E*, 325).

As usual in this novel, the narrator closely imitates
the rhythms of the heroine's consciousness; even the privileged view of the historian seems compatible with her finite
sense of things at this time: "The ball proceeded pleasantly.
The anxious cares, the incessant attentions of Mrs. Weston,
were not thrown away. Every body seemed happy; and the
praise of being a delightful ball, which is seldom bestowed till
after a ball has ceased to be, was repeatedly given in the very
beginning of the existence of this" (*E*, 326). Miss Bates's ex-
clamation, "This is meeting quite in fairy-land!—Such a trans-
formation!" (*E*, 323), is prophetic; and in running off to her
usually recessive mother she extends the festive spirit even
beyond the Crown room. Under these ideal circumstances,
therefore, Mr. Knightley's heroic action is not just for Harriet's
sake but to preserve the communal happiness from the Eltons'
rudeness.

Since any encounter is a kinetic arrangement of intentions lasting only for the moment, its historical existence is
subject to doubt even for those who had directly experienced
it. That the event is ultimately a phenomenon created in the
minds of the participants rather than something objectively
"out there" is the emphasis of the narrator's peculiarly ontic
description: "after a ball has ceased to be . . . the very beginning of the existence of this" (*E*, 326). Maybe the whole thing
has been an illusion in the first place, the magic of Aladdin's
lamp, to use Miss Bates's figure; and like most occasions in
daily life it has little or no significance to the nonparticipant:

"Of very important, very recordable events, it was no more productive than such meetings usually are" (*E*, 326). Yet, strangely enough, not only this entire chapter but nearly all the chapters, from the first anticipation of Frank Churchill and Jane Fairfax in the story, are preoccupied, directly or indirectly, with this one social occasion.

Despite its momentous importance to Highbury at the time, nevertheless, the encounter is doomed to oblivion, as the following anticlimactic chapter reveals, when the blissful mood of the community gives way abruptly to hysteria over Harriet's scrape with an alien reality beyond the shrubbery: "It was the very event to engage those who talk most, the young and the low; and all the youth and servants in the place were soon in the happiness of frightful news. The last night's ball seemed lost in the gipsies" (*E*, 336). The fanfare over this melodramatic incident gives edge to the narrator's "very important, very recordable events" and illustrates again the easy transition from play to seriousness, and vice versa, in daily life.

4. *"Every Savage Can Dance"*

Since play often connotes a childish indulgence, a nonproductive activity enjoyed by the leisured classes, even in comic fiction the ascetic voice may sound most authoritative and put a damper on the gamboling mood. Furthermore, if for one reason or another the game separates the participants too exclusively from the rest of the community, it is likely to be held in suspicion by those without the franchise. In contrast to most encounters in Austen's novels, the ball at the Crown Inn reduces the divisions in the community for its duration and proves costly to the malcontents who would interrupt its progress. Like the more explicit attack on Churchill's frenchified amiability, this village diversion, organized around a centuries-old form of group dancing, alludes tendentiously to the traditional national character threatened by the new urban wealth and manners.

Because the English country dance evolved to simplify the movements of address between the sexes, by the end of the eighteenth century it had become a national institution and an almost unavoidable ritual of courtship.[19] Not surprisingly, therefore, it is an important activity for several Austen heroines—Catherine, Elizabeth, Fanny, and Emma—who discover their marriage partners in the shared experience. Although the English country dance usually included persons of all ages and ranks, married or unmarried, Austen's novels give the impression that it is intended only for the eligible singles; small wonder, then, that both Darcy and Knightley prefer to remain on the sidelines, not wanting to perform with "strangers" and risk unwanted entanglements. Once they do engage in the dance, however, to judge by the effect on their partners, they perform with all the felicity of motion expected of trueborn English gentlemen.

Since the country dance had declined, at least in Austen's novels, to a mating game rather than a diversion for the whole community, at times it is almost incumbent on the heroine to refuse a partner, if only to assert her personal freedom. But then, by a wry twist, the refusers themselves may form an alliance against the indiscriminate herd. Darcy's and Elizabeth's dislike of performing gratuitously, we have noted, turns out to be a bond between them. Although most readers stress the memorable crisis at the Meryton ball when Darcy scandalizes the company by his unwillingness to dance with anyone except Bingley's sisters, the action at the Lucases' party soon afterward more than redeems his "pride," though even more than usual in Austen the narrative omits any explicit interpretation. A subtle refinement of the dance motif in the novel's discourse, this scene brings out at once Darcy's first attraction to Elizabeth by the discovery of their mutual contempt for the London trend-setters (Sir William Lucas is the local Beau Brummel), metonymically represented by the new wave of Scottish and Irish dance forms.

The Lucas party foregrounds masterfully the principal dialogue to counter the mindless diversions elsewhere in the room. After Elizabeth has been forced by Charlotte to play the piano ("pleasing, though by no means capital" [the narrator's judgment, but presumably Darcy's and Elizabeth's as well]) and to sing a few songs, her sister Mary, "always impatient for display" (*PP*, 25), ostentatiously interrupts the mood established by a good attitude in a weak performer:

> Elizabeth, easy and unaffected, had been listened to with much more pleasure, though not playing half so well; and Mary, at the end of a long concerto, was glad to purchase praise and gratitude by Scotch and Irish

airs, at the request of her younger sisters, who with some of the Lucases and two or three officers joined eagerly in dancing at one end of the room.

Mr. Darcy stood near them in silent indignation at such a mode of passing the evening, to the exclusion of all conversation, and was too much engrossed by his own thoughts to perceive that Sir William Lucas was his neighbour, till Sir William thus began.

"What a charming amusement for young people this is, Mr. Darcy!—There is nothing like dancing after all.—I consider it as one of the first refinements of polished societies."

"Certainly, Sir;—and it has the advantage also of being in vogue amongst the less polished societies of the world.—Every savage can dance." (*PP*, 25)

The narrator renders Mr. Darcy's point of view toward Mary's pedantic performance and especially the younger Bennet and Lucas sisters' capers with the officers "to the exclusion of all conversation"; at the same time, moreover, we are free to assume that Elizabeth shares his "silent indignation" at this noisy exhibitionism and has thus already entered his mind-set.

But a crux occurs when Sir William intrudes like Polonius upon the melancholy hero, "too much engrossed by his own thoughts" to be in rhythm with the sham world without. The rejoinder "Every savage can dance" cuts right through the metaphysical illusions of politesse to the primal urges of bodily motion; and even if it is a sign of his excessive shyness in public, Darcy's remark is probably not intended as an attack on "savages" or on dancing as a recreation. In the context of social history, Darcy is witnessing a provincial version of the latest fad at Almack's which, besides pretentiously aping the folkways of Scotland and Ireland (much like Beau Brummel's adoption of the miners' long trousers), is wholly indifferent to the rest of the company and is being performed "at one end of the room" by a few individuals. By contrast, the traditional country dance could include as many as thirty couples in a long room and allowed both exercise and conversation.[20] Whatever thoughts engrossed Darcy at this point will be forever unknown: but perhaps Edmund Burke's worst fears came to his mind: "All the decent drapery of life is to be rudely torn off."[21] Besides displaying proud contempt, Darcy appears from the beginning to resent the disruptive motions that threaten to destroy village culture. Sir William Lucas, who has grown ashamed of that culture, fully deserves the sarcasm his fatuous comment receives. Under the circumstances of the regent's well-known interest in fashions, when Sir William, failing to understand the previous remark, only smiles and asks whether he dances often at St. James's, Darcy's impatience with his fawning interlocutor is comparable to Mr. Bennet's toward Collins:

> "Never, sir."
>> "Do you not think it would be a proper compliment to the place?"
>> "It is a compliment which I never pay to any place if I can avoid it." (*PP*, 25–26)

To judge by the positioning of characters in the scene, this dialogue is tête-à-tête; its privacy, however, makes all the more grotesque the distance between alazon and eiron.

Immediately afterward, a third person arrives to join forces against the common enemy: Sir William, upon seeing Elizabeth moving toward them, attempts to do "a very gallant thing" by steering Darcy into dancing with her; the latter "with grave propriety requested to be allowed the honour of her hand; but in vain" (*PP*, 26). Free indirect discourse here spares the hero some embarrassing verbiage, and we may infer Elizabeth's amused recognition of the anomaly. Rather than a spiteful return for his proud behavior at the Meryton ball, her declining to dance, "Mr. Darcy is all politeness," seems actually to enhance her role as a kindred spirit opposing the master of ceremonies.

Darcy's gentlemanly behavior here involves a risk that usually escapes notice. Given his open attack on any dancing that prevents conversation, when we remember that the music in progress calls for the modish reel or jig, his offer to Elizabeth shows the pluck of a hero. Later, at Netherfield, it is Miss Bingley's turn to be playing as much out of character as the bookish Mary, again "a lively Scotch air," which prompts Darcy to tease Elizabeth as someone with whom he has already reached an understanding:

> "Do not you feel a great inclination, Miss Bennet, to seize such an opportunity of dancing a reel?"

> She smiled, but made no answer. He repeated
> the question, with some surprise at her silence.
> "Oh!" said she, "I heard you before; but I
> could not immediately determine what to say in reply.
> You wanted me, I know, to say 'Yes,' that you might
> have the pleasure of despising my taste; but I always
> delight in overthrowing those kind of schemes, and
> cheating a person of their premeditated contempt.
> I have therefore made up my mind to tell you, that I
> do not want to dance a reel at all—and now despise
> me if you dare."
> "Indeed I do not dare." (*PP*, 52)

Perhaps as her silence implies, Elizabeth may not see the
connection between the music of the moment and the reels
played at the Lucases' when she declined to dance with him;
but doubtless still grateful for her having spared him the ordeal before, Darcy now assumes an intimacy with her on that
account. Best of all, for one who abhors any dancing that rules
out conversation, Elizabeth's witty repartee in the process of
the music answers his taste exactly.

Polite conversation, then, supported by the unaffected
bodily movement of the country dance, is what distinguishes a
civilized society. Characters, we know, are valued by what
they say or by what is said about them; and no matter what
else they do, they come to us mainly through discourse of
some kind. Both Darcy and Elizabeth prevail over the other
characters in the story by the power of their speech; yet they
would be amiss as English types if they did not perform together in the country dance.[22]

Rather than allegorize moral seriousness over play,
then, it is more pertinent to Austen's comic aesthetic to grasp
the characters while they are in motion and at risk in an encounter. Against all the self-conscious, deliberate intentions in
the story, some of the most significant moments reveal the character swept up in the performance, the dancer at one with the
dance, and yet feeling a rare intimacy with another. Through
this bond, discovered in the temporary control over situations
that play gives, characters stand apart from their peers who
uncritically accept the everyday world and remain entrapped
as stereotypes of parody.

II. Desire

When characters play games in Austen's fiction, we are led to believe, they may be sublimating "real-life" conflicts or actually revealing quite serious, even dangerous, intentions within the encounter. As we ponder their behavior, moreover, we are subscribing to a more fundamental game that the author has initiated in her parodic text—namely, the metaphor of lived experience. In this quixotic reflexivity, as the reader watches characters play tricks on other characters, he or she forgets about being manipulated within the linguistic frames arranged by Austen. Without quite knowing it, once our curiosity about the players is aroused, we fall into the role of spectators at an event and project our wishes onto the story.

To begin with, even before the reader himself can become actively engaged with the text, characters are already shown to be prying into each other's affairs and thus stirring up trouble; and almost at once patterns of discourse are set in motion to elicit a finite set of responses among the actors and external witnesses involved. At one level of abstraction, the narrative text insinuates itself like a crossword puzzle, providing just enough information to stir the reader's interest in filling in the empty spaces. Similarly, the charades in *Emma* function reflexively as a play-within-a-play, imitating in miniature the whole enterprise of constituting the text of the novel. In their textual roles, then, narrators/characters intentionally or unintentionally speak in fragments—revealing themselves sufficiently to attract attention yet all the while concealing some part, not merely to keep the story going but because the *whole* story can never be told. In this way parody brings us to a solipsistic standstill in our efforts to fathom the truth of what is said.

Just as it is the precondition of reading, so desire is inherent in the discourse of character. Not surprisingly, therefore, novels tend to stress knowledge as the protagonist's goal; and to this extent the modern detective story answers a primary need of realistic fiction. Of Austen's novels, *Emma* is most obviously plotted on the heroine's ignorance of a central mystery; and her discovery of the truth coincides, we are to understand, with a new self-awareness leading to her own engagement to marry. In the other novels some element of knowledge is also at stake: Marianne Dashwood comes to see that passion is suicidal; Catherine Morland learns the real evil of General Tilney's greed; Elizabeth Bennet sees Darcy in a new light on her visit to Pemberley; Fanny Price comprehends the full impact of Mansfield during her exile in Portsmouth; and Anne Elliot finds at last that Wentworth still loves her. Knowledge and character development, essentials of the bildungsroman formula, are important to Austen's method; and Tory interpretations generally press hard the lessons the errant heroine must learn, as if this didactic gratification itself were not part of the author's game plan.

But in past readings this epistemological emphasis has ignored the dialogical text, which articulates the language of human consciousness in a rhythm of desire and boredom without end. While one part of the story satisfies the appetite for the resolution of conflict, another brings into doubt not only the possibility of fulfillment but even the freedom of the character engaged in the process of willing. It is this primary concern with the state of being that the Austen narrator/character articulates in one form or another throughout the story. Rasselas's demand, "Give me something to desire," implies the fundamental paradox of narrative dynamics: the subject cannot exist literally without *some* intention, and of course the subject is no more than a cipher without the reader's prior act of conjuring her up from the printed page. As it already expresses a desire, Rasselas's demand is tautological; and Imlac's moral psychology is in keeping with the quest motif of the romance: "Some desire is necessary to keep life in motion, and he, whose real wants are supplied, must admit those of fancy." [1] In practice, however, the fictional subject is no more free to choose his terms of desiring than the victim of passion is to alter his feelings. [2]

Desire is not merely a theme in, say, Johnson's and Austen's texts: it is inextricably woven into the fabric of narrative itself; and some authors call attention to this fact more than others, deliberately frustrating the reader's impatience for closure. Recent semiotics help to explain the phenomenon:

> Because signs are used to communicate not only a finished product, the message, but also the processes which make the ongoing production of that message

possible, a text functions much like a painting, which communicates a clearly identifiable narrative message, while also displaying the diacritical marks of that message all across the canvas without allowing a clear distinction of what is form and what is substance.[3]

If the distinction between tenor and vehicle is illusory, Blanchard further points out, the dual structure of showing and telling, axiomatic in any representational theory, no longer obtains; instead of a single, unified text imaging an original, authoritative consciousness, narrative reveals the usual vagaries of overlapping codes and omissions intrinsic to speech.

Programmed within an erotic field, characters sometimes emerge to reflect on the tenuous source of their being and even to complain of their textual fate, as in Don Quixote's allusions to the evil enchanter (the author) who holds him in thrall: "I am in love, for no other reason than that it is incumbent on knights-errant to be so."[4] Austen's parodic narrators take a similar predeterministic stance toward their subject. Marianne Dashwood is duty bound as sentimental heroine, we are told, to match feelings to her situation and "would have thought herself very inexcusable had she been able to sleep at all the first night after parting from Willoughby" (SS, 83). By contrast, opposing texts jostle for control of Catherine Morland's mind:

> Whether she thought of him so much, while she drank her warm wine and water, and prepared herself for bed, as to dream of him when there, cannot be ascertained; but I hope it was no more than in a slight slumber, or a morning doze at most; for if it be true, as a celebrated writer has maintained, that no young lady can be justified in falling in love before the gentleman's love is declared, it must be very improper that a young lady should dream of a gentleman before the gentleman is first known to have dreamt of her. (NA, 29–30)

Although "falling in love" is an attitude imitative of romance and is thus inevitably suspect, not all language of undying devotion is insincere simply because it has been used before; indeed, as Thackeray recognized,[5] there are conditions when acting a role becomes identical with the role itself, when all the world becomes truly a stage. In another context, free indirect discourse obviates the lover's standard aria and thereby communicates deep feeling without any hint of posturing. What matters is Anne Elliot's heartfelt reception of his words:

> Of what he had then written, nothing was to be re-tracted or qualified. *He persisted in having loved none but her. She had never been supplanted. He never even believed himself to see her equal. Thus much indeed he was obliged to acknowledge—that he had been constant unconsciously, nay unintention-ally; that he had meant to forget her, and believed it to be done. He had imagined himself indifferent, when he had only been angry; and he had been unjust to her merits, because he had been a sufferer from them. Her character was now fixed on his mind as perfection itself, maintaining the loveliest medium of fortitude and gentleness.* (P, 241; my emphasis)

Wentworth's actual speech at the time may have been the out-pouring of the individual soul, and nothing in the passage raises doubts about his sincerity; but it also belongs to a literary type, a category of the lover's discourse that Roland Barthes identifies as "The Intractable."[6]

Love is more a situation than a sentiment; and in Austen the situation is nearly always triangular, mediated through a variety of rival claims on the protagonists. Although characters appear to move at random and undergo encounters by happenstance, even the everyday world turns out to be regulated by kinetic contraries. Despite the illusions of the moment, therefore, desire is not free and unconditional; rather, as characters discover by hindsight, it arises from certain op-posing tensions in discourse, subject to no higher authority than the laws of motion. As we see in the same context quoted above, for instance, Wentworth frankly acknowledges the im-pact a rival has in enhancing his desire for Anne in the last hours before his declaration:

> She had not mistaken him. Jealousy of Mr. Elliot had been the retarding weight, the doubt, the torment. That had begun to operate in the very hour of first meeting her in Bath; that had returned, after a short suspension, to ruin the concert; and that had influ-enced him in every thing he had said and done, or omitted to say and do, in the last four-and-twenty

hours. It had been gradually yielding to the better hopes which her looks, or words, or actions occasionally encouraged; it had been vanquished at last by those sentiments and those tones which had reached him while she talked with Captain Harville; and under the irresistible governance of which he had seized a sheet of paper, and poured out his feelings. (*P*, 241)

In this passage, rendered entirely in free indirect discourse, emotion is found to be the work of the moment, a product of energy generated from impetus and resistance, tension and release. Despite the "serious" tone of this confession, moreover, the mechanical forces involved are reminiscent of Pope's epigrammatic style:

> When bold Sir *Plume* had drawn *Clarissa* down,
> *Chloe* stept in, and kill'd him with a Frown;
> She smil'd to see the doughty Hero slain,
> But at her Smile, the Beau reviv'd again.[7]

Again, the parodic disclosure of character, with all its finite dependence on signs for its existence, operates uneasily with the narrative presentation of a moral consciousness, free and unconditioned. But it is this peculiar contradictory sense of character that is distinctive of Austen's comic art.

Because it is most outspokenly "French" in spirit, a fulfillment of the promise shown already in *Lady Susan*, *Emma* is our set piece for the interpretation of desire in Austen. Daring in its untrammeled will-to-power, the narrative of self here moves through one situation after another in an amoral dialectic usually embraced by the villainous characters in the other novels and openly avowed by the Crawfords. As in the other novels where the triangular situation culminates in an ordeal testing the heroine's strength to surrender her desire, Emma must suffer pain and humiliation before she attains the pleasure of at last dominating her world; but she differs from all the other Austen heroines in having a voice in her world from the outset.

From the analysis of the magnitude and direction of desire in *Emma* our inquiry turns to the "body language" of desire, mainly references to food and drink as signs of intentionality. Generally speaking, Austen places a Fieldingesque emphasis upon the appetite as a measure of good or bad nature, as well as of good or bad physical health; and though the motif of food appears in the earliest novels, it is most symbolic in *Mansfield Park* and *Emma*. As the opening metaphor in *Tom Jones* suggests, the reader's primary role is to cannibalize the character, to taste his humor directly on the palate after the narrator-chef has dressed it: "we shall represent Human Nature at first to the keen Appetite of our Reader, in that more plain and simple Manner in which it is found in the Country, and shall hereafter hash and ragoo it with all the high *French* and *Italian* Seasoning of Affectation and Vice which Courts and Cities afford."[8] Processing the text, to extend the metaphor, incorporates language emotively, just as eating food incorporates the object into the self: appetite and consuming (tasting, mastication) are primary impulses, whereas critical judgment, the finesse of comparison, is secondary.

In contrast to desire, which is verbally structured on social relations, appetite, often to our embarrassment, is a basically visceral, nonsituational, and nonverbal urge of the body. Neither wish-making nor hunger is entirely subject to the conscious will, however, but is partly autonomous in the character's emotional life. It is such blind forces within the "real-life" encounter that Austen recognizes in her intriguing phrase "the work of a moment," a sudden release of energy after a period of tension that may seal the character's fate without further ado. Textually these moments lie beyond the margins of words and are represented as interruptions—silence. Without some fragmentation of the character's speech there is no apparent energy behind the words. Of course, not all instances of fragmentation are indubitable proof of "real feeling" but may simply indicate mindlessness, as in Mrs. Allen's nervous ejaculations by the window (*NA*, 60) or in Mr. Elton's feeble attempt to defend Emma's portrait of Harriet (*E*, 48). Hence, by a tactical shift in narrative direction, the parodic voice not only signals the artificiality of representing the self but also the inadequacy of words to convey the *lived* self.

1. *Emma in Love*

Emma is probably the most Gallic novel in English, imbued with the acuity of La Rochefoucauld, Diderot, and Laclos, even to the extent of warping the rural English into caricatures of plain dealers, vulnerable to the sly cynicism from across La Manche. It is not Austen's particular attitudes toward French culture that matter, however, but rather the convenience of this intertextual locus for a discourse on the radical egoism of desire called for in her undercutting of romantic situations. One announced game within the narrative concerns getting the heroine to fall in love the way attractive young women are supposed to do when courted by attractive young men; and, given the strategies of the interlopers in the story, only the exertion of a penetrating intelligence (emulating the author's and external reader's)—and of course the happenstance that conditions *any* moment—will preserve her from her predicted textual fate. Mary Crawford's jocular remark that selfishness needs to be forgiven because it is incurable (*MP*, 68) ignores, to be sure, the positive alternatives of egoism often borne out by Fanny who, besides exercising prudence, also feels compassion toward those who deserve it. In contrast to Fanny, Emma Woodhouse seems to have everything in her favor for the pursuit of happiness; and at times her self-esteem amounts to Mary's version of egoism. If Fanny's project is to become important to someone, Emma's is no less than that of being "first." The converse of Fanny in physical health, emotional temperament, social privilege, and worldly ambition, Emma nonetheless must undergo the same struggle for self-esteem in an environment felt to be competitive and often hostile; and whatever the advantage of her material comfort, she lacks her little predecessor's flawless judgment of others, which is finally the self's best defense. Yet despite her quixotic fantasies involving others, she is surprisingly accurate in assessing her own state of mind—at least more so than Mr. Knightley ever perceives. His project toward the heroine, moreover, ironically parallels Henry Crawford's toward Fanny: "I should like to see Emma in love, and in some doubt of a return; it would do her good" (*E*, 41). He is wrong, we know, in suspecting Frank Churchill to be the one to make her fall in love; and for all his perspicacity in the many offices he performs in the community, right down to the moment of his proposal to Emma he underestimates his own hold over her mind. In many ways Emma's selfishness is no more than her effort to be assertive as an individual, free from his authority; and the momentous events in Highbury are usually beyond her control.

Despite the narrator's introductory judgments of the heroine, Emma's situation from the beginning is anything but secure, as her behavior subsequently implies: her dependence on her father and her competitiveness with Mr. Knightley, her hatred of Jane Fairfax and Miss Bates, her vicarious pleasure as matchmaker, and her continual anxiety over social class. The project of being "first" entails at once a sufficient degree of self-esteem and a belief in the inferiority of the other, and to her credit Emma often has the honesty to admit her failure to meet these requirements. Even in moments of euphoric egoism, moreover, Emma appears uneasy that her own ambitions contradict the Woodhouse ideal of fixed hereditary order.

Her pervasive concern with social rank, reflected throughout the narrative, leads inevitably to making Miss Bates the *pharmakos* of the action. As Northrop Frye explains this ritual scapegoat: "The *pharmakos* is neither innocent nor guilty. He is innocent in the sense that what happens to him is far greater than anything he has done provokes, like the mountaineer whose shout brings down an avalanche. He is guilty in the sense that he is a member of a guilty society, or living in a world where such injustices are an inescapable part of existence."[9] The pressure for something like Emma's violence to Miss Bates that fateful day at Box Hill had been mounting from the outset of the story: "Emma could not resist" (*E*, 370); and notwithstanding Mr. Knightley's lecture on how she should comport herself toward the pitiable old maid, the trauma of this scene surpasses anything the hero, heroine, or narrator can formulate in language.

According to Bernard Paris, the irresistible pressure involved her dislike of Miss Bates for constantly lauding Jane, her fear of being associated with the lower elements of her society, her hatred of the woman for being too good-natured and silly, and for being a spinster burdened with a senile mother and yet apparently content in spite of it, approving of everything and everyone indiscriminately.[10] But to invoke Johnson's Hobbesian point (in *Rambler* no. 166) about the dangers of obsequiousness in receiving charity,[11] Miss Bates clearly brings the violence on herself by talking too much about gratitude, an interpretation that will be elaborated upon in my fourth chapter. Briefly stated, a lack of self-esteem is universally contemptible, whether in the giver or in the receiver. It goes without saying that all this anxious discourse on patronage and subordination reflects the unsettling effects of the new economic and political order that accompanied the French Revolution and the Napoleonic Wars.

A youthful urge to be free of a tiresome society is enough to account for Emma's abhorrence of Miss Bates, but the poor woman's obsessive speeches only make matters worse by reflecting embarrassingly on the giver/receiver roles in egoistically motivated charity. Emma especially resents the woman's fulsome gratitude and even mimics her manner (*E*, 225), as does the narrator, eliciting the reader's own aggressions toward the scapegoat. Again, the situation automatically generates responses from the various participants in the encounter. Knightley's reprimand, however, implies that one is free to feel sympathy when called upon: "She is poor; she has sunk from the comforts she was born to; and, if she live to old age, must probably sink more. Her situation should secure your compassion" (*E*, 375). But in spite of this lofty instruction, Emma is *not* free to choose the appropriate emotions for the circumstance, especially since as a woman it is her burden, after all, to have to enter into conversation with this garrulous fool. The *pride of the moment* had possessed her.

Although the narrator informs us that Emma "was very compassionate; and the distresses of the poor were as sure of relief from her personal attention and kindness, her counsel and her patience, as from her purse" (*E*, 86), the heroine's dialogue with Harriet immediately after visiting the sick cottagers reads like an antidote to the modish sentimentalism: "If we feel for the wretched, enough to do all we can for them, the rest is empty sympathy, only distressing to ourselves" (*E*, 87). Her delight at seeing Mr. Elton on his way to the same poor family drives home again the eighteenth-century moralists' stress on the superior pleasures of giving as opposed to those of receiving: "'To fall in with each other on such an errand as this,' thought Emma; 'to meet in a charitable scheme; this will bring a great increase of love on each side. I should not wonder if it were to bring on the declaration'" (*E*, 87–88). The meditation is self-serving and made at the expense of the poor as well as of the imagined lovers. To be fair, however, except for some religiously inspired selflessness, the alternative to this crisply rational "scheme" is the maudlin discourse on the poor that Austen shunned. Whatever the actual feelings involved, muddled as they must be over such a hopelessly vague and perennial evil, there is a language commensurate with what one can do to alter real circumstances. Furthermore, if her tone seems glib on this occasion, Emma at other moments is sincere enough to send the "whole hind-quarter" of the Hartfield porker to the Bateses' without consulting her father beforehand (*E*, 172); and the "child from the cottage, setting out, according to orders, with her pitcher, to fetch broth from Hartfield" (*E*, 88) also testifies to her genuine charity, comparable to Mr. Knightley's own quiet ministry. Mute actions, rather than banal senti-ments, are the best evidence of charitable feelings. Thus his lecture on her duty to the poor was hardly necessary; what is more to the point is whether *anyone* in Emma's situation could honestly avoid expressing contempt for Miss Bates. In an un-usually probing conversation Harriet herself ventured the com-parison between Emma and Miss Bates:

> "That is as formidable an image as you could present, Harriet; and if I thought I should ever be like Miss Bates! so silly—so satisfied—so smiling—so pros-ing—so undistinguishing and unfastidious—and so apt to tell every thing relative to every body about me, I would marry to-morrow. But between *us*, I am convinced there never can be any likeness, except in being unmarried."
>
> "But still, you will be an old maid! and that's so dreadful!"
>
> "Never mind, Harriet, I shall not be a poor old maid; and it is poverty only which makes celibacy contemptible to a generous public!" (*E*, 84–85)

As Emma goes on about the crucial difference between being a single woman with means and one without, her vindictiveness toward Miss Bates is clear-cut ("she is only too good natured and too silly to suit me" [*E*, 85]) and yet guarded at the same time: "Poverty certainly has not contracted her mind: I really believe, if she had only a shilling in the world, she would be very likely to give away sixpence of it; and nobody is afraid of her: that is a great charm" (*E*, 85). It is a strange concession for Emma to make, the most positive ever in the story, after ridiculing her enemy's behavior; and she may indeed fear some likeness between themselves other than in being unmar-ried. Whatever the hidden motives, Emma cannot exercise the requisite charity unless she is confident that her wealth distinguishes her from the poor woman; and Knightley never recognizes this instability.

Emma's situation resembles that described by Stendhal, who explored the structure of egoism against the cataclysmic changes of the Napoleonic era and identified the stock character of the *vaniteux*. Raised by sycophants who had flattered him into the belief that he should be happier than others, the *vaniteux* enters the world with a metaphysical handicap: "It is because the *vaniteux* feels the emptiness mentioned in Ecclesiastes growing inside him that he takes refuge in shallow behavior and imitation. Because he cannot face his nothingness he throws himself on Another who seems to be spared by the curse." [12] If in orthodox Christian morality pride and vanity are illusory states produced by a turning away from God and a withdrawing into the self, the major European novelists from Stendhal to Proust, as Girard states, have shown that the contrary conditions of other-directedness are imitative to the extreme of self-abandonment known as *bovaryism*. [13] While Emma Woodhouse's possessive desire may culminate only in painful embarrassment in contrast to Emma Bovary's suicidal narcissism, both characters nevertheless experience the need to transcend their circumscribed conditions ("so absolutely fixed, in the same place" [*E*, 143]) and to seek escape in a mediator of some kind. If Emma Bovary is shown to have read the wrong material for dealing with the everyday situations, Emma Woodhouse is no less romantically inclined when it comes to "reading" the movements of others. Her fantasy of Jane Fairfax's erotic link with Mr. Dixon, for instance, plays upon the conventional triadic arrangement of romantic passion.

Perhaps the clearest tie between the two Emmas is their bourgeois malaise of snobbism. The antithesis of good citizenship, snobbery is, ironically, a problem arising from a more or less egalitarian society, where class distinctions no longer protect the individual from the anxiety of status: significantly, the age of the prince regent and Beau Brummell abounded with controversy over dress and manners. [14] The faithful medieval mind, absorbed with the vanity of human existence, could look upward to the divine mediator for deliverance; after the collapse of the ancien régime, the desiring subject was reduced to making a god of others in the finite world while still condemned to self-contempt. Since the mediator was no longer divine but merely possessed of some intangible social advantages like nobility, the snob was likely to hate himself in the person imitated: "Hatred is individualistic. It nourishes fiercely the illusion of an absolute difference between the Self and that Other from which nothing separates it." [15]

Deprived of the means of skirting this illusion, Emma tacitly shares her father's phobia toward social mobility in principle; and like Mrs. Elton's Maple Grove snobbery, Emma's resentment of any aspirant among the middle ranks contradicts the same ambitious individualism which both women endorse for themselves. Their emulation of Mr. Knightley is symptomatic: while Mrs. Elton tries to vulgarize him by breaching decorum of address, thus pretending an unwarranted familiarity, Emma values him all the more as a role model by keeping him on a pedestal for the public to admire at a distance. Despite the wishful thinking embodied in the comic plot, which finally assigns appropriate places to the various female contenders, there is a lingering suspicion to the very end that not even an exemplary gentleman like Mr. Knightley can protect the social hierarchy from the egalitarian rhetoric, on the one hand, and from the elitist overreaching of the nouveau riche, on the other. [16]

Emma's disapproval of Robert Martin for being a farmer, of the Coles for their former connections in "trade" (her father refuses their invitation on the grounds of his health and Mr. Cole's temperament, but clearly it is the presumption of upstarts that bothers him most), of Mrs. Goddard for being merely a teacher, and of Miss Bates for having nothing but the memory of her clergyman father, shows her own dread of the second- and third-rate; simultaneously, it betrays her own lack of a clear identity in this society. An exception to this behavior is her kindness toward Mr. Weston and an attractive loyalty to the woman who married him; nevertheless, in later scenes she privately resents his indiscriminate affability.

Throughout this story the language of desire is emphatically based on difference and hierarchy. Mr. Elton's proposal shocks Emma into evaluating her present status as the heiress of thirty thousand pounds: "Perhaps it was not fair to expect him to feel how very much he was her inferior in talent, and all the elegancies of mind. The very want of such equality might prevent his perception of it; but he must know that in fortune and consequence she was greatly his superior"

(*E*, 136). Though acknowledging the inferiority of her talent to
Jane's, whose social life otherwise seems predetermined to fall
well below hers, Emma needs everything at her disposal to
condemn Elton's presumptuous claim on her. In the midst of
what the narrator terms her "raving," however, is the important revelation that the Woodhouses stem from the "younger
branch" of an old family, that Hartfield is only a "notch" in the
Donwell Abbey estate, and that "their fortune, from other
sources," [that is, from trade] made them "scarcely secondary
to Donwell Abbey itself, in every other kind of consequence."
Scarcely secondary, but *secondary* nonetheless! Not fully apparent to the heroine is her deep-seated rivalry with the hero
on account of his greater power derived from family, fortune,
talent, and male prerogative, even as she paradoxically upholds
his standards for her own strivings. In spite of her outward
self-assurance, therefore, Emma yearns with other womanly
aspirants, including Mrs. Elton and Mrs. Churchill, to find
the means of her own personal legitimacy in a man's power
structure; and the consequence is her neurotic fear of bearing
any resemblance to a disturbingly nimble, if impoverished,
old maid.

Implicit in the dynamics of desire is a falling-off of
energy, when the mind becomes temporarily depressed by
nothing to wish for; and, again, the character must exert herself if only to prevent redundancy and oblivion. The failure of
the Box Hill scheme, in sharp contrast to the brief happiness
attained at the Crown Inn ball, is simply a moment of truth
revealing the spiritual anarchy of the Highbury world, which
threatens to sink under its own ennui; and not even the audacious gamesters can stem the contagion: "At first it was down-
right dulness to Emma. She had never seen Frank Churchill
so silent and stupid. He said nothing worth hearing—looked
without seeing—admired without intelligence—listened without knowing what she said. While he was so dull, it was no wonder that Harriet should be dull likewise, and they were both
insufferable" (*E*, 367).

Since blaming Churchill for Harriet's dullness only
shows how far afield Emma's perception can stray, a moralist
might take the view that this ennui is an evil of egoism and
that the hero's stoic rationalism provides immunity from this
disease. Thus Mrs. Weston's earlier remark could serve as the
norm here: "I do not think Mr. Knightley would be much dis-

turbed by Miss Bates. Little things do not irritate him" (*E*, 225–26). Yet elsewhere Emma's mind can also be provident toward little things, and without any assistance from Knightley. While waiting for Harriet to finish her purchases at Ford's, Emma converts all the trivial activities outside the door into a picturesque townscape: "A mind lively and at ease, can do with seeing nothing, and can see nothing that does not answer" (*E*, 233). But neither reason nor the imagination can save Emma from the paucity of objects to contemplate on that particular day; the very necessity of mingling with unwanted company has a claustrophobic effect, forcing her into aggressive speech for release. Until this moment, access to her hostile feelings was mainly the privilege of the dilatory Harriet or of the narrator. As her own recommendation to Frank Churchill on self-command (*E*, 364) assures us, Emma knows painfully well her duty at Box Hill but cannot resist her attack anyway.

Emma is not to blame, however, for the ennui that brought on the offending words. At Donwell the day before, we recall, not even Mr. Knightley's flawless hospitality could prevent the comic world from falling apart; and Emma's most enjoyable moment was spent alone in reverie over a pastoral, harmonious world: "It was a sweet view—sweet to the eye and the mind. English verdure, English culture, English comfort, seen under a sun bright, without being oppressive" (*E*, 360). This is the daytime equivalent to Fanny Price's nocturnal repose by the window, away from the madding crowd; thus, rather than polar opposites, both heroines respond to the "luxury of silence" (*MP*, 278) and to the "comfort of being sometimes alone" (*E*, 363).

In another context, for instance in Marianne Dashwood's narcissistic moods, Austen might have invoked Johnson on activity as therapy against the insatiable desires spawned in solitude and idleness; but Emma is no solipsistic dreamer and attempts to carry out her social duties. Lacking the opportunity of private indulgence in the scenery at Box Hill, a pleasure that seems unaccountably lost on the others, she enters the play of conversation as a modus vivendi to cope with the existential emptiness felt from the beginning of the day. Emma's problem here is not self-deception, nor is it an uncritical love of games, but rather the disturbing absence of a saving illusion: "She laughed because she was disappointed;

and though she liked him [Churchill] for his attentions, and thought them all, whether in friendship, admiration, or play- fulness, extremely judicious, they were not winning back her heart" (*E*, 368). In the predicament of having nothing to de- sire, Emma resorts to a familiar aristocratic text, to erotic play, "glad to be enlivened" (368) for the moment by imagining (self-consciously) her part as female libertine, with Miss Bates as the prescribed petit bourgeois victim of her wit. It was Mary Crawford's predicament as well; but Emma, in contrast, shares Fanny's concern, if not her talent, for feeling the emo- tion appropriate to the situation.

No matter that the plot's didactic contour requires it, Emma's humiliation by Knightley's rebuke discloses yet an- other French text in her erotic pleasure derived from pain. Despite the requirement by the Protestant ethic of a conver- sion, her visceral hatred of Miss Bates remains constant to the end of the novel; and her real change of heart appears mainly in the mediating friendship formed with Jane Fairfax after her discovery of the engagement, a friendship anticipated at vari- ous moments in the heroine's consciousness earlier in the story. What is most significant about the energy released in this encounter, however, is that Mr. Knightley's angry words arouse a new feeling in her that neither she nor the narrator ever interprets: *the thrill of being punished.* As long as she can remain detached, Emma's relationships with others, when not merely boring, involve mainly vicarious pleasure. Harriet, for instance, is a delightful plaything, a "walking companion," perhaps a David Hamilton daydream, with "those soft blue eyes and all those natural graces" (*E*, 23). But in contrast to her usual lackadaisical interest in others, Emma's response to Mr. Knightley's wrath is passionate—a rare feeling of ecstasy, a complete surrender of the self to the other on the model of Christian agape:

> In this ecstatic love, then, we are far from egocentric love. The lover has no thought of himself, except that he would willingly give his all for the other. Secondly, this love is almost a dark passion; it is a fire and a wound; it is violent and sacrificial; it cares nothing for reason, because it is a madness and a rapture, and lastly it has no ulterior purpose; it seeks no reward;

love is the end and consummation. Love, therefore, of this kind is above all; it looks outside itself to another person, and it is beyond reason and nature.[17]

The "wound" inflicted drives her on a mission of "penitence" to Miss Bates; and during Knightley's farewell before going to London she experiences something akin to rapture (a word usually bracketed in Austen's text for feelings imitative of romantic texts) at his slightest gesture of approval:

> —It seemed as if there were an instantaneous impression in her favour, as if his eyes received the truth from her's, and all that had passed of good in her feelings were at once caught and honoured.—He looked at her with a glow of regard. She was warmly gratified—and in another moment still more so, by a little movement of more than common friendliness on his part.—He took her hand;—whether she had not herself made the first motion, she could not say—she might, perhaps, have rather offered it—but he took her hand, pressed it, and certainly was on the point of carrying it to his lips—when, from some fancy or other, he suddenly let it go. (*E*, 385–86)

There are few scenes anywhere in Austen that come as close to depicting the heroine's utter trust in the male counterpart, without the least hint of ridicule, as this one of unfulfilled desire. Although oblivious to the fact, Mr. Knightley, in contrast to Henry Crawford's experiment on Fanny, has succeeded in his project of making Emma fall in love and be in doubt of having it returned.

The violence of this encounter has unleashed new energies and refined the heroine's awareness of herself as a sexual being through reference to quasi-religious texts on suffering and humiliation. Emma Woodhouse, of course, is not Emma Bovary; and it may be that she is simply exaggerating her guilt and indulging in masochistic dreams as an alternative to the ultimate crisis of Box Hill, the utter dearth of eros at the moment. Having savored this frightening experience of ritual bondage, however, she readily snaps back to her former self and overcompensates for her brief defeat by dreams of grandeur, feeling most in command of events just before discovering Harriet's love for Knightley. Armed with the knowledge of

Jane's and Frank's engagement, she mitigates her anger at having been used by considering what the news will mean for "Harriet, poor Harriet!"—now presumably reduced to the carrion of dark passion. Furthermore, though having been duped all along by Churchill, she takes comfort in the thought that her vain flirtation had given her real power over Jane: "—Emma could now imagine why her own attentions had been slighted. This discovery laid many smaller matters open. No doubt it had been from jealousy.—In Jane's eyes she had been a rival; and well might any thing she could offer of assistance or regard be repulsed" (*E*, 403).

Emma is an imaginist, as many readers have said, but the narrative only superficially declares her need of abandoning this talent. On the contrary, she emulates her author's own intertextuality as she "reads" Jane's story. Mock heroic metaphors of torture imply all the sadism of imagining the Gothic heroine's writhing agonies: "An airing in the Hartfield carriage would have been the rack, and arrow-root from the Hartfield storeroom must have been poison" (*E*, 403). It was only a passing thought; but nevertheless, to the narrator's secret delight, it could not be stifled. The next sentence weighs the degree of power gained by her newfound knowledge against the quantity of charity to be allotted to either Jane or Harriet under the circumstances: "She understood it all; and as far as her mind could disengage itself from the injustice and selfishness of angry feelings, she acknowledged that Jane Fairfax would have neither elevation nor happiness beyond her desert. But poor Harriet was such an engrossing charge! There was little sympathy to be spared for any body else" (*E*, 403). As if rewound all the more tightly after her momentary selflessness and dependence, Emma's ego glories in the knowledge of the secret engagement and its apparently dire consequences for her protégée.

While deriving self-esteem from her exclusive grasp of events ("She understood it all"), Emma can rise to being charitable toward her rivals; but with the return of self-contempt at Harriet's traumatic declaration, she loses control and suffers the deepest jealousy ever. Like Victor Frankenstein confronting the monster of his own creation, Emma panics at the metamorphosis of the sweet, docile, and selfless object into a discriminating judge of gentlemen, who repeats the very words of an earlier lesson on the differences between a farmer and a man of quality. Now, in imitation of other Austen heroines, strength in defeat is all that Emma can hope for as she endures Harriet's detailed account of her romance with Knightley until they are happily interrupted by Mr. Woodhouse's entrance; but after all the compression of outward demeanor, when finally alone, "this was the spontaneous burst of Emma's feelings: 'Oh God! that I had never seen her!'" (*E*, 411). At this point one may surmise that she actually regrets Harriet's recovery from the "putrid sore throat." Now that the distance in triangular desire has dangerously narrowed and brought the three participants almost face to face, there is no brooking the usurper ("there would be no need of *compassion* to the girl who believed herself loved by Mr. Knightley").

Whatever her personal loss in this matter, Emma resorts to a snobbish elevation of the beloved to vindicate her hatred of the rival; and the whole reverie is in free indirect discourse:

> Mr. Knightley and Harriet Smith!—It was an union to distance every wonder of the kind.—The attachment of Frank Churchill and Jane Fairfax became commonplace, threadbare, stale in the comparison, exciting no surprise, presenting no disparity, affording nothing to be said or thought.—Mr. Knightley and Harriet Smith!—Such an elevation on her side! Such a debasement on his!—It was horrible to Emma to think how it must sink him in the general opinion, to foresee the smiles, the sneers, the merriment it would prompt at his expense; the mortification and disdain of his brother, the thousand inconveniences to himself. (*E*, 413)

Aside from her obvious rivalry with her female charge, Emma dreads the possibility that the man she had always admired from a sexual distance, without the threatening necessity of marriage in adult life, should stumble into the mill of the conventional and deprive her of further imitative desire: his sterling class is her only assurance of that "absolute difference" to distinguish herself from the second- and third-rate. Her eventual sympathy with Jane, however, shows a liberal impulse that contradicts this obsession with hierarchy and assures us that the sentiments toward Harriet are greatly distorted by jealousy.

A major twist to this novel, nevertheless, is its refusal to bow to conventional plot solutions to restore a neat equilibrium between the heroine and her rival. Characters have no way of escaping the "evil of their situation." If Emma's feelings toward Harriet immediately after the fateful discovery are unrelievedly selfish, they do not improve even after Knightley's proposal abruptly allays her worst fears. Upon his spontaneous words of love, Emma's immediate reaction is to gloat over her enemy's defeat: "to see . . . that Harriet was nothing; that she was every thing herself" (*E*, 430). With a perverse gush of egotism, she hugs herself for not having revealed to him the truth about Harriet's error: "there was time also to rejoice that Harriet's secret had not escaped her, and to resolve that it need not and should not." Although her self-esteem had enabled her to take a charitable view of Jane's fortune, here it requires a persistent rejection of Harriet as a friend because of the imagined rivalry between them. While listening to Knightley's proposal, Emma can think only of Harriet's demise and her own determination to withhold any assistance: "for as to any of that heroism of sentiment which might have prompted her to entreat him to transfer his affection from herself to Harriet, as infinitely the most worthy of the two . . . Emma had it not" (*E*, 431). Then, in a parody of religious sacrifice, which warns us against taking too seriously the whole business of the heroine's moral reform: "She felt for Harriet, with pain and with contrition; but no flight of generosity run mad, opposing all that could be probable or reasonable, entered her brain" (*E*, 431). As in the conjunction of Mars and Venus, sexual love is warfare; and the narrative leaves few doubts about how deeply felt were the "pain" and "contrition" for her vanquished enemy.

Although from this stage on Harriet is merely "dead weight" to Emma, a continually irksome reminder of past errors, the former is still full of surprises: for instance, her quick return to Robert Martin ("it really was too much to hope even of Harriet, that she could be in love with more than *three* men in one year" [*E*, 450]); and the discovery of her humble origins ("The stain of illegitimacy, unbleached by nobility or wealth, would have been a stain indeed" (*E*, 428]). Hence, as Emma's self-esteem reaches new heights by the end of the story: "—The intimacy between her and Emma must sink; their friendship must change into a calmer sort of good will;

and, fortunately, what ought to be, and must be, seemed already beginning, and in the most gradual, natural manner" (*E*, 482). A question never raised in the text is whether Emma would ever have gone so far as to become engaged had it not been for Harriet's misapprehension of Mr. Knightley's love; in any case, the heroine is too caught up in the mechanics of triangular desire to see that her power over the rival has obviated her former detachment. Emma's ego now depends precariously upon Mr. Knightley's favor, and the alternative is too frightening to contemplate—an utter void equivalent to death.

In view of her entrapment in the text, therefore, Emma could readily say, with Don Quixote, that she is in love because it is incumbent upon the heroine of romance to be so. If love proves to be more a situation than an idea, perhaps La Rochefoucauld best describes the motive: "It is difficult to define love; what can be said is that in the soul it is a passion to dominate another, in the mind it is mutual understanding, whilst in the body it is simply a delicately veiled desire to possess the beloved after many rites and mysteries."[18] Another maxim of the great French egoist suggests why desire is inevitably triangular in Austen: "Jealousy is in some measure just and reasonable, since it merely aims at keeping something that belongs to us or we think belongs to us, whereas envy is a frenzy that cannot bear anything that belongs to others."[19] Compassion, charity, and friendship are surely possible in Austen's fictional world; but what is most remarkable about her comic art is the moral neutrality it shows toward such traditional vices as hatred, jealousy, envy, pride, and other modes of self-aggrandizement condemned by Christian tradition. From our brief analysis of Emma as desiring subject, the reason for this neutrality should be clear: emotion (the *character*'s emotion, to give it a place in the text) is not free and spontaneous but inherently contextual and triadic in structure. "Some desire is necessary to keep life in motion"; unless a character is given the situation necessary for desire, however, there is no life. This is the vicious circle that Emma comprehends in the end and exploits unconscionably to be first. Throughout her struggle to avoid the pitfalls of romantic passion and the degradation of being among the second- and third-rate heroines of pulp fiction, Emma nevertheless emulates other texts, especially from the eighteenth-century French libertine tradition; and thus without always knowing it, she has no choice but to play the game prescribed for her.

2.   *"The Power of Eating and Drinking"*

As events prove, Emma's following remark is dramatically ironic: "There does seem to be a something in the air of Hartfield which gives love exactly the right direction, and sends it into the very channel where it ought to flow" (*E*, 75). At the moment, her words are derisive of Mr. Elton's "falling in love" as a ridiculous loss of selfhood. When she herself falls, as we have seen, the experience is not the self-destructive desire, the "dark passion" that de Rougemont traces to medieval cults;[20] rather, it is a form of agape, an ecstatic surrender of ego to the beloved that seems both sacred and sexual. It does not take long, of course, for Emma to revert to her old self and "bad faith" roles; nevertheless, the evocation of desire and renunciation in her narrative has a quasi-religious intensity that sets her apart from the other characters. It is this mythical deliverance from the ritual bondage that A. O. J. Cockshut observes when citing Austen, along with Richardson and D. H. Lawrence, as a writer who renders sexual conflict with unusual candor.[21]

Yet because of censorship, literary decorum, and other historical restraints, in Austen's text the body is scarcely described at all, whether clothed or naked. It is known or "lived," however, through certain metonyms, especially those of food and drink; and, as in Fielding and Sterne, even these references sometimes depend on innuendo to avoid the viscera. Although *Don Quixote* is usually regarded as the prototype of the novel, its attack on conventions of romance employs the digestive tract more boldly than any fiction before Joyce; to a large extent its form resembles what Frye calls the anatomy of satire, which tends "to become what the world calls obscene," forcing us to contemplate "excretion, copulation, and similar embarrassments."[22] Like Don Quixote and Sancho, Gulliver is disarmingly frank about urination and defecation, though all are reticent about sexual intercourse and, together with Uncle Toby, Walter Shandy, and Leopold Bloom, may be impotent.

By contrast, the romance usually has such "high" norms of reality that not only bodily functions but even the mention of food seems inappropriate. The witty narrator in Gottfried von Strassburg's *Tristan*, for instance, distinguishes between everyday reality and the erotic world:

> Some people are smitten with curiosity and astonishment, and plague themselves with the question how these two companions, Tristan and Isolde, nourished themselves in this wasteland! I will tell them and assuage their curiosity. They looked at one another and nourished themselves with that! Their sustenance was the eye's increase. They fed in their grotto on nothing but love and desire. The two lovers who formed its court had small concern for their provender.[23]

Lacking such passionate abandonment, however, Austen's characters do have physical appetites; and their interest in food belongs to the text of festive comedy.

Mimetic criticism, as seen in Frye and Cockshut, assumes an Aristotelian hierarchy of mind over body and thus credits realism to a text that refers to "low" aspects of physical and social existence not mentioned in other genres. Although limited for the most part to investigations of a privileged class, Austen's novels do reveal by innuendo and symbolic allusion a surprising frankness toward the human body; and occasionally there are traces of the Augustan satirist's voice anatomizing characters as fundamentally material beings subject to blind appetites. A basic element of exchange, the concrete nexus of subject and object, food initiates a variety of behavior among donors and recipients alike, ranging from simple gustatory impulses to the most neurotic fixations in self-affirming, from such stock comic humors as gluttons and hypochondriacs to discriminating gourmets and good providers. Although stereotypes exist independently and invite predictable responses, the discourse involving food and drink has a wide range of intentions in the Austen text.

For the early-nineteenth-century woman writer especially, the allusion to appetite had political significance. Set against the ascetic moralists of the time, who, like Dr. Gregory, believed that the "luxury of eating" for a woman "is beyond expression indelicate and disgusting,"[24] Austen's cheerful reference to food in her letters and novels betrays a meaningful aplomb. Even before the Victorian period, when angel worship reached its peak, the mores of woman's "delicacy" made it unthinkable for her to have any appetite at all—whether sexual or gustatory; and thus Austen seems puckish in reporting an acquaintance's aberration: "Mrs. F. A. has had one fainting fit lately; it came on as usual after eating a hearty dinner, but did not last long."[25]

While overeaters come in for attack in her fiction, the ones without a real zest for food seem the least sympathetic; and, of course, her satire on the cult of sensibility ridicules neurotic pretensions concerning diet. Rather than take laudanum to settle the nerves, as her hypochondriacal mother was used to doing, Austen held the commonsensical view that eating well was the best remedy. When her brother Edward arrives in Bath looking "fagged," she trusts that the "bustle of sending for tea, coffee, and sugar, &c., and going out to taste a cheese himself, will do him good."[26] Similarly, when Frank Churchill came "out of humour" to the party at Donwell, Emma "knew that eating and drinking were often the cure of such incidental complaints, she recommended his taking some refreshment; he would find abundance of every thing in the dining-room—and she humanely pointed out the door" (*E*, 364). As a stereotype of sensibility, Marianne Dashwood is unwilling to dance and becomes quickly exhausted by the exercise; and true to form, she has no appetite for days on end. Likewise Jane Fairfax, while enduring the uncertainty of her secret engagement, has special dietary problems; and Mr. Woodhouse's dread of food, above all of the wedding cake, seems to imply his morbid repression of sexual desire.

Aside from its more narrowly feminist implications, food can generally be a means of expressing power and influence in society. Despite all her other faults, Mrs. Bennet redeems herself near the end of the story by providing a festive board for her well-to-do guests: "she did not think any thing less than two courses, could be good enough for a man, on whom she had such anxious designs, or satisfy the appetite and pride of one who had ten thousand a-year" (*PP*, 338). The result of her good sense is propitious: "The dinner was as well dressed as any I ever saw. The venison was roasted to a turn—and everybody said, they never saw so fat a haunch. The soup was fifty times better than what we had at the Lucas's last week;

and even Mr. Darcy acknowledged, that the partridges were remarkably well done; and I suppose he has two or three French cooks at least" (*PP*, 342). In *Mansfield Park* the food service seems identified less with any particular person (Lady Bertram is too indolent to provide comfort herself) than with the house as an institution. Thus, while entrapped like Clarissa by an unwanted suitor, Fanny feels joy upon being interrupted by a domestic ritual: "The solemn procession, headed by Baddely, of tea-board, urn, and cake-bearers, made its appearance, and delivered her from a grievous imprisonment of body and mind" (*MP*, 344). In contrast, she perceives the misery at Portsmouth, "the boys begging for toasted cheese, her father calling out for his rum and water, and Rebecca never where she ought to be" (*MP*, 387). Whereas Mansfield's Baddely can minister such a sumptuous ritual, Portsmouth's Rebecca codifies the utter despair of poverty:

> She [Fanny] was so little equal to Rebecca's puddings, and Rebecca's hashes, brought to table as they all were, with such accompaniments of half-cleaned plates, and not half-cleaned knives and forks, that she was very often constrained to defer her heartiest meal, till she could send her brothers in the evening for biscuits and buns. After being nursed up at Mansfield, it was too late in the day to be hardened at Portsmouth. (*MP*, 413)

At least in consciousness, Fanny is safely removed from T. S. Eliot's typist, who "lays out food in tins"; she is also hardly Trilling's ascetic Christian heroine when envying Henry Crawford's freedom to enjoy the "best dinner that a capital inn afforded" (*MP*, 412).[27]

For transparent economic reasons, epicurean indulgence is regarded as a male prerogative; but it appears to be more a compulsive disorder, not a pleasure, as in Sir John Middleton's manic hospitality as compensation for his wife's cold aloofness. Similarly, Mr. Weston's married life, in Mr. John Knightley's view, depends "much more upon what is called *society* for his comforts, that is, upon the power of eating and drinking, and playing whist with his neighbours five times a-week, than upon family affection, or any thing that home affords" (*E*, 96). Taxed by another chronic mingler, the Dashwoods decline Middleton's aggressive hospitality: they had "no curiosity to see how Mr. and Mrs. Palmer ate their dinner, and had no expectation of pleasure from them in any other way" (SS, 108–09). Not having such power of their own to bolster selfhood, the visit would be only a punishment to the Dashwood women. Yet, even the Middletons' company is more welcome than that of the John Dashwoods: "The dinner was a grand one, the servants were numerous, and every thing bespoke the Mistress's inclination for shew, and the Master's ability to support it" (SS, 233). At this ostentatious event, there was "no poverty of any kind, except of conversation." Again, the power of eating and drinking is ruthlessly exploitative of the disenfranchised.

In other contexts, besides sheer self-aggrandizement, behavior associated with food reveals less conscious forms of giving and taking. Because of political inequality, Mary Wollstonecraft asserts, one sex is more prone to gourmandizing than the other:

> Men are certainly more under the influence of their appetites than women; and their appetites are more depraved by unbridled indulgence and the fastidious contrivances of satiety. Luxury has introduced a refinement of gluttony which is so beastly, that a perception of seemliness of behaviour must be worn out before one being could eat immoderately in the presence of another, and afterwards complain of the oppression that his intemperance naturally produced.[28]

Austen's humorous gluttons, in keeping with this contemporary view, reflect some of the traditional harangues against luxury; but, of greater interest to the modern reader, they embody nuances that go beyond such tendentiousness. Besides addressing a social evil, her overeaters are mainly ciphers in a pattern of frantic acquisitiveness. Although General Tilney, for instance, is not the Gothic villain that Catherine had imagined, nevertheless his voracious appetite signifies the shameless greed subsequently demonstrated. At Woodston, Henry triumphs in offering his father a meal good enough to eat but falls short in the quantity of food expected:

> She could not but observe that the abundance of the dinner did not seem to create the smallest astonishment in the General; nay, that he was even looking at the side-table for cold meat which was not there. His

son and daughter's observations were of a different
kind. They had seldom seen him eat so heartily at any
table but his own; and never before known him so
little disconcerted by the melted butter's being oiled.
(*NA*, 214–15)

Unlike her friends, who are accustomed to their father's eating
habits, Catherine feels a Gothic "astonishment" toward the
giant masticator, a monster almost on the scale of Kronos and
equally capable of consuming his own children.

Among all the overindulgers in Austen's repertory,
Dr. Grant is self-destructively hedonistic and of course a disgrace to his profession; yet, compulsively driven in his vice, he
is too easy a target for the alazons in the story. Not only is Mrs.
Norris's criticism of him superfluous, but her own niggardli-
ness is a worse evil because it is hypocritically represented as
thrift. Besides alluding to the stereotype defined by Wollstonecraft, Austen doubtless has in mind the eighteenth-century
moralist's topic of the "contempt of the clergy," which culmi-
nated in the Evangelical movement;[29] and with such a help-
meet as Fanny, Edmund, by contrast, will become an exemplary preacher.

So much is clear. But if Dr. Grant lacks any real
authority in his calling, he nevertheless "talks for victory"
against Mrs. Norris on a subject he knows best—*food*, after
her pious remark about the apricot tree planted by her deceased husband:

> "The tree thrives well beyond a doubt, madam," re-
> plied Dr. Grant. "The soil is good; and I never pass it
> without regretting, that the fruit should be so little
> worth the trouble of gathering."
>
> "Sir, it is a moor park, we bought it as a moor
> park, and it cost us—that is, it was a present from Sir
> Thomas, but I saw the bill, and I know it cost seven
> shillings, and was charged as a moor park."
>
> "You were imposed on, ma'am," replied Dr.
> Grant; "these potatoes have as much the flavour of a
> moor park apricot, as the fruit from that tree. It is an
> insipid fruit at the best; but a good apricot is eatable,
> which none from my garden are." (*MP*, 54)

Like most other references to food, the conversation here occurs without any narrative interpolation; and the reader is on

his own to determine its significance. At the level of allegory, the spiritually barren Mrs. Norris is not only childless but, as is implied by her preoccupation with the price of the tree, a blight on her husband's husbandry as well (Chaucer's "shiten shepherde").[30] Dr. Grant's own marriage is also sterile; and his gluttony seems to have displaced his sexual drive, as Tom Bertram, who should know, shrewdly observes to Fanny while Mrs. Grant is dancing with Mr. Yates: "'between ourselves, she, poor woman! must want a lover as much as any one of them. A desperate full life her's must be with the doctor,' making a sly face as he spoke towards the chair of the latter" (*MP*, 119). This motif of gourmandizing as a perversion of the sexual appetite already appeared in the character of Mr. Hurst, whose motions include ragouts, claret, or cards as alternatives to sleeping on the sofa.[31] What is particularly interesting about the conversation above, however, is the way an otherwise negative stereotype like Tom can suddenly gain a voice in the text and direct our attention to meanings neglected in the "normative" commentary.

Curiously, a related stereotype, the drunkard, far from the impotence of the glutton, seems to have a dangerously overactive sexual appetite, and is not only given to producing, like Mr. Price, a number of unwanted children but is also callous, withdrawn, and hostile toward women as companions. Tom Bertram himself cannot take Fanny seriously because from the first she exhibits, more than his sisters, a feminine vulnerability. In general, Austen's topers are coarsely physical toward women and assume that their whole purpose in life is to catch rich husbands. The uncertain sexual connotation of "tumble" implies that the female is a mere object of appetite, without any mind of her own.[32] While advising Elinor about Willoughby's potential, Sir John Middleton remarks bluffly: "if I were you, I would not give him up to my younger sister in spite of all this tumbling down hills" (*SS*, 44); and on their way to Claverton Down, John Thorpe makes a similar jest to Catherine: "They want to get their tumble over" (*NA*, 61). Thorpe's allusion to the quantity of drinking at Oxford further implies the sort of masculine bawdy that his inebriated conversation would involve.

At the opposite extreme of the gluttons, though sometimes just as compulsive, are the good providers, usually jovial and healthy nurturing parental types. Mrs. Jennings is an amiable host on the journey to London, "only disturbed that she could not make them choose their own dinners at the inn, nor extort a confession of their preferring salmon to cod, or boiled fowls to veal cutlets" (*SS*, 160). During Marianne's crisis this maternal surrogate tries a "variety of sweetmeat and olives, and a good fire" (*SS*, 193) to raise her spirits, but to no avail: "And I declare if she is not gone away without finishing her wine! And the dried cherries too!" (*SS*, 194). Finally, when the ultimate medicine is proffered, "some of the finest old Constantia wine in the house" (*SS*, 197–98) that Mrs. Jenning's husband used to imbibe for his gout, Elinor herself takes it, "its healing powers on a disappointed heart might be as reasonably tried on herself as on her sister" (*SS*, 198).

Like Goldsmith's endearing philanthropists,[33] the most exemplary providers in Austen work behind the scenes to reduce the onus of giving as well as of receiving. Moreover, it is the action itself, not the personal donor, that finally impresses the recipient. Without himself overcoming the stigma of a flannel waistcoat, Colonel Brandon nevertheless has power in his country estate; and if Lucy Steele is in raptures over his Grandisonian beneficences (*SS*, 293), Mrs. Jennings is on hand to register the happiness Marianne is destined to enjoy at Delaford: "exactly what I call a nice old fashioned place, full of comforts and conveniences; quite shut in with great garden walls that are covered with the best fruit-trees in the country: and such a mulberry tree in one corner! Lord! how Charlotte and I did stuff the only time we were there!" (*SS*, 196–97). Appetite is primal, obviating all sexual and social distinctions, and thus "irrational" and blind in its intent. The two women "stuff" themselves to visceral content and then feel gratitude toward the place more than toward the owner per se.

Although Mr. Darcy's secret beneficence saves Lydia and her family from disgrace, previous to that action his estate already spoke for itself, not merely in the testimonies from Lambton of his charity to the poor (*PP*, 265) but directly on the palate in the abundance of his trees and vines: "There was now employment for the whole party; for though they could not all talk, they could all eat; and the beautiful pyramids of grapes, nectarines, and peaches, soon collected them round the table" (*PP*, 268). The narrator's rendering of Elizabeth's point of view here imparts again the feelings beyond words: "though they could not all talk, they could all eat." In his nurturing role Darcy gains for the first time what he had lost abruptly at Hunsford in his blunt proposal.

Austen's unabashed sensuousness about food and drink is not far from Keats's pagan "beaded bubbles winking at the brim, / And purple-stainéd mouth." Like the air at Hartfield, there is something contagiously erotic in the exchange of food: pyramids of fruit can do what no words can. Mr. Martin walks three miles to oblige Harriet with walnuts, her favorite; and with less self-interest, his mother had given a "beautiful goose" to Mrs. Goddard (*E*, 28). In spite of her conscious stance as a stiffly detached egoist, Emma herself is as quiet a provider as Mr. Knightley, with his famous apples. Besides recommending the "minced chicken and scalloped oysters" (*E*, 24), as well as other luxurious dishes, to old Mrs. Bates and Mrs. Goddard, who can enjoy eating well if nothing else in their physical state, Emma, the narrator informs us, has also instructed the cottagers to send their child up to Hartfield with a pitcher for some broth (*E*, 88). Whatever the barely mentioned social and economic evils threatening this pastoral Eden, the benefactions of the privileged spread a warmth throughout the community that, at least temporarily, closes the distance between self and other. When Mr. Knightley invites the Highbury society to Donwell, "Come, and eat my strawberries," he offers the delights of "English culture" (*E*, 354, 360), and in a sense he is equivalent to the bounty of the land.

Food, then, is an important metonym in Austen's text for reifying the character as body and positioning the reader toward the action. Just as the word *taste* connoted moral qualities in the Shaftesburyan ethos of the eighteenth century, so the objects of appetite themselves take on surprising nuances of a character's intention, often ignored by the narrator. Desire, as most of the quotations above suggest, occurs mainly in the form of direct discourse, with little or no narrative interpretation. A character responds to another without the mediation of language, and moral taste is quite literally an experience to be gained at the table. On one of those admittedly rare occasions (Elizabeth at Pemberley, Emma at Ford's shop, Anne at Lyme), Austen abandons dialogue and approaches Flaubert's descriptive technique by allowing objects a life of their own in a character's perception—as in the scene where Fanny Price enters alone after her brother and bogus suitor have departed Mansfield:

> After seeing William to the last moment, Fanny walked back into the breakfast-room with a very saddened

heart to grieve over the melancholy change; and there
her uncle kindly left her to cry in peace, conceiving
perhaps that the deserted chair of each young man
might exercise her tender enthusiasm, and that the
remaining cold pork bones and mustard in William's
plate, might but divide her feelings with the broken
egg-shells in Mr. Crawford's. (*MP*, 282)

Table scraps, as any garbage collector knows, tell their story of
the particular appetite involved; and William's "cold pork
bones and mustard" and Henry's "broken egg-shells" may be
read as a contrast between a robust masculine nature and one
that needs to destroy things for the sake of amusement. The
description here effectively collapses the dualism of tenor and
vehicle, of subject and object, much as in Flaubert's description of Emma Bovary after she reads Rodolphe's farewell letter
that had been hidden in a basket of apricots. When Charles
samples one of the apricots and tries to tempt Emma to taste
them, she identifies the fruit so intensely with her lover that
at the sight of her husband eating she is overwhelmed with
nausea.[34] The letter has been made flesh in her imagination,
and this reaction to the husband's cannibalizing of the lover
also implies the same double bind of loathing and desire that
Fanny suffers that morning at Mansfield.

By capturing the thingness of the perceiver's environment, Austen's text renders emotion on almost any page, turning the subject into object, and the object into subject. While
desire reveals the individual self to be the product of impersonal forces in an encounter, appetite renders objects as
food—hence as erotic extensions of the self.

3.   *"The Work of a Moment"*

So far I have been discussing Austen's narrative erotics
in geometric (triangular desire) and biological (appetite) terms.
Another text for describing the impersonal forces involved in
any encounter alludes to classical physics. Once again, it is a
way of talking about character as part of an autonomous system. Even if, presumably, the individual has a choice and can
move at will, it is the material rather than efficient cause that

is stressed: "There is nothing which energy will not bring one to."[35] Austen's remark to her sister in 1801 stems as usual from a commonplace of domestic life, in this case the need to overcome the disappointment of not having Cassandra for company on the journey to Bath; but this brave assertion is about something primordial to the self—energy.[36] How this resource becomes available to motivate the self is another matter, and hardly a topic to discuss with Cassandra.

Energy held a certain political mystique for the times, and Austen was sensitive to its cant appeal. In 1813, when victory over Napoleon seemed imminent, Austen read Sir Charles William Pasley's *Essay on the Military Policy and Institutions of the British Empire* (1810) and confessed: "—the first soldier I ever sighed for—but he does write with extraordinary force & spirit."[37] Pasley's vigorous exhortation to his country to achieve world supremacy by military conquest had an understandable appeal to a reader with two brothers in the Royal Navy, but his zeal in the national will carried with it a behavioral psychology that seems especially pertinent to her characters' conflict:

> It is not always however, perhaps seldom, that the ambition of a nation has been directed with a permanent degree of *energy* towards any object, before the necessity of succeeding in that pursuit has been deeply felt. This strong sense of necessity will often precede, or lead to ambition; and when that *ardent passion*, the spirit of *exertion* arising from it, have once been called forth in bodies of men, and have been confirmed by habit, so as to *grow into principles or rules of conduct*; they will generally survive the causes which may at first have given birth to them. Hence a nation may go on *increasing its power*, after the necessity which first compelled it to adopt that policy may no longer exist.[38]

Not only Pasley's atomistic differentiation of what causes national policy but also his particular terms *energy, ardent passion*, and *exertion* are characteristic of Austen's style. Even if her remark to Cassandra about energy is partly ironic, alluding to the more awesome contexts for the term, nevertheless, the idea of exertion as a means of affirming the self in the world is familiar enough throughout her novels.

A related term, *power*, is much more pervasive in Austen's text, carrying several discrete meanings. The first has to do with a person's ability to act, and for the woman the power of refusal may be an answer to the man's freedom of choice (*NA*, 77; *E*, 208; *PP*, 183). Not surprisingly, the female is more subject to the loss of this power to act: trapped in the Thorpes's carriage and prevented from joining the Tilneys in the promised walk, Catherine "had no power of getting away" (*NA*, 87); later, while under the Radcliffean spell of terror at Northanger, "She had no power to move" (*NA*, 194). With the intrusion of Mary Crawford at Mansfield, Fanny is denied the "power of riding" (*MP*, 74); but when called upon to demonstrate her clandestine lover's gift of the Broadwood piano, Jane Fairfax "must reason herself into the power of performance" (*E*, 240).

Another meaning of power contains the idea of acting forcibly and even automatically, as in Mr. Darcy's retort to Mr. Bingley: "The power of doing any thing with quickness is always much prized by the possessor, and often without any attention to the imperfection of the performance" (*PP*, 49). Despite this debunking of effortless motion, however, it is the involuntary process itself that is repeatedly at issue, irrespective of the agent involved. After her raptures over Edmund's expression of love, Fanny is then depressed to find the "superior power of *one* pleasure [Mary] over his own mind" (*MP*, 262). Henry's proposal forces her into another dilemma: "She could not have supposed it in the power of any concurrence of circumstances to give her so many painful sensations on the first day of hearing of William's promotion" (*MP*, 303). Again, it is the triadic structure of desire, the "concurrence of circumstances," not the personality of the agent or patient in a given situation, which is the motivating force.

Finally, because it is detachable from the self and operative in a kinetically charged universe, power is an elusive commodity to be valued for its own sake, the gaining of dominion over another being only the originating purpose (Pasley's theory). In the business of attracting a man, for instance, it is the woman who wields power. As a quick matchmaker, Mrs. Jennings "enjoyed the advantage of raising the blushes and the vanity of many a young lady by insinuations of her power over such a young man" (*SS*, 36). After seeing Darcy's behavior at Pemberley, Elizabeth wondered "how far it would be for the

happiness of both that she should employ the power, which
her fancy told her she still possessed, of bringing on the renewal of his addresses" (*PP*, 266). Not only is Lydia reprehen-
sible for having "'thrown herself into the power of—of Mr.
Wickham'" (*PP*, 277); but what is worse, Elizabeth's "power
was sinking; every thing *must* sink under such a proof of family
weakness" (*PP*, 278). When Maria Bertram is excluded from
the invitation to the parsonage, "As Mr. Rushworth did *not*
come, the injury was increased, and she had not even the relief of shewing her power over him" (*MP*, 70). In the scene
where Edmund tries to persuade Fanny into accepting Henry:
"Full well could Fanny guess where his thoughts were now.
Miss Crawford's power was all returning" (*MP*, 349). After his
infatuation with Fanny, Henry's abrupt return to Maria, we
are to believe, was a circumstance of seducing himself while
engaging her affections: "but in triumphing over the discre-
tion, which, though beginning in anger, might have saved
them both, he had put himself in the power of feelings on her
side, more strong than he had supposed" (*MP*, 468). Free indirect discourse renders Anne Elliot's despair after the more
than seven years since her engagement have left her haggard:
"He had been most warmly attached to her, and had never
seen a woman since whom he thought her equal; but, except
from some natural sensation of curiosity, he had no desire of
meeting her again. Her power with him was gone for ever"(*P*,
61). A major contradiction between the narrator's opening
claims and the actual working out of the story in *Emma*, however, is that despite the heroine's alleged "power of having
rather too much her own way" (*E*, 5), most of the events prove
to be coincidental and for the most part beyond her control;
she is the last to fathom Mr. Elton's and Frank Churchill's real
intentions.

If power is circumstantial and continually in flux, selfhood is hardly a birthright in Austen's world. In fact, given the
ultimate standard of social perfection implicit in *Emma*, characters are ever in peril of annihilation. After Emma explained
her objections to the engagement to Robert Martin, for instance, "Harriet had not surmised her own danger, but the
idea of it struck her forcibly" (*E*, 53). Similarly, although jealousy of Frank Churchill taints his observations, Mr. Knightley
does feel a genuine concern, according to the narrator, to protect Emma's reputation when he detects his rival's intimacy

with Jane: "He could not see her in a situation of such danger, without trying to preserve her. It was his duty" (*E*, 349). *Without trying to preserve her*: threatened with loss of power, the Austen character, even the first in rank, faces instant death on every page of consciousness.

Yet somehow the heroine prevails. Austen's world no longer reflects the providential teleology still apparent in the eighteenth-century novel, and skepticism toward the individual's grandiose plans for the future is chronic in the narrative tone. No amount of energy will suffice to carry the self through impossible situations, and since eros is blind, even the best intentions may come to naught unless events take place fortuitously. It is the unforeseen place and timing of circumstances that give the moment long-range consequences. Originating in the Latin *momentum*, with its sense of movement, moving power, and measurement of time, moment associates energy with the time spent in producing the effect; hence, Austen's alazons usually make false claims about the duration of an event and the work accomplished.

In general, there are at least three discernible meanings of *moment* in the novels. The first is simply a measure of time, as in Isabella Thorpe's pretended difficulty with clocks because of the pleasure she derives from the Morlands' company: "to have doubted a moment longer *then*, would have been equally inconceivable, incredible, and impossible; and she could only protest, over and over again, that no two hours and a half had ever gone off so swiftly before" (*NA*, 67). A second category denotes a turning point in the story; and since rapid attachments are always suspicious, the romantic convention of love at first sight comes under particular scrutiny, though for Mrs. Jennings the swiftness of Marianne's passion is what authenticates it: "Don't we all know that it must be a match, that they were over head and ears in love with each other from the first moment they met?" (*SS*, 182).

Rather than a neutral measure of time or a turning point in the consciousness of events, "moment" in Austen often refers to the juncture of circumstances that results in an important change; and this meaning brings together the ideas of kinetic energy, exertion, force, and work within a temporal dimension. Hence, when Marianne Dashwood and her sister Margaret are caught in the rain, a negative event becomes linked with a positive: "One consolation however remained for them, to which the exigence of the moment gave more than usual propriety; it was that of running with all possible speed down the steep side of the hill which led immediately to their garden gate" (*SS*, 41). In a more ironic juxtaposition, the narrator describes how Lady Middleton's polite indifference came as a relief to Elinor after her sister's jilting: "Every qualification is raised at times, by the circumstances of the moment, to more than its real value; and she [Elinor] was sometimes worried down by officious condolence to rate good-breeding as more indispensable to comfort than good-nature" (*SS*, 215).

From classical physics, "moment" as the product of forces acting at a point represents yet more specifically the way a phenomenon occurs without human interference; and this autonomy of the process itself creates wonder in the thinking agents on hand, who resemble the fascinated observers of a scientific experiment in the well-known painting by Joseph Wright of Derby. Marianne's remark on Willoughby's abrupt departure from Barton focuses defensively on the action instead of on its disturbing motives: "It is all very strange. So suddenly to be gone! It seems but the work of a moment" (*SS*, 77). When a letter imagined to be from him turns out to be from her mother, the narrator describes the sequence abstractly: "The work of one moment was destroyed by the next" (*SS*, 202). The description implies a mind primarily interested in the phenomena themselves, as if tinkering with the way things work could compensate for one's inability to control events.

Like those infrequent occasions of agape, when the heroine entrusts herself to another unconditionally, the work of a moment comes about freely, without deliberation. At the least significant level, it may reveal simply mechanical behavior, as in Darcy's convincing Bingley of Jane's indifference—"'scarcely the work of a moment'" (*PP*, 199). In an environment where spontaneous overflow of emotion is highly valued, to be persuasive requires at least the appearance of the moment; hence, Mr. Bennet's question to Mr. Collins: "May I ask whether these pleasing attentions proceed from the impulse of the moment, or are the result of previous study?" (*PP*, 68). Since not only the juncture of events but the energy expended goes into the work done, the turning point in the Austen story, especially the making of a tryst, depends on a chance encounter that begins with quite opposite expectations:

> "I had gone a few steps, Fanny, when I heard the door open behind me. 'Mr. Bertram,' said she. I looked

back. 'Mr. Bertram,' said she, with a smile—but it
was a smile ill-suited to the conversation that had
passed, a saucy playful smile, seeming to invite, in
order to subdue me; at least, it appeared so to me. I
resisted; it was the impulse of the moment to resist,
and still walked on. I have since—sometimes—for
a moment—regretted that I did not go back; but I
know I was right; and such has been the end of our
acquaintance!" (*MP*, 459)

A major obstacle to Fanny's happiness, we know, has been
Edmund's almost spineless admiration of Mary's energetic
mind; in this scene, however, the concatenation of a dire family crisis and an inappropriate smile triggers for once a defini-
tive response that even the speaker fails to understand afterward. Had it not been for the electricity of this fateful moment,
Fanny may well ask, could Edmund ever have resisted Mary's
power?

Austen's comic text reveals character both as a consciousness generated by triangular relations with other persons and things, and as a material body moved by impulses of
the moment. Instead of the traditional hierarchy of mind over
body, her narrative implies a psychosomatic doubleness about
one's being that recalls Tristram's equating of the jerkin with
the jerkin's lining. Rumple the one and you rumple the other.
During peaks of e/motion in an encounter, characters undergo
sudden changes of energy and often become strangers to themselves; and, as in Fielding's world, the mechanics of intention
proves benevolent in the end. Rather than an absolute duality
between spirit and matter, there is one continuum of energy
giving rise to phenomena. At one extreme, to render consciousness, Austen's free indirect discourse fuses the perceiver
with the thing; at the other, to render the thing devoid of an
individual perceiver, her "objective" voice describes the moment of an encounter in impersonal, quasi-scientific terms.

III. Character (Written)

In the foregoing discussion, my emphasis has been on Austen's situating of characters within temporary but regulated activities. Erving Goffman's behavioristic model of the encounter describes the largely unconscious role-playing in everyday communication, which has remarkable parallels in the more explicitly controlled conditions of playing games. Although Austen's educational theme generally articulates a dichotomy between play and work, with the flawed heroine finally discovering her duties to family and community, elsewhere her text implies that writing the story itself is a form of play and that the imagination transforms all the world into a stage for comic revelations. The many scenes involving play—card games, charades, piano-playing, singing, acting, dancing—are focused situations that reflect the larger enterprise of representing the lived self within typographical space.

From this play-within-the-play reflexivity, characters gain or lose in their competing discourses. With *Emma* as the paradigm of this activity in creating the self at the expense of the other, we have explored the intertextual structures of represented consciousness. Giving a character something to desire is tantamount to giving her life, the kinetic principle within any narrative that reflects the external reader's design on the story as well as the protagonist's alleged disposition. As if wary of readers—whether within or without the story—trying to entrap her in the convention of falling in love, Emma Woodhouse patterns her defenses on the antiromantic texts of the eighteenth-century French tradition. To demonstrate the variety of manifesting desire in Austen's narrative, our focus moved from a character's conscious willing to the implicit intentionality of her object world, where the description of physical things reflects the mind perceiving them.

Until now our interpretation of Austen's narrative strategies has been mainly local and empirical, while the whole concept of novelistic character remains elusive. Having reached its apogee during the Victorian period, character as an element of fiction has been deprecated among postmodern experimenters. As Thomas Docherty sees it, "Cartesian selfhood, 'I

am that which thinks,' is replaced here by the Todorovian
homme-recit, 'I am that which speaks.'"[1] In contrast to the uncritical positing of a noumenal being, often initiated simply by
a proper name, say Pip or Jane, who supposedly exists independently of author and reader, a writer like Robbe-Grillet
shuns such pretense of godlike authority and shifts the burden
of illusion-making onto the reader.[2] The Cartesian dualism of
self and other has been so axiomatic in the early realistic novel
and in the mimetic criticism traditionally associated with the
genre that until recently Austen's novels have always seemed
immune to the modern neurosis of ambivalent attitude and in-
decisive action. Yet, as Scott recognized immediately, her
writing is not of the "bow-wow" kind that sweeps across time
and distance without questioning the author's privilege.[3] Moreover, notwithstanding their ostensibly insistent Cartesian selfhood, Austen's characters also have a way of being that which
speaks.

But what is character in fiction? To begin with, it is a
noun or pronoun, as Chekhov's advice to his brother suggests:
"Don't try for too many characters. The center of gravity should
reside in two: he and she."[4] At the most fundamental linguistic
level, these subjects take on life as patients or agents when
joined to a predicate and qualified by adjectives and adverbs.
In general, there are two mutually opposed ways of understanding character: the semiotic and the mimetic. According
to the first, characters are no more than textual segments,
"patterns of recurrence," whose meanings shift with their contextual motifs.[5] In contrast to our illusions of a continuous personality while reading linearly, this approach, which comes
naturally to the parodist, alerts us to the limitations of the text
itself and to the "dissolution" of all those relationships that initiated our responses. The second and more familiar way of
reading simply regards characters as individuals with a unique
history and personhood, as imitations of real life to be comprehended by all the means available to the human sciences.

Once forced back to its originating logos, character
may blend readily with its context to the extent of disappearing altogether. As we shall see, for example, the line between
narrator and character is at best often tenuous in Austen; and
this marginality is itself an important stylistic feature to be
considered in any interpretation of the story, on a par with her

reflexive conclusions that wrench the illusive beings from
their plot conventions:

> I purposely abstain from dates on this occasion, that
> every one may be at liberty to fix their own, aware that
> the cure of unconquerable passions, and the trans-
> fer of unchanging attachments, must vary much as to
> time in different people.—I only intreat every body
> to believe that exactly at the time when it was quite
> natural that it should be so, and not a week earlier,
> Edmund did cease to care about Miss Crawford, and
> became as anxious to marry Fanny, as Fanny herself
> could desire. (*MP*, 470)

As the parodic narrative voice reminds us, aesthetic closure not
only reduces the variables of real life but also taxes the reader's
complicity in shaping a character's behavior. Yet breaking the
illusion of flesh-and-blood life by this editorial interference is
only another mimetic subterfuge, which momentarily elevates
the narrator as a presence at the expense of the storytelling.

Our concern in this chapter, then, will be to examine
the peculiar locution that gives rise to the Austen character.
Although finally a composite of written language, no more
than ciphers on a printed page depending on certain conventional responses, what the reader takes for living beings in a
story are the effect of represented speech within selective contexts. Just as Austen's reflexive narratives may abruptly call attention to the fictional methods elsewhere quietly assumed, so
throughout this book my approach to her characters will alternate the psychological model of consciousness/unconsciousness
with the semiotic model of signifier/signified. For instance,
sometimes Catherine Morland is a young woman in love and
determined to have her way against all familial, social, and fi-
nancial obstacles; at other times, she is only a satirical persona
intended to undermine the generic roles of the "heroine"
in romance, and thus speaks, or is spoken about, in a self-
deprecating language. For many readers of *Northanger Abbey*,
of course, these separate functions pose no difficulties at all
but become blurred as the desire to articulate the character's
personhood prevails over any other consideration.[6]

Whether regarded primarily as psychological entities
or as linguistic artifacts, however, Austen's characters exist as

modes of represented speech; and our analysis should begin with four categories of discourse that interlock to render the individual voice: the dualities (1) of self and other; (2) of inner and outer self; (3) of narrative authority and readerly freedom; and (4) of subjective and objective description.

1. Self and Other

The dualism of self and other verges between the "classical" notion that the self must be balanced by social norms and traditions or suffer from the delusions of pride (Pope) and the "romantic" notion that the *real* self is essentially opposed to the public sphere (Wordsworth). The one stresses the need of subordinating the individual's desires to the general wisdom of the community; the other exalts the value of original insight that can only be gained in solitude and usually includes hostility toward the status quo. Although both extremes appear in early fiction, the critical realists emphasize the former pattern and define the person's identity in terms of his social function. In its absolute physical isolation of the main character, *Robinson Crusoe* brought into relief, Ian Watt argues, man's inherently social nature. According to Hume, "We can form no wish which has not a reference to society"; and it is this tenet that the realistic novel presumably implements in opposition to Defoe's allegory of individualism.[7] Contrary to Watt, however, though Crusoe may discover unexpected resources, especially his Protestant conscience, in his loneliness, he never forgets that he is an English property owner with certain rights and privileges in relation to anyone who encroaches on *his* island; and thus, if in the end he has no difficulty in returning to "civilization" it is because he never really ever left it. In the novels after Defoe, the protagonist—whether Pamela or Parson Adams, Clarissa or Tom Jones, Yorick or Primrose, Evelina or Matt Bramble—may stand apart from the unthinking crowd but ultimately relies, nevertheless, on the approval of worldly opinion. Not even Clarissa is content to make her exit without first receiving her earthly father's forgiveness for her original disobedience.

Under the spell of the female quixotic motif, conservative readers of Austen have exaggerated some form of external authority as a norm for selfhood. Wayne Booth formulates the reader's moral responsibility in judging Emma Woodhouse's flawed character: "We have been privileged to watch with her [Austen] as she observes her favorite character climb from a considerably lower platform to join the exalted company of Knightley, 'Jane Austen,' and those of us readers who are wise enough, good enough, and perceptive enough to belong up there too." [8] Similarly, Marilyn Butler's recent thesis about an explicitly anti-Jacobin roman à clef posits the heroine's education within a historically specific political context: "The theme, then, is the struggle towards a fixed and permanent truth external to the individual; and chastening, necessarily, to individual presumption and self-consequence." [9] Opposite to this approach, the "regulated hatred" school of D. W. Harding, Marvin Mudrick, and Barbara Hardy stresses the integrity of selfhood vis-à-vis the community. Hardy observes: "Within her social groups, Jane Austen frequently shows a serious restlessness, critical and even subversive, which looks beyond social limits." [10] Clearly, no matter what versions of the Austen text commentary may produce, one assumption remains intact—the duality of self and other as the basis of realistic presentation.

Yet Austen's fictional world resists either/or solutions. E. M. Forster, we have noted, observed that even her minor characters are round. Likewise, Gilbert Ryle places her outside the Christian ideology of saints and sinners; in place of the old faculty psychology describing the hierarchy of reason over the passions, she renders human nature with the wine connoisseur's sensitivity to barely discernible gradations of feeling. [11] But these fine shadings of character are mainly implicit in behavior; Austen seldom attempts the elaborate narrative analyses given by George Eliot or Henry James. As Martin Price states, "Manners . . . are supremely important for Jane Austen because they are the field in which the moral self is revealed and defined. Manners are a form of role-playing. We use them to order our relations with each other; we can use them for disguise and deceit; or we can make them a game, an end in themselves, mere empty formalism." [12] Since in both real life and fiction the self interacts with others in all this role-playing, to a large extent the old dichotomy vanishes in actual practice: character is nothing without intention toward another person or thing—its emotional existence is inseparable from its field of action.

The "otherness" of the Austen character, especially when intoned in the narrative, has sometimes attracted notice. As if excited by his discovery, R. W. Chapman pointed out coincidences in language between hero and heroine in *Emma:* "I venture, at the risk of exceeding my editorial function, to call attention to this and some other places in which Mr. Knightley comes unbidden, and sometimes unrecognized, into Emma's thoughts."[13] Although Chapman was satisfied that this coincidence anticipated the marriage of true minds eventually borne out in the plot, there is actually a more pervasive sharing of language in Austen's narratives than his few egregious examples would suggest.

Character is inseparable from its field of action; and in Austen, we have said, this action is mainly speech represented with varying levels of directness. Just as the narrator may absorb the character's point of view in telling the story, so one character may appropriate another character's language at certain moments to become effectually one voice. Emma feels so completely Mrs. Weston's state of excitement at meeting Frank Churchill for the first time that in a deep reverie she projects herself onto Randalls:

> "My dear, dear, anxious friend,"—said she, in mental soliloquy, while walking down stairs from her own room, "always over-careful for every body's comfort but your own; I see you now in all your little fidgets, going again and again into his room, to be sure that all is right." The clock struck twelve as she passed through the hall. "'Tis twelve, I shall not forget to think of you four hours hence; and by this time tomorrow, perhaps, or a little later, I may be thinking of the possibility of their all calling here. I am sure they will bring him soon." (*E*, 189–90)

In terms of the story, Emma's wishful daydream is unnecessary, as Frank Churchill had arrived in Highbury a day early and is in fact sitting at this very moment with her father in their parlor. But in terms of Austen's narrative technique, the passage illustrates how readily the character's consciousness appropriates another character's field and, at least for a brief duration, loses all sense of apartness.

Still more importantly, it illustrates how thinking in Austen is, after considerable refinement of narrative technique, only a matter of talking. As scholars have pointed out, Austen is the first English novelist to have grasped the full range of effects produced by what is commonly known as "erlebte Rede," "le style indirect libre," or "free indirect discourse."[14] To some degree this hybrid form of representing speech may have been an accident of eighteenth-century printing history, the result of attempts to standardize typographical marks for dialogue. Thus until about the time of Dickens quotation marks could be used for reported as well as direct speech, and it is likely once again that the medium was the message.[15]

Private thoughts often have the same status as dialogue in Austen's text, the assumed psychological/rhetorical dichotomy softening in the grey area of reported speech:

> "You will stay, I am sure; you will stay and nurse her;" cried he, turning to her and speaking with a glow, and yet a gentleness, which seemed almost restoring the past. —She coloured deeply; and he recollected himself, and moved away. —She expressed herself most willing, ready, happy to remain. *It was what she had been thinking of, and wishing to be allowed to do. —A bed on the floor in Louisa's room would be sufficient for her, if Mrs. Harville would but think so.*" (*P*, 114; my emphasis)

As if consciously seeking a privileged space for her character's mental life somewhere between direct and indirect discourse, Austen depicts Anne Elliot's thinking/speaking to be simultaneous with Captain Wentworth's thinking/speaking: the two principals are united here in one field of discourse set in process by an unforeseen event.

Not only does free indirect discourse merge the self with the other, but once the field is established it can reduce the self to a mere atom, to an allusion that assures us minimally of the character's presence:

> This topic was discussed very happily, and others succeeded of similar moment, and passed away with simi-

> lar harmony; but the evening did not close without a little return of *agitation*. The *gruel* came and supplied a great deal to be said—*much praise* and many comments—undoubting decision of *its wholesomeness for every constitution*, and pretty severe Philippics upon the many houses where it was never met with *tolerable;*—but, unfortunately, among the failures which the daughter had to instance, the most recent, and therefore most prominent, was in her own cook at South End, a young woman hired for the time, who never had been able to understand what she meant by *a basin of nice smooth gruel, thin, but not too thin*. Often as she had wished for and ordered it, she had never been able to get any thing *tolerable*. Here was a dangerous opening. (*E*, 104–05, my emphasis)

Until the middle of this passage ("the failures which the daughter had to instance") the report avoids identifying any speaker at all but instead focuses on how the physical object—the gruel—prompts nervous responses with embedded stances, the vocal proponents dominating over the quiescent dissenters. Obviously the speaker herself has no opinions of her own to express but essentially simulates her father's in order to humor him and if possible to stave off any attack from her increasingly annoyed husband, an impression wrought by his conspicuous silence during verbal explosions from the others. Although the conversation is superficially about gruel, the real issue, we discover fully by the end of the chapter, is whether the hypochondriacal father can uphold his will over his daughters and ally them against his male rivals. Yet Mr. Woodhouse himself is never mentioned by name as in a conventional report; instead, the motif of the gruel alone implies the character's idiosyncrasies and fears without the least interference from the narrator. In a linguistic sense, the gruel not only alludes to, but *is* Mr. Woodhouse in this scene. His otherness is all.

2. Inner and Outer Self

Besides questioning the character's viability in isolation from others, Austen's speech-oriented style also tends to challenge the hallowed assumption of an internal, "real" self as opposed to an other-directed, role-playing self. Although the ideal of sincerity may have the highest value among the romantic poets, it does not come easily to a parodic artist like Austen; hence, even *Mansfield Park*, a novel sometimes praised for its Wordsworthian spirit, presents a main character who rebels against acting *Lovers' Vows* but lacks the inner strength to resist Henry Crawford's eloquent reading of Shakespeare even while doubting his good intentions in the encounter.[16]

But whence the illusion of inner and outer self? M. M. Bakhtin (Volosinov) sees language as the most elemental basis of the personality, which is no more than a pattern of language: "Consequently, *a word is not an expression of inner personality; rather, inner personality is an expressed or inwardly impelled word.*"[17] Instead of plumbing the depths of psychoanalysis to account for a character's motivation, Bakhtin suggests that we begin with what we know—the actual text of personality; and his conception of the polyvocal novel underscores the arbitrary spaces of mimetic characterization. Bahktin's *heteroglossia* involves both the direct discourse and the free indirect discourse that imply points of view.[18] Unless we are to disregard entirely the wealth of analysis in Freud, Jung, and their numerous successors, however, it seems facile to suggest that mental life is only a verbal phenomenon; and despite the inconsistency with the linguistic approach to character, as already indicated above, our discussion will take into account psychological models of behavior as well.

Nevertheless, if we give primacy to the word, the illusion of "inner" and "outer" self derives from constrasting narrative voices. The opening chapter of *Emma*, for example, is approximately three thousand words long, more than half of which takes the form of dialogue; and however the voices are named—the narrator, Emma, Mr. Woodhouse, or Mr. Knightley—all converge on the theme of triangular relationships.

The first ten paragraphs of narrative, which Graham Hough calls objective,[19] set in motion two very different, even contradictory, attitudes toward the heroine. The initial stance is ironic and promises a story about an affluent, attractive, and egocentric woman destined for trouble: "The real evils of Emma's situation were the power of having rather too much her own way, and a disposition to think a little too well of herself" (*E*, 5). A second voice, beginning in the sixth paragraph, is sympathetic, however, and closes ranks with Emma's perspective. While the first narrator introduces a female quixote, the second creates a protagonist with a mature insight into her situation: "she was now in great danger of suffering from intellectual solitude. She dearly loved her father, but he was no companion for her. He could not meet her in conversation, rational or playful" (*E*, 7). Although presumably "outside" the character, the point of view is identical with her perspective: under no delusion of being free and powerful, she feels trapped in her situation and for the moment lacks any hope of finding a worthwhile social role. Rather than maintaining a detached, judgmental role, the second narrator merges continually with the character in the process of free indirect discourse; hence, the overall effect is to collapse the distinction between thought and speech, between inner and outer communication.

Sometimes reverie anticipates dialogue. After being privy to Emma's quiet assessment of the change ("that great must be the difference between a Mrs. Weston only half a mile from them, and a Miss Taylor in the house"), the reader can sympathize with her valiant "exertions" to cheer her father by emphasizing the proximity to Randalls; and the scene immediately bears out the narrator's (and surely the character's) judgment that "He could not meet her in conversation, rational or playful." Besides absorbing her father's objections to the change, Emma, in an instant of agape, takes sincere pleasure in her friend's happiness and ingenuously applauds the marriage in words that Mr. Knightley repeats later in the scene.

What is not articulated in conscious thought or direct speech may be significant. Although father and daughter talk at cross purposes concerning the departure of Miss Taylor, both are depressed by the loss of a congenial household companion. Furthermore, Mr. Woodhouse's humor against marriage may, under the cover of senility, possibly betray the darker aspects of the institution—the violence of sexual intercourse and the dangers of childbirth. Because of her adherence to "rational or playful" discourse, therefore, Emma disregards the import of her father's words and, confident of her superior understanding, talks mainly to pacify him.

As the embodiment of the "rational or playful" talker desired to replace the father, Mr. Knightley enters the scene just when there was "no prospect of a third to cheer a long evening" and the ubiquitous backgammon table seemed impending. His cryptic remark, "it must be better to have only one to please, than two," the first of many riddles in the discourse of this novel, puts the Woodhouses immediately on the defensive and elicits humorously predictable responses:

> "Especially when *one* of those two is such a fanciful, troublesome creature!" said Emma playfully. "That, is what you have in your head, I know—and what you would certainly say if my father were not by."
>
> "I believe it is very true, my dear, indeed," said Mr. Woodhouse with a sigh. "I am afraid I am sometimes very fanciful and troublesome."
>
> "My dearest papa! You do not think I could mean *you*, or suppose Mr. Knightley to mean *you*. What a horrible idea! Oh, no! I meant only myself. Mr. Knightley loves to find fault with me you know— in a joke—it is all a joke. We always say what we like to one another." (*E*, 10)

In accordance with their established game plan, Emma freely gives the requisite interpretation in deference to Mr. Knightley's familiar role as her mentor and accepts the riddle as an attack on herself. But the term *joke* is always suspect in Austen's vocabulary, implying something unstable in the speaker's motives and alerting us to the more serious quarrels to come later in the story, culminating in Emma's humiliation at Box Hill. Thus, after having caused both father and daughter to acknowledge themselves "fanciful, troublesome creatures," Mr. Knightley innocently explains his original intention: "I meant no reflection on any body. Miss Taylor has been used to have two persons to please; she will now have but one." If this solution comes as an anticlimax, the riddle nevertheless succeeded in forcing each of the Woodhouses to make public their respective self-images; and after their confessions Mr. Knightley plays his trump card by pretending that his only meaning was a tautology.

By drawing out each character's subjective response, this verbal encounter illustrates J. L. Austin's basic distinction between constative and performative speech acts—the first having to do with the truth or falsehood of statements, the second, with the success or failure of utterances toward the auditor.[20] In conversation the denotative aspect of language weighs very little compared to what it *does*, whether persuade, warn, surprise, deceive, command, and so on. To judge by their effectiveness in triggering self-deprecating replies, Mr. Knightley's words, we may infer, were carefully chosen for their performative value; and his dullish explanation of himself here undercuts his interlocutors' own guilt feelings. To invoke a psychological speculation at this point, despite his aplomb in the repartee, however, perhaps not even the triumphant hero is conscious of yet another meaning to his cryptogram: unconsciously he is defending the idea of marriage not only for Miss Taylor but for Emma as well. Given the treacherous ambiguity of speech acts, as attested here, the dialogue has a tendency to behave much like the narrative in denying any clear division between a character's private and public stance.

Because of its thoroughgoing dialogicity, Austen's text may balance sincere feeling with epigrammatic undermining without any serious damage to either purpose. Among the high points of her use of free indirect discourse are those scenes where some vital information is communicated after a period of increasing tension and doubt:

> He had found her agitated and low.—*Frank Churchill was a villain.*—He heard her declare that she had never loved him. *Frank Churchill's character was not desperate.*—*She was his own Emma*, by hand and word, when they returned into the house; and if he could have thought of Frank Churchill then, he might have deemed him a very good sort of fellow. (*E*, 433; my emphasis)

This passage reveals the complex distancing effects possible in Austen's narrative. The underscored clauses indicate the usual free indirect discourse mode of reporting, and if transposed to conventional indirect discourse could be worded as follows:

> Mr. Knightley felt that *Frank Churchill was a villain.*
> Mr. Knightley felt that *Frank Churchill's character was not desperate.*
> Mr. Knightley felt that *she was his own Emma.*

To avoid the monotonous repetition of the introductory formula is perhaps sufficient reason for taking the shortcut of free indirect discourse; but, clearly, it is the antithesis between simple declaration of fact and the hero's instantaneous response to it that represents the very rhythm of desire. In contrast to these closeups, the last conditional and main clauses, it will be noticed, imply a narrator's distant perspective, with the question of what Mr. Knightley was in fact thinking at this moment left unanswered. Although superficially the dialogical structure registers his thoughts in response to each stage of enlightenment concerning Emma's feelings, the staccato sentences allow us to *hear* his actual words, whether or not they were actually spoken to her in this scene.

3. Narrative Authority and Readerly Freedom

Given the kinetic nature of Austen's polyvocal text, it should be evident by now that character is not something rigid and detachable, but rather is equivalent to a field of related intentions that may be shared with a narrator and other discourses signaling different speakers. From the standpoint of the Austen novel's linguistic structure, therefore, the humorous matchmaking so explicit in each plot does not merely reflect the English gentry's preoccupation with marriage settlements but parallels nicely the whole jostling for communicative authority in the text itself. Whenever the storytelling relies heavily on scenic rather than narrative presentation, characters appear to act autonomously, entering freely into alliances or rivalries while pursuing their own ends. Although never very far from the participants, Austen's narrator, unlike Fielding's or Sterne's, only intermittently interferes in our daydream of the story and instead usually fades into the central character's point of view, becoming identical with it through free indirect discourse.

Despite her reputation among Tory readers, then, Austen takes surprising risks in the storytelling process. It is a commonplace of modern criticism that the author can no longer play God. We see this fact in Sartre's well-known attack on Mauriac's indiscriminate use of omniscience: "He takes God's standpoint on his characters. God sees the inside and outside, the depths of body and soul, the whole universe at once. In like manner, M. Mauriac is omniscient about everything relating to his little world."[21] Roland Barthes's apothegm, "The birth of the reader must be at the cost of the death of the Author," is only a drastic metaphor of the same critical preference for allowing the text its autonomy, or to be more exact, for allowing the reader his freedom to constitute the text.[22] In condemning the modern writer's and critic's abnegation of authority, W. J. Harvey is quite open about his preference of a mimetic model of character; and of course such a model presupposes a reality about which there is general agreement.[23]

But Sartre's attack on authorial omniscience and Harvey's dread of textual autonomy are both anachronistic in claiming too much for modern theory. By tracing the "birth of the author" to the lives of Renaissance artists as witnessed in Vasari's biographies, Mukařovský shows that despite personal, even petty, reasons for identifying himself with his work (Michelangelo's signature on the Virgin's girdle in the Pietà) the autonomy of his product was never in doubt: it was always for the perceiver rather than for the originator to generate meaning from the object:

> The perceiver's active participation in the formation of intentionality gives the intentionality a dynamic nature. As a resultant of the encounter between the viewer's attitude and the organization of the work, intentionality is labile and oscillates during the perception of the same work, or at least—with the same perceiver—from perception to perception. It is a common experience that the more vividly a work affects a perceiver, the more possibilities of perception it offers him.[24]

What follows in Mukařovský's argument is something resembling Hutchinson's principle of "co-operative conflict" between author and reader: a dialectic between the aesthetic displeasure of unintentionality (what is perceived to contradict meaning) and the aesthetic pleasure of intentionality (what is perceived as a unity but always as partial). To understand the experience of "reality" in art, therefore, we need to recognize its essential openness.[25]

Just as the author's intentionality has a history of only a few hundred years in Western culture, so the problem of accounting for the unconscious or unintentional element of art dates mainly from the aesthetic controversy over the "rules" in the French neoclassical academies.[26] Leonardo, for instance, while subscribing to a thoroughgoing scientific approach to artistic representation, nevertheless anticipated the elusiveness of aesthetic grace that Boileau, Pope, and others emphasized against rigid conventions: "When the work is equal to the knowledge and judgment of the painter, it is a bad sign; and when it surpasses the judgment, it is still worse, as is the case with those who wonder at having succeeded so well."[27] In the eighteenth century, when aesthetics and literary criticism became firmly established disciplines, this principle of unintentionality in art underlay the concept of grace, which evolved from the "je ne sçai quoi" of the rationalistic academicians to a quality of movement perceived.

A witness to an era that amused itself with the trompe l'oeil, Jonathan Richardson advised against a fully determinate representation in general: "So far should the Painter be from inserting any thing Superfluous, that *he ought to leave something to the Imagination.* He must not say all he can on his Subject, and so seem to distrust his *Reader,* and discover he thought no farther himself."[28] Similarly, Diderot observes: "True taste fastens on one or two characteristics, and leaves the rest to the imagination. . . . If an artist shows us everything, and leaves *us* nothing to do, he leaves us weary and impatient."[29] Hogarth, as Ronald Paulson remarks, applied his aesthetic theory of lines to a practice of sketching an object with the barest essentials, for the perceiver to complete.[30] Perhaps not despite, but *because* of, the abiding concern of the Enlightenment with freeing the mind of superstition and fear, Edmund Burke stresses the effectiveness of obscurity as a means of communication in language and art: "so far is a clearness of imagery from being absolutely necessary to an influence upon the passions, that they may be considerably operated upon without presenting any image at all."[31] Throughout the eighteenth century, then, unintentionality, far from being an aesthetic flaw, went hand in hand with the artist's conscious purpose and became a basic principle of romanticism.[32]

Another context for this dialectic between the known and unknown in the dynamics of perceiving the object is in the late-eighteenth-century theory of the picturesque, which compared the principles of landscape painting with those of landscape gardening. Not only does Austen allude to the picturesque in her letters and novels, but her brother Henry's

"Biographical Notice" specifically mentions her admiration of Gilpin on this subject. Though the "improvers" themselves sometimes admitted to being despots in sacrificing cottages, orchards, and gardens to carry out their ends, the idea was to give expression to a landscape; and again the principle of the unfinished is at work in the aesthetics of *intricacy: "that disposition of objects,"* according to Uvedale Price, *"which, by a partial and uncertain concealment, excites and nourishes curiosity."* Because of its power to motivate the perceiver, artificial torsos and classical or medieval follies have special value as fragments: "A temple or palace of Grecian architecture in its perfect entire state, and with its surface and colour smooth and even, either in painting or reality is beautiful; in ruin it is picturesque."[33] Likewise, the rough symmetry of Gothic architecture is picturesque as opposed to the symmetry of classical styles, which are paradigms of beauty.

Neither one quality nor the other, however, is in itself sufficient; rather, each reciprocates psychologically to offset the other. Price argues that deformity is to ugliness as picturesqueness is to beauty; the main difference is in their communicative effect. Like the picturesque, deformity "corrects" the cloying regularity of beauty and the monotony of ugliness by making a "quicker impression" and arousing interest in the mind after a state of passive enjoyment. In view of the constant stress on the active role of the perceiver, whether the "reader" of art objects, including landscapes, or the reader of written texts, it is astonishing to find Roland Barthes's assertion: "Classic criticism has never paid any attention to the reader; for it, the writer is the only person in literature."[34] While it may be true that earlier periods had a lower threshold for realism than ours and hence risked relatively much less in surrendering the artifact to the viewer's imagination, nevertheless the authority of the artist, we have seen, was hardly absolute in any way.

In view of the long history of the reader's role in completing the author's purposely fragmented work, therefore, it is not surprising that Austen grasped the principle implied in Keats's "Heard melodies are sweet, but those unheard / Are sweeter." As we shall see in the final chapter, reading her novels is very much an encounter, an action that often tests the full mental powers of her characters to constitute the text, and is hence on par with writing. Austen's well-known comment on *Pride and Prejudice* should serve as a warning to those un-creative readers who insist on allegorical reductions of her comic playfulness: "The work is rather too light, and bright, and sparkling; it wants shade; it wants to be stretched out here and there with a long chapter of sense, if it could be had; if not, of solemn specious nonsense, about something uncon-nected with the story."[35] Clearly, in admitting that her work is unfinished and resistant to closure, Austen agrees with Tristram's theory of narrative: "no author who understands the just boundaries of decorum and good-breeding, would pre-sume to think all: The truest respect which you can pay to the reader's understanding, is to halve this matter amicably, and leave him something to imagine, in his turn, as well as your-self."[36] If Austen acknowledged this principle of the unfinished regarding *Pride and Prejudice*, she became all the more ven-turesome, as we shall see, in *Emma*. The author's advice to her niece Anna, written during the composition of *Emma*, hints at the many omissions she had to decide upon in the in-terest of engaging the reader: "You describe a sweet place, but your descriptions are often more minute than will be liked. You give too many particulars of right hand and left."[37] Doubt-less, it was this finely honed narrative language, in contrast to his own habit of telling everything, that impressed Walter Scott most about Austen's "exquisite touch, which renders ordinary commonplace things and characters interesting."[38]

It is an irony of literary history, then, that, unlike many of her twentieth-century admirers, Austen trusted the tale and eschewed the narrative authority often attributed to her novels. As in other Tory interpretations, Graham Hough supports a widely held view of closure in her art and educes her familiar Johnsonian cadences without seeing their reflex-ively subversive contexts.[39] The famous opening sentence of *Pride and Prejudice*, for instance, mimics the aphoristic man-ner of the Augustan moralist to ridicule the mercenary atti-tudes toward marriage in the period: "It is a truth universally acknowledged, that a single man in possession of a good for-tune must be in want of a wife" (*PP*, 3). Superficially, the propo-sition appears to describe the actual desires of rich bache-lors in any society; but the absoluteness of the "truth" falling abruptly on the periodic "wife" makes the tone suspicious, no longer a mere statement of fact. It suddenly discloses the motives for courtship to be integral to the prevailing economic system, which made daughters the pawns of their families in settling property. With this situation brought to mind, the proposition, far from being universal, applies specifically to parents burdened with unmarried daughters, who look upon any rich bachelor as the one hope of deliverance. Finally, in the ensuing dialogue, we quickly see that what began as an assertion about life in general has narrowed to the blinkered vision of Mrs. Bennet. Not authority, therefore, but only the threadbare authoritarian manner is what the narrative tone implies.

By contrast to Austen's mock dogmatism, Johnson's style in *Rambler* no. 85 has the strategy of making an opinion seem deductively true: "It is certain that any wild Wish or vain Imagination never takes such firm Possession of the Mind, as when it is found empty and unoccupied."[40] Why is it certain? On the authority of the "old peripatetick Principle, that *Nature abhors a Vacuum*," Johnson infers a universal mechanism to account for daydreaming as well as for atmospheric pressure. Since the mind "will embrace any Thing however absurd or criminal rather than be wholly without an Object," Johnson concludes that work of any kind, if only embroidering or knitting, is therapeutic against this natural tendency. The essayist's persuasive authority seems incontrovertible, and Austen presses its declamatory voice into comic service while pursuing her errant characters' ambitions. As Reuben Brower observes, Austen's style is a triumph of combining the "traditions of poetic satire with those of the sentimental novel."[41] Thus, rather than attribute the "voice of the author" to Johnson, it is more accurate to trace the influence to the Augustan mock-heroic: "All human things are subject to decay, / And when fate summons, monarchs must obey." Closer to home, Austen universalizes a less awesome fate: "Human nature is so well disposed towards those who are in interesting situations, that a young person, who either marries or dies, is sure of being kindly spoken of."[42]

A striking quality of her narrative is its self-conscious undermining of the artistic illusion to create a yet deeper impression of reality, the onion-peeling effect first exploited in *Don Quixote*. By this strategy the "voice of the author" itself is bracketed in Austen, inevitably related to some character's point of view and hence only another fictional element. Paradoxically, Austen gains authority in her narrative by seeming to renounce any claim to it, allowing her characters to speak for themselves and her readers to indulge in vicarious virtue or naughtiness, whatever the textual encounter calls for. Occasionally the "voice of the author" is invoked to implicate the reader in a character's private sarcasm at the expense of another, unsuspecting character.

Perhaps the most embarrassing example of this technique is in chapter 8 of *Persuasion,* when Anne is relishing an intimate glimpse of Captain Wentworth's secret contempt for the deceased Richard Musgrove while outwardly showing "the kindest consideration for all that was real and unabsurd in the parent's feelings" (*P,* 68). On numerous other occasions two characters confide in attacking a third, usually a loquacious one—Catherine and Henry versus Mrs. Allen; Elinor and Marianne versus Mrs. Jennings; Elizabeth Bennet and her father versus Mr. Collins; and Emma and Mrs. Weston versus Miss Bates. But in this scene the "voice of the author" adds support to the heroine's rare moment of triumphant egotism while shielded on the sofa by the corpulent Mrs. Musgrove, whose "large fat sighings over the destiny of a son, whom alive nobody cared for" are presumably a test of Wentworth's self-restraint from laughter: "Personal size and mental sorrow have certainly no necessary proportions. A large bulky figure has as good a right to be in deep affliction, as the most graceful set of limbs in the world. But, fair or not fair, there are unbecoming conjunctions, which reason will patronize in vain,—which taste cannot tolerate,—which ridicule will seize" (*P,* 68). If this moment of Johnsonian sententiousness seems out of place here, remote from the spirit of Mr. Rambler, it is owing largely to Austen's very different aesthetic purpose. Mrs. Musgrove, we are being reminded, is only a comic character, not a flesh-and-blood creature entitled to genuine grief and thus to our human compassion. The issue is nevertheless confused because Anne Elliot otherwise never expresses such nastiness toward even foolish characters and generally maintains a tone of high seriousness. To the carnivorous author—and reader—even a character who has exerted a certain hold on life as a free individual with a private history becomes fair game as a textual stereotype, to be devoured as food at the narrator's table. Again the semiotic model of representation competes with the psychological one.

4. Subjective and Objective Description

Inclusive particularity, "thingness" as an end in itself, reduced scale, "low life"—these have been features of description usually conducive to the illusion of the lived character. Together with the bifurcations of self and other, of inner and outer awareness of self, and of dominant author and passive reader, minute presentation of the character's mental and physical environment has seemed generic to the novel's form. Moreover, as opposed to narrative, description is usually taken to be static language from the omniscient author and hence without voice, often dead weight in the storytelling process and most safely skipped if one is in a hurry. Austen's caution to Fanny against describing too much recognizes this fact, and her own novels exemplify an Augustan economy in this respect. Unlike Radcliffe, Scott, or the great Victorian novelists, Austen rarely attempts to paint a scene with words and is likewise sparing in describing her character's emotions. Always the spectre of Tristram's blank, black, or marbled page prompts her to leave something for the reader to do.

Description in Austen's world has generally appeared to reflect a limited but solid grasp of things, a welcome relief from the modern condition; and until recently her playful irreverence, most conspicuous in *Pride and Prejudice* and in *Emma*, could be dismissed as a temporary aberration. Yet, despite the reassurance of the Olympian narrative manner, the Austen environment is remarkably circumstantial and fragmented; consequently, not only is sentimental love anathema, but even the most positive attachments have some degree of distrust and tend to occur by accident. Daniel Cottom observes: "As opposed to the providential pattern of communication which proceeds from a loss of truth through various confusions and errors to a final reclamation of that original truth, communication in Austen's novels generally proceeds by half-measures and half-truths."[43] In Cottom's view, Austen marks the end of the eighteenth-century scheme of subordinating everyday events to a universal plan; and although she preserved the convention of happy endings in her comic plots, she differs from her predecessors in stressing the minute complications of story rather than their formal resolutions. The fragility of individual judgments and the evident incoherence of the social background are what her selective description invites the reader to see.

Description in Austen, however, serves two primary and opposite functions: to render emotional states by means of a "scientific," disinterested vocabulary and to render the physical world by means of an individual perspective. To paraphrase the authors of the *Lyrical Ballads*, Austen's aesthetic works toward making the private feelings part of communal experience and toward revealing the ordinary outside world to be capable of unexpected perceptions.[44] In the first instance, she uses a commonplace diction based on the eighteenth-century sensationism deriving from Hobbes, Descartes, Locke, Hume, Hartley, and others; in the second instance, she positions the character in a scene with remarkable exactitude and then plays upon the vagaries of the lonely mind that images the reality.

For tracing the character's linear movement of feelings in a one-to-one causality of stimuli, Ann Radcliffe is probably an important source:

> Her mind was, at length, so much agitated by the consideration of her state, and the belief, that she had seen Valancourt for the last time, that she suddenly became very faint, and, looking round the chamber for something that might revive her, she observed the casements, and had just strength to throw one open, near which she seated herself. The air recalled her spirits, and the still moonlight, that fell upon the elms of a long avenue, fronting the window, somewhat soothed them, and determined her to try whether exercise and the open air would not relieve the intense pain that bound her temples.[45]

The mind/body interaction here may be reduced schematically: agitation (caused by the aunt's interference and the lover's departure) produces faintness; revived spirits (under the influence of fresh air and moonlight) result in the desire for exercise to overcome headache. Although mechanically applied in

Radcliffe, this nomenclature from eighteenth-century physiology gained new force in Sterne's comic fiction; and Austen assimilates it in a style parallel to the economic and arithmetical language of measurement recognized by Mark Schorer and Dorothy Van Ghent.[46]

Just as the mock-heroic "voice of the author" plays against omniscient authority, however, so the descriptive matrix in Austen helps to bolster up provisionally the threatening circumstantiality by alluding to forces that operate according to universal laws, though its obsolescent epistemological basis also raises doubts about the long-term effect of these forces in human affairs. Deriving from what Foucault understands as one of three avenues to knowledge in the classical *episteme*— *Taxinomia*, the science of finding identities and differences— this matrix of classification already had a quaintly archaic connotation in the period of Wordsworth.[47]

A few categories of Austen's affective description will suffice to show the implicit hierarchy of values in the nomenclature. "Agitation" (*agitare*, "to put in motion") is a word reserved for the most crucial moments in her novels and almost always is applied to a character when unobserved except by the privileged narrator and reader. Inevitably the emotion results from a conflict with another person. After the first news of Edward Ferrar's disinheritance, for instance, "Elinor had heard enough . . . to agitate her nerves and fill her mind" (*SS*, 297). Catherine Morland's "agitation as they entered the great gallery was too much for any endeavour at discourse" (*NA*, 191). The thought of the breach between Bingley and Jane is traumatic to Elizabeth: "The agitation and tears which the subject occasioned brought on a headach [*sic*]" (*PP*, 187). Since agitation is an involuntary motion produced by some outside force, in an ethical world that places the highest value on the freedom of the will, it is always met as a danger to the self; and the Austen protagonist usually has to *exert* herself to overcome it.

In terms of the novel's overall textuality, as opposed to the individual character's psychology, however, agitation is a stimulus to perceive the world of minute things being put into motion and acquiring an autonomous life in the narrative: bed curtains, door locks, pens, pencils, scissors, pianos, watches, toothpick cases, spectacles, and carriages suddenly become equivalent to the nerves and spirits, reminding us of Burke's idea taken from Stoic philosophy "that the influence of most

things on our passions is not so much from the things themselves, as from our opinions concerning them."[48] Alan McKillop
has noted how both Richardson and Sterne reduced the scale
of perception, the latter even to a microscopic extreme; and
Barbara Hardy has shown that this focus on everyday objects
is shared by all the major writers of the genre: "The novel can
create a second coming of *things*, beautiful or functional, lucid
or inscrutable, friendly or obstructive, outside ourselves but
connected with us for better or worse."[49] It is this materi-
alistic/kinetic thingness in Austen's description that renders
fully public the character's innermost feelings.

"Animation" is Austen's principal term for the overcoming of rest, the ennui inevitable to sensationist beings
caught in the flux of stimuli. As Newton remarked soberly:
"[M]otion is much more apt to be lost than got, and is always
upon the Decay."[50] This biological sign tends to be invoked in
social contexts to register an individual's energy level, and
often the aristocratic character is perceived to be deficient.
Pamela's conquest of Mr. B. is a likely paradigm for Elizabeth's
advantage over Mr. Darcy, who "seldom appeared really ani-
mated" (*PP*, 180). Elizabeth's function is to make him smile
more, just as his is to make her smile less. In contrast to these
complementary spirits, Mrs. Bennet's and Lydia's laughter
suggests an animal energy that endangers polite society. Yet,
as Fielding implies through the character of Blifil, a dearth of
libido results in sinister behavior; and thus Anne Elliot's first
judgment about her cousin's polished demeanor is ominous:
"There was never any burst of feeling, any warmth of indignation or delight, at the evil or good of others" (*P*, 161).

Even the most lively temperaments, however, are
subject to depression, though readily activated again by the
least change in the environment: Frank Churchill's return to
Randalls "was a most delightful re-animation of exhausted
spirits. The worn-out past was sunk in the freshness of what
was coming" (*E*, 188). If humors at a fixed, low energy cannot
be reanimated, they can be altered by external events: Mr.
Woodhouse's acceptance of Emma's marrying comes about not
by "any wonderful change of his nervous system, but by the
operation of the same system in another way" (*E*, 483). The
raiding of the poultry houses ("Pilfering was *housebreaking* to
Mr. Woodhouse's fears") poses a somewhat worse threat than
the marriage contract to his wombed space.

"Flutter of spirits" or simply "nerves" denotes the

involuntary operations of the mind, with "fidgettiness" at the bottom of the scale of meaningful motions. Marianne's "spirits still continued very high, but there was a flutter in them which prevented their giving much pleasure to her sister, and this agitation increased as the evening drew on" (*SS*, 161). Elizabeth's "spirits were in a high flutter" as her carriage approaches Pemberley (*PP*, 245); but after contemplating the house and grounds, hearing Mrs. Reynolds's account, and seeing Mr. Darcy's picture in the gallery amidst his ancestors, her opinion rises: "There was certainly at this moment, in Elizabeth's mind, a more gentle sensation towards the original, than she had ever felt in the height of their acquaintance" (*PP*, 250); then, just before Mr. Darcy himself appears unexpectedly, "she thought of his regard with a deeper sentiment of gratitude than it had ever raised before" (*PP*, 251). Harriet's "all flutter and happiness" (*E*, 73), by contrast, is as mechanically reflexive as Mr. Woodhouse's "peculiarities and fidgettiness" (*E*, 93), Isabella Knightley's "little nervous head-aches and palpitations" (*E*, 103), and Mr. Elton's and Emma's "irritation of spirits" (*E*, 132). A similarly unconscious mind goes through the same movements: Maria Bertram's "spirits were in as happy a flutter as vanity and pride could furnish" (*MP*, 83) at Sotherton, while the machinelike Mrs. Norris "fidgetted about" (*MP*, 104) without more purpose than supplying herself with some eggs and cheese from the kitchen, niggardly behavior for one associated with Mansfield Park. Anne Elliot was "quite ashamed of being so nervous" in the scene when Wentworth rescues her from little Walter's clutches (*P*, 81); but at the time of Louisa's accident she resembles Captain Harville, who "brought senses and nerves that could be instantly useful" (*P*, 111). In this last context, it will be noticed, "nerves" denotes purposeful energy, in contrast to the neurotic behavior of Mary Musgrove or the hysterical fits of Henrietta.

A singular term that implies the interest at the time in galvanism as containing the secrets of life occurs early in *Persuasion:* Anne Elliot meets Mrs. Croft "full of strength and courage" until she is "electrified" by the first mention of Wentworth. The word *electrified* used to describe Anne's instantaneous metamorphosis recalls Erasmus Darwin's experiments on electrifying a strand of vermicelli thus giving it the appearance of life, an experiment that inspired Mary Shelley to write a tale about animating a corpse. The static electrical "bath" treatment, which Austen's brother Edward tried for his gout, is also a probable analogy to the shock Anne feels in that moment. In contrast to this au courant image, used only once or twice in all of Austen's writing, a traditional allusion conveys the moment of recognition in *Emma:* "It darted through her, with the speed of an arrow" (*E*, 408). Characters who lack this force, the product of the impetus on a body that resists the movement, die off before the end of the novel: Mrs. Churchill, who had "no more heart than a stone to people in general" (*E*, 121); Mr. Norris, who "could no more bear the noise of a child than he could fly" (*MP*, 9); Dr. Grant, who, as Tom Bertram said, "was a short-neck'd apoplectic sort of fellow, and, plied well with good things, would soon pop off" (*MP*, 24); and Mr. Elliot, whose cold politeness is metaphorically rewarded by his union with Mrs. *Clay.* In sum, Austen's nomenclature for describing a character's emotion and bodily changes implies a whole microcosm of kinetic forces that operate at different moments and intensities. Though her minor characters are comically limited to a few behavioral tics, her central characters are rendered as beings with a complex consciousness who struggle against their circumstantiality.

From this brief review of her sensationist taxonomy, it should be evident that Austen's descriptive purpose is hardly to render a visual image of her character but rather to provide a zone of kinetic energy, an environment in which communication of some sort is possible, ranging from the lowliest twitching to the most ecstatic impulse. In contrast to such details of movement, the Austen character's physical appearance—her hairstyle, complexion, physiognomy, manner of dress, and the like—is left significantly vague for the reader to "fill in"—one reason why attempted dramatizations on stage and in films are especially difficult with this novelist. It should also be evident, furthermore, that this system of vectors obviates the character's individuality by showing her to be participating in impersonal and universal forces, and hence not wholly responsible for her behavior.[51]

At the other end of the spectrum from this "objective" description, the Austen character projects herself in the act of perceiving and experiences her environment as a phenomenon. In the earliest novels this technique mostly delineates a culpable intentionality, an idea brought home when the

Dashwood sisters disagree about the identity of a man seen in the distance:

> Amongst the objects in the scene, they soon discovered an animated one; it was a man on horseback riding towards them. In a few minutes they could distinguish him to be a gentleman; and in a moment afterwards Marianne rapturously exclaimed,
> "It is he; it is indeed;—I know it is!"—And was hastening to meet him, when Elinor cried out,
> "Indeed, Marianne, I think you are mistaken. It is not Willoughby. The person is not tall enough for him, and has not his air."
> "He has, he has," cried Marianne, "I am sure he has. His air, his coat, his horse. I knew how soon he would come." (*SS*, 86)

Of course, Elinor is right as usual: the figure turns out to be the lacklustre, commonsensical Edward instead of the dashing Willoughby; and the narrative does not suggest that *her* intentionality is involved in spotting *her* lover. Presumably, here the ideal of disinterested observation has its own reward; and the reader will never be the wiser about the air, coat, and horse of either man.

Elsewhere, in less morally tendentious encounters, positional description renders a character's timbre along with the object perceived. Thus Emma's daydreaming at Ford's is a tour de force to illustrate how "A mind lively and at ease, can do with seeing nothing, and can see nothing that does not answer" (*E*, 233). Although Mr. Knightley maintains Elinor Dashwood's ideal of objectivity, Emma provides a deeper insight concerning the inevitable subjectivity of vision; the attempt to describe things, she recognizes, is always positional, and ultimately circular. Despite Tory insistence on his voice as norm throughout the story, Mr. Knightley is not flexible enough to see that Emma deliberately improves Harriet's picture for Mr. Elton's benefit:

> "You have made her too tall, Emma," said Mr. Knightley.
> Emma knew that she had, but would not own it, and Mr. Elton warmly added,
> "Oh, no! certainly not too tall; not in the least too tall. Consider, she is sitting down—which

naturally presents a different—which in short gives
exactly the idea—and the proportions must be preserved, you know. Proportions, fore-shortening.—
Oh, no! It gives one exactly the idea of such a height
as Miss Smith's. Exactly so indeed!" (*E*, 48)

What is important here is not that Mr. Knightley is right and
Emma knows it, but that they are each approaching the object
from different perspectives: the one, moral; the other, aesthetic.[52] Mr. Elton, we may safely assume, is merely spouting
the jargon of art appreciation classes without seeing anything.
But Mr. Knightley insists on a scientifically objective duplica-
tion, no matter what the cost to Harriet's self-esteem and interest as a subject (also, of course, as a possible object of desire); and Emma insists on the artist's prerogative to enhance
nature and create something suitable for the mantelpiece, a
point Mr. Elton confusedly supports in his misguided designs
on the artist. Thanks to the author's own designs, again the
reader will never find out whether Harriet is relatively tall
or short, or merely average, in her particular society: the
hard scientific information of whether she is 5'4" or 5'6" would
be wholly irrelevant and even destructive to the narrative
purpose.

    With the help of such dramatized encounters involv-
ing problems of intentionality, Austen seems almost at pains to
align her taut descriptions of place with the lessons provided
by Fielding and Sterne before her. The narrator of *Tom Jones*,
for example, refused to paint the landscape on the journey to
London in any detail but instead focused on the disposition of
the observer:

The same Taste, the same Imagination, which luxu-
riously riots in these elegant Scenes, can be amused
with Objects of far inferior Note. The Woods, the
Rivers, the Lawns of *Devon* and of *Dorset*, attract the
Eye of the Ingenious Traveller, and retard his Pace,
which Delay he afterwards compensates by swiftly
scouring over the gloomy Heath of *Bagshot*, or that
pleasant Plain which extends itself Westward from
Stockbridge, where no other Object than one single
Tree only in sixteen Miles presents itself to the View,
unless the Clouds, in Compassion to our tired Spirits, kindly open their variegated Mansions to our
Prospects.[53]

In the same vein, Austen abrogates her narrative privilege and assigns the reader the task of knowing the places alluded to: "It is not the object of this work to give a description of Derbyshire, nor of any of the remarkable places through which their route thither lay; Oxford, Blenheim, Warwick, Kenelworth, Birmingham, &c. are sufficiently known. A small part of Derbyshire is all the present concern" (*PP*, 240). When we arrive at Pemberley immediately after this passage, the narrator cites only broad architectural features to register the datum of Mr. Darcy's sound Augustan taste, features reminiscent of Squire Allworthy's estate or those of the Man of Ross.[54]

At first glance the description of Pemberley itself may appear to stem from an omniscient narrator's point of view; but if we recall the explicit fact that it is seen from the heroine's perspective, even the few details given take on a positional significance:

> Elizabeth's mind was too full for conversation, but she saw and admired every remarkable spot and point of view. They gradually ascended for half a mile, and then found themselves at the top of a considerable eminence, where the wood ceased, and the eye was instantly caught by Pemberley House, situated on the opposite side of a valley, into which the road with some abruptness wound. *It was a large, handsome, stone building, standing well on rising ground, and backed by a ridge of high woody hills;—and in front, a stream of some natural importance was swelled into greater, but without any artificial appearance. Its banks were neither formal, nor falsely adorned.* Elizabeth was delighted. She had never seen a place for which nature had done more, or where natural beauty had been so little counteracted by an awkward taste. They were all of them warm in their admiration; and at that moment she felt, that to be mistress of Pemberley might be something! (*PP*, 245; my emphasis)

Who is speaking the words emphasized in this passage? Ostensibly the impartial narrator; but the context indicates that these judgments may be read as free indirect discourse, to be attributed primarily to Elizabeth and seconded by the Gardiners. Once individualized, the description becomes appropriated to the temporal scheme of the heroine's musings on the scene; and so every detail suddenly takes on a personal significance, a heightened awareness of Mr. Darcy as perceived through the metonyms of the building and grounds. Apart from their being proof of the owner's good taste, the details symbolize masculine power, in the stone edifice as well as in all the rising and swelling of the ground and stream. Almost as if awed by this immediate sexual apprehension and supported by her parental surrogates' admiration, Elizabeth's lips cannot resist forming the words in silence: "To be mistress of Pemberley might be something!"

Another example of how positional description fuses place and personhood in the viewer's mind appears in Emma's reverie at Donwell:

> She felt all the honest pride and complacency which her alliance with the present and future proprietor could fairly warrant, as she viewed *the respectable size and style of the building, its suitable, becoming, characteristic situation, low and sheltered—its ample gardens stretching down to meadows washed by a stream, of which the Abbey, with all the old neglect of prospect, had scarcely a sight. . . .*
>
> *It was a sweet view—sweet to the eye and the mind. English verdure, English culture, English comfort, seen under a sun bright, without being oppressive.* (*E*, 358–360; my emphasis)

Unlike Elizabeth at Pemberley, Emma does not discover anything new about the hero in her perception of this landscape, and the abrupt sight of him together with her young friend only increases the pleasure of the place rather than arousing any jealousy at this stage. Instead, Mr. Knightley and the Donwell estate are perceived as a unity, connoting all that is good in an agrarian culture; his attention to Harriet is part of his nurturing role in the scene. The positional description moves from this state of tranquil receptivity to a more aggressive, judgmental intentionality:

> There had been a time also when Emma would have been sorry to see Harriet in a spot so favourable for the Abbey-Mill Farm; but now she feared it not. *It might be safely viewed with all its appendages of prosperity and beauty, its rich pastures, spreading flocks, orchard in blossom, and light column of smoke ascending.* (*E*, 360; my emphasis)

With complete confidence that Mr. Knightley belongs to her, Emma never questions the tête-à-tête before her but gloats instead on her having separated her protégée from Robert Martin, represented by Abbey-Mill Farm. Conveyed by free indirect discourse, the few attributes of the picturesque scene, however, are enough to assure us not only of what Harriet Smith is in danger of losing, thanks to her friend's overreaching, but also of a mind open to pastoral beauty, a mind worthy of Mr. Knightley. The details themselves, it will be seen, are the barest essentials of almost any landscape painting of the day, with its requisite column of smoke rising from the cottage chimney. What matters is that Emma perceives it under the particular conditions of the moment: and at this moment the place is infused in her mind with the spirit of Mr. Knightley.

Character in Austen, we have seen, is an image of individual life stemming from a variety of represented speech within meaningful contexts. Although singled out in the story as a person with a particular name and a certain history, when not merely referred to but actually doing something, the character is a voice within a multiple structure of discourse. She may be reified and given psychological motives in the reading process, but her textual existence is linguistic, subject to the limits of words and empty spaces, with intentional and unintentional mimetic effects. Austen's parodic art mixes uneasily with her "serious" moral realism, and consequently at times the sincere ideal appears to conflict with role-playing as a way of being.

Traditional dichotomies for understanding the individual consciousness are still useful; but Austen's reflexive text shows the provisional otherness of self called forth in her original use of free indirect discourse. Instead of having rigid identities, characters in her novels inhabit a field and often quite literally speak the same language as well as share the same mind-set. Although the narrators may project authority and normative stances, their main function is to render the character's finite point of view without invoking the privileges of authorial omniscience; and in free indirect discourse the storyteller and the subject become indistinguishable. Through the same positional strategy, Austen turns even description into a kinetic language, which merges subject and object in the phenomenon of the encounter.

IV. Speech

Like dancing, playing cards, or writing a novel, conversation is a structured event, usually involving three roles—a speaker, a listener, and an observer of the exchange. Tristram addresses the reader while recording his mother's interruption of his father, and likewise Walter addresses his wife while spying on Toby and Mrs. Wadman at close quarters. In Austen, except for occasional narrative interference, the third role goes unnoticed for long stretches, as the external reader quietly eavesdrops on direct discourse. Although the topics of conversation may vary from the weather, travel time and distance, food and health, gardening, novels and poetry, preaching, the navy, the poor, and entailments, gossip is what exercises the participants the most; and so a fourth part in conversation may be filled by the person spoken about, who is usually identified by certain roles each time he or she is mentioned.

Numerous characters, especially servants, owe their existence in the text solely to the way they are perceived by other characters. Robert Martin, for instance, does "actually" make a brief appearance but never says a word himself; his function throughout the story is mainly as a referent; even his letter to Harriet is used as a text (without any specimens reproduced) for a lesson on the writing style of a gentleman. A far more peripheral character like Hannah, the daughter of the Woodhouses' servant, James, owes her textual life to a single item—her exemplary deference to authority and poor nerves alike: "'Whenever I see her, she always curtseys and asks me how I do, in a very pretty manner; and when you have had her here to do needlework, I observe she always turns the lock of the door the right way and never bangs it'" (*E*, 9). Similarly, the Bennet's housekeeper, Mrs. Hill, attains existence when Mrs. Bennet wants to speak to her about the scarcity of fish on the day that Mr. Bingley is mistakenly supposed to dine with them (*PP*, 61); at a later point, this same referent is allowed a few words of joy over Lydia's wedding plans (*PP*, 301, 307); and finally, without being named or credited, this good woman is doubtless to be thanked for the succulent roast venison served to Mr. Bingley and Mr. Darcy (*PP*, 342). Not just servants but many other voiceless members of the community, including the deceased, exert a significant hold on the discourse at center stage.

Not words per se but the expressed intentions of the principals are what structure conversation: the whole encounter depends on cooperation between the speaker and the listener to permit the rhythm of stimulus and response. Without a partner who agrees to interact appropriately, not only remaining silent out of deference, but also reciprocating with the corresponding sounds and gestures when called upon, the speaker is at a loss in the performance; and hard feelings ensue. Because of their primordial rivalry for control over the drawing room, Austen's older women especially have difficulties in conversation and often depart from an encounter in deep discontent. By contrast, the heroines, as we have seen, are both model speakers and listeners, capable of repartee or moral sentiment, depending on the situation; and if they do not know exactly how to cajole their counterparts in the heat of the moment, they are lucky enough to produce an effective response anyway, as in Catherine Morland's disarmingly ingenuous replies to Henry.

Amidst the variety of speaking in Austen's novels, besides conversation as an experience having a direct impact on the character's thoughts, there are moments of unstructured talk, discourse run wild in the text like mutational sports that lacks proper listeners. Humors appear who assert their presence by the energy of sheer ejaculation, often without the least concern for a response from an interlocutor. Like the useful instruction given by bad actors, who by breaking the rules reveal what is requisite of art, their unedited flow creates a needed waste in the text to put into relief the highly selective language used to etch the central characters. Despite their inconsequential talk in dramatic situations, these comic humors season the narrative feast, particularly when mimicked by another character in free indirect discourse.

Among all of Austen's heavy talkers, Miss Bates is the most capacious source of meaning not only for the story but, more importantly, for the author's technique of representing speech in general. Although Mary Lascelles pointed out years ago the importance of Miss Bates's speeches in letting the reader in on the secret engagement of Jane Fairfax and Frank

Churchill, their value as discourse of the mind has usually escaped notice, though Marilyn Butler comes close to the point by recognizing the essential isolation of this character.[1] In studying the way in which characters perceive each other, Susan Morgan probably declares a widespread assumption about this loquacious humor: "Miss Bates tells everybody everything; facts, feelings, details jumbled together, as fast as she thinks of them. . . . Unlike those who perceive according to preconceived structures, Miss Bates doesn't shape or select or distinguish at all."[2]

On two important occasions, however, Miss Bates surprises us by showing that indeed she does shape, select, and distinguish: during the visit to Hartfield, when she almost perversely insists on the truth in contrast to Frank Churchill's flimsy alibi about Mr. Perry's plans to set up a carriage; and, of course, on Box Hill when she suddenly penetrates Emma's witticism and confronts the heroine with her tactlessness. At times this prolific word-maker acts like the author's fifth columnist by stepping into a scene and playing havoc with the "clever" talkers in the story; and among Miss Bates's various functions, perhaps the most intriguing is the expression of an existential loneliness that no other characters can voice in their polite conversation. Through direct discourse, unfiltered by the narrator and usually ignored by the other characters, a voice enters the text to disclose the possibility of an "inner" life omitted in the story proper.

In contrast to the speech acts of real-life situations, with all the variables of physical sound, gesture, and countenance, a fictional character's direct discourse needs to be rigorously contextualized to have meaning; and in Austen there are some surprisingly indeterminate moments because of the spare narrative economy. To help read Miss Bates's humor, it will be useful to examine less complex talkers in the repertory. Mrs. Jennings comes closest to Miss Bates as a good-natured talker, whereas Mrs. Bennet's language rarely includes noncontingent relationships. Though not presented as a humorous talker, Mrs. Allen has stretches of unforgettable discourse and surely belongs to the archetype of monologist that is most complete in Miss Bates. One liability shared by all these characters is the unwillingness of others, doubtless including many external readers, to listen to their prattle.

1. Mrs. Allen: "No Real Intelligence to Give"

Among the many samples of pointless talk in *North-anger Abbey*, Mrs. Allen's discourse reveals the most narrow form of associationism: "Dress was her passion" (*NA*, 20); and on every occasion without fail she is the materialistic half of Pope's antithesis, "Or stain her honour, or her new brocade," oblivious to the moral significance of events: "With more care for the safety of her new gown than for the comfort of her pro-tegée [sic], Mrs. Allen made her way through the throng of men" (*NA*, 21). Besides not having children of her own, she is hopelessly incompetent as a foster-parent to Catherine during their visit to Bath. The most serious problem of her obsession with clothes, in brief, is its utter replacement of normal hu-man relationships, which is evident in her inane effort at con-versation. When Catherine is dejected by being alone at the dance, "Mrs. Allen did all that she could do in such a case by saying very placidly, every now and then, 'I wish you could dance, my dear,—I wish you could get a partner.' For some time her young friend felt obliged to her for these wishes; but they were repeated so often, and proved so totally ineffectual, that Catherine grew tired at last, and would thank her no more" (*NA*, 21). What makes Mrs. Allen's speech acts "so totally inef-fectual" is their schizoidal separation from the other's pres-ence, a handicap underscored summarily by the narrator, for instance, in the meeting with Mrs. Thorpe, "talking both to-gether, far more ready to give than to receive information, and each hearing very little of what the other said" (*NA*, 32). Over-whelmed by the latter's plethora of information to give, thanks to a numerous family, Mrs. Allen "was forced to sit and appear to listen to all these maternal effusions, consoling herself, how-ever, with the discovery, which her keen eye soon made, that the lace on Mrs. Thorpe's pelisse was not half so handsome as that on her own" (*NA*, 32). Despite this fundamental barrier, however, the two women come together almost daily "in what they called conversation, but in which there was scarcely ever any exchange of opinion, and not often any resemblance of subject, for Mrs. Thorpe talked chiefly of her children, and Mrs. Allen of her gowns" (*NA*, 36). In its transparent reductionism, the humorous split between the two contending speakers highlights other individualized discourses in the story that pretend to express real feeling by emulating sentimental and Gothic texts.

Mrs. Allen's total withdrawal from any concern with others is one of Catherine's early discoveries about her environment, and the woman's speech habits are the means to this truth:

> from habitude very little incommoded by the remarks and ejaculations of Mrs. Allen, whose vacancy of mind and incapacity for thinking were such, that as she never talked a great deal, so she could never be entirely silent; and, therefore, while she sat at her work, if she lost her needle or broke her thread, if she heard a carriage in the street, or saw a speck upon her gown, she must observe it aloud, whether there were any one at leisure to answer her or not. (*NA*, 60–61)

Conversely, later in this same chapter Catherine tries to give a signal for help from Mrs. Allen while fending off John Thorpe's Claverton Down scheme; but it is in vain, for the woman "not being at all in the habit of conveying any expression herself by a look, was not aware of its being ever intended by any body else" (*NA*, 61). If Mr. Allen, among the first of the sullen counterparts to loquacious humors in Austen's gallery, objects to "young men and women driving about the country in open carriages" on grounds of impropriety, his wife objects simply because "a clean gown is not five minutes wear in them" (*NA*, 104). Yet neither one shows any emotion upon the announcement of James's engagement to Isabella: "It was to Catherine the most surprising insensibility" (*NA*, 125). Apparently the Allen marriage "works," we are to understand, because it is based on a mutual insensibility and psychological isolation, an arrangement implied by La Rochefoucauld: "Good marriages do exist, but not delectable ones."[3] After her ultimate crisis of expulsion from Northanger to Fullerton, Catherine can expect even less consolation from the Allens than from her own parents: while Mrs. Morland at least looks for an appropriate text of morality to suit her daughter's situation, Mrs. Allen can only repeat her husband's "wonder," "conjectures," and "explanations" (*NA*, 237).

Since Mrs. Allen is radically cut off from her environment in all but the instrumentality of clothes, she has little to communicate, not even whether the Tilneys are dead or alive: "Catherine inquired no further; she had heard enough to feel that Mrs. Allen had no real intelligence to give" (*NA*, 69). Though the primary meaning here of "intelligence" is "information," the narrator may also be invoking Henry's sense of "intellectual poverty." Emma Woodhouse is often in a parallel position with Miss Bates as Catherine is with Mrs. Allen; but there is one very significant difference: Miss Bates's speech, as we shall see, almost always offers information to anyone who cares to listen.

No real intelligence to give: Mrs. Allen's discourse fails both as constative and as performative speech, but the narrator emphasizes the former specifically. It is for Catherine, however, to register firsthand the boredom Mrs. Allen's monotonous conversation elicits; and her discernment here aligns her perfectly with Henry when he pronounces on the quality of life at Fullerton: "What a picture of intellectual poverty!" (*NA*, 79).

2. Mrs. Jennings: "A Voice of Great Compassion"

While Mrs. Allen is the ejaculating solitary self, Mrs. Jennings, in *Sense and Sensibility*, introduced misleadingly as "full of jokes and laughter" (*SS*, 34), is vicariously involved in the lives of the young—whether in their throes of courtship or their fears during pregnancy—and immediately feels compassion when called upon, as in the jilting of Marianne: "Poor soul! I am sure if I had had a notion of it, I would not have joked her about it for all my money" (*SS*, 195). Despite first appearances, her busy talk is never really malicious, as Elinor comes to learn and later instructs her sister, but shows a genuine interest in others and always has something to communicate.

Devoid of any illusions concerning herself, she is "invariably kind" (*SS*, 168) and exposes the egocentric blindness of Marianne, who "expected from other people the same opinions and feelings as her own, and [who] . . . judged of their motives by the immediate effect of their actions on herself"

(*SS*, 202). Unlike other matchmakers, particularly Mrs. Bennet and Emma Woodhouse, Mrs. Jennings is remarkably observant and often lucky in guessing at the potential outcome of the action. Her power of instilling fear in Elinor as well as in Marianne is a function of her penetrating curiosity and quickness in discovering relationships in reflexive imitation of the author. Far from being incidental to the action like Mrs. Allen, Mrs. Jennings serves at least three important functions in this novel: (1) as a comic humor to ventilate the presumed opposition between "sense" and "sensibility," or between rational judgment and emotional response; (2) as a maternal figure to give support, rarely shown in Austen, against the status quo; and (3) as a dramatized reader whose responses to the story are a proximate version of the outside reader's.

From the beginning, Mrs. Jennings's loquacious presence helps to free the narrative from the rigid eighteenth-century dichotomy implied by the title of this novel and thus to allow a broader range of ethical language than Elinor's conduct-book vocabulary provides.[4] Both characters demonstrate that perception must involve both the feelings and the intellect in order to interact with others fully, but the good widow also shows a visceral response to Marianne's pathos that would be unthinkable in the exemplary heroine. Against the narcissistic sensibility of Marianne, Mrs. Jennings's honest self-deprecation is a welcome antidote of common sense: "Aye, it is a fine thing to be young and handsome. Well! I was young once, but I never was very handsome—worse luck for me. However I got a very good husband, and I don't know what the greatest beauty can do more" (*SS*, 163).

Likewise, her ebullient speech relieves the sententious exactitude in Elinor's discourse. Perhaps spoken on her sister's as well as on her own behalf, nevertheless Elinor's refusal ("a grateful but absolute denial") to accompany Mrs. Jennings to London may be a trifle self-complacent and may warrant the volley of parental advice that follows: "I am sure your mother will not object to it; for I have had such good luck in getting my own children off my hands, that she will think me a very fit person to have the charge of you; and if I don't get one of you at least well married before I have done with you, it shall not be my fault" (*SS*, 153–54). If the sentiment sounds absurdly coarse to the delicate ears of the Dashwood sisters, nevertheless it represents not only the way of the world but probably the author's buried aggression against literary paragons of virtue. Elinor herself offers no argument against the woman's well-intentioned pragmatism; and thus Mrs. Jennings's prediction turns out to be right, her voice fulfilling the implied reader's desires in comedy.

In a society where "female sensibility" prohibited allusions to the body, Mrs. Jennings's frankness about sexuality and pregnancy brings some fresh air to the stuffy drawing room. Pamela, we recall, was deeply embarrassed by Mr. B.'s slightest hint of their expecting a child;[5] similarly, Mrs. Jennings's pointed references to Mrs. Palmer's condition shocks her more correct daughter: "Lady Middleton could no longer endure such a conversation, and therefore exerted herself to ask Mr. Palmer if there was any news in the paper" (*SS*, 108). Later, however, her proud speculation, "I warrant you she is a fine size by this time" (*SS*,163), fails to disturb Colonel Brandon, thereby proving his ingenuousness. Ironically, by rumoring him to be the natural father of little Eliza, her fantasy hints of a sex life otherwise unthinkable in this virtuous bachelor, and hence spices up the dullish Grandisonian *ur*-text.

A humorous composite of both sense and sensibility, Mrs. Jennings can alternate effortlessly between the economic advantages of a match and the claims of the heart; but in serving eros she can also substitute one partner for another without any qualms. For instance, she mistakes Colonel Brandon's remark to Elinor ("I am afraid it cannot take place very soon") for a postponement of their marriage. Earlier, she had matched him to Marianne: "Astonished and shocked at so unlover-like a speech, she was almost ready to cry out, 'Lord! what should hinder it?'—but checking her desire, confined herself to this silent ejaculation. 'This is very strange!—sure he need not wait to be older'" (*SS*, 281). Her jumbling together fragments of conversation to spin out yet another romantic match is not merely quixotic, however, for Elinor herself feels such gratitude for his beneficence that their interview does have the emotional intensity of a proposal scene. As a festive spirit secretly urging the couple toward union, Mrs. Jennings reflects impatiently on Colonel Brandon's age and presumably weak libido ("This is very strange!—sure he need not wait to be older"). Thus her role here is to say what neither the narrator nor any character other than Marianne is allowed the honesty to say.

Remnants of a medieval folk tradition about garrulous and concupiscent widows survive in Mrs. Jennings's matchmaking role, but her indiscriminate benevolence and democratic championing of virtue in distress probably owe something to the eighteenth-century vogue of Don Quixote, represented most successfully in Fielding's Parson Adams.[6] Being a mixture of quite different ethical and psychological attitudes, Mrs. Jennings at times evokes the aggressive sexuality of a Wife of Bath or a Mrs. Jewkes; and at other times she can suddenly become the surrogate mother of the Dashwood sisters, replacing the ineffectual, even harmful, guidance of their own sentimental mother. Already on the road to London she is the jovial benefactress, ever solicitous toward the girls' physical comfort and "only disturbed that she could not make them choose their own dinners at the inn" (*SS*, 160). Although Elinor does grow to love this woman by the time of Marianne's critical illness, when the widow risks her own health to assist with the nursing (*SS*, 308), nevertheless it is not clear in the structure of the story what impact, if any, this awakened sensibility is to have on the heroine. Likewise, the narrator hastily notes Marianne's changed feelings toward Mrs. Jennings (*SS*, 341), but again without indicating their consequences. Some of this ambiguity, it seems safe to assume, reflects the author's own unfinished business in working out all the details of the story.

Perhaps most remarkable is the resistance, sometimes hostility, felt toward Mrs. Jennings's nurturing offices. Quite apart from all her unwanted conviviality in previous scenes, upon discovering that Marianne has been jilted, Mrs. Jennings suddenly speaks "in a voice of great compassion" (*SS*, 192), but to no avail. That Mrs. Jennings is perfectly sincere is never in doubt: the interpretative problem is the Dashwoods' reluctant acceptance of her effort to comfort them, as if someone who talks too much is irredeemable under any circumstances; the same problem reappears in Emma Woodhouse's implacable hatred of Miss Bates.

The narrative renders suspicious how the recipients of charity are to comport themselves under the circumstances: the emphasis on "all the indulgent fondness of a parent towards a favourite child on the last day of its holidays" (*SS*, 193) is hardly reassuring to a wounded ego like Marianne's; and the beneficence of "sweetmeats and olives, and a good fire" is secondary to what poor Elinor endures on behalf of her mute sister in properly acknowledging the widow's services, whose "effusions were often distressing, and sometimes almost ridiculous" (SS, 193). Given their social deprivation at the moment, something seems askew in Elinor's tone toward one who is trying to salvage what little is left to them. When Mrs. Jennings produces her ultimate remedy, "'some of the finest old Constantia wine in the house that ever was tasted,'" for Marianne's indisposition, the report that it was her husband's favorite tonic for "his old cholicky gout" causes Elinor to smile "at the difference of the complaints for which it was recommended" (SS, 198). Within the matrix of giving and receiving, Elinor, as well as her more obviously indulgent sister, cannot help but resent the power they must surrender to the donor.

Minor characters can be useful indicators for confronting the text; in fact, they are texts themselves, blue books for reading the larger fabric of the novel. Mrs. Jennings's penchant for matchmaking is humorously reflexive of the reader's own prying into the narrative and into the characters' cryptic messages; and at some moments she, like the narrator, observes more of the story than Elinor herself, no matter how self-disciplined. The widow may be "a great wonderer," but her uninhibited gusto counters the delusions of sensibility. On the contrary, her discourse always expresses a genuine humility at the cost of an outspoken earthiness: and if its "form" may cause Elinor to smile, its substance is often worthwhile. Without suspecting Lucy Steele's secret engagement, for example, she nevertheless fathoms her character: "but as for Lucy, she is such a sly little creature, there is no finding out who *she* likes" (SS, 148). Described from the beginning of the story as "remarkably quick in the discovery of attachments" (SS, 36), she is the first to detect Colonel Brandon's falling in love with Marianne and to find out that the latter has been with Willoughby to Allenham (SS, 67).

Mrs. Jennings is so observant, indeed, that until Marianne's emotional collapse in London, a large part of the story's suspense involves Elinor's careful maneuvering to keep the truth hidden from her; and after that crisis, all three women, like a trio in a Mozart opera, vie with one another in interpreting the events leading up to Willoughby's stormy confession at Cleveland. Mrs. Jennings's most telling humor, therefore, is in her privilege to the truth that those with either an excess of reason (Elinor) or an excess of emotion (Marianne) are bound to distort. From the perspective of the 1790s, it is tempting to see her as the author's parodic foil to the tired eighteenth-century debate over which was essential to human perception (reason versus the imagination).[7] If Austen herself never theoretically resolved the problem so brilliantly discussed by her contemporaries Wordsworth and Coleridge, at least she could find a voice, no matter how secondary, to express the anxiety of human existence in general. Mrs. Jennings is not to be ignored on this account.

3.   Mrs. Bennet: "A Complete Victory"

Talk as oral aggression and silence as defense, a frequent pattern in *Sense and Sensibility,* are keyed in the structure of *Pride and Prejudice,* where the conflict between parents and children becomes a major subject in the narrative. Introduced flatly as a "woman of mean understanding, little information, and uncertain temper" (*PP,* 5), Mrs. Bennet's discourse promises to be tedious and yet unexpectedly throws light on the central agon. Though not so repetitive as Mrs. Allen's preoccupation with clothes, the same refrain of material/moral dichotomy appears in her good opinion of Mrs. Hurst's gown (*PP,* 13), of Colonel Forster's regimentals (*PP,* 29), of Mrs. Gardiner's information about long sleeves (*PP,* 140), and of Lydia's marriage once "all the particulars of calico, muslin, and cambric" (*PP,* 307) are decided. Unlike Mrs. Jennings's matchmaking pursuit, Mrs. Bennet's obsessive interest is in the economic disposal of her children without any sentimental lingering: "If I can but see one of my daughters happily settled at Netherfield . . . and all the others equally well married, I shall have nothing to wish for" (*PP,* 9). An insensitive manipulator, she interferes even to the extent of commanding her daughter to accept a ridiculous marriage proposal: "Lizzy, I *insist* upon your staying and hearing Mr. Collins"(*PP,* 104). Possessing few redeeming qualities, this character functions mainly as an obstacle, a *sena irata* of comedy, whose tactless words threaten the progress of romance.

Though outré in the manner of Mrs. Allen and Mrs.

Jennings, Mrs. Bennet's principal role in the novel is to compensate for woman's inferior social position by wielding power through offensive speech and by resorting to her "nerves" as a defense whenever convenient. Often she is a mouthpiece to spew out ideas prohibited in civil conversation but relevant to the circumstances, as is demonstrated emphatically in the scene upon Elizabeth's return from Hunsford:

> "And so, I suppose, they often talk of having Longbourn when your father is dead. They look upon it quite as their own, I dare say, whenever that happens."
>
> "It was a subject which they could not mention before me."
>
> "No. It would have been strange if they had. But I make no doubt, they often talk of it between themselves." (*PP*, 228)

To suspect the Collinses of gloating over their eventual inheritance of Longbourn may betray a "mean understanding" and "little information," but granted the egocentric norm of this comic world it is distinctly possible that they *do*, after all, "often talk of it between themselves." Mr. Collins's previous gesture of "atonement" to the Bennets made plain that the entail was very much on his mind, and Mrs. Bennet has good reason to believe that the "Lucases are very artful people indeed" (*PP*, 140).

Despite her muddled reasoning in an argument, Mrs. Bennet is at times disquietingly right about other characters; and her talk has the advantage of filling in many empty spaces in the dialogue and narrative, and of thus imitating the reader's activity. As is already clear from the opening chapter of the novel, her speech has two basic functions: to play alazon to the other's eiron[8] in dialogue, and to demonstrate the false intent of polite conversation. But indirectly, her free talk is useful in expressing the various moods of frustration that arise from woman's subjugation in a male-dominated society; hence, as if to reify a self perpetually disappearing in a void, her words explode spontaneously to release energy and create a presence.

The Bennets' humorous dialogue plays upon the motif of marital asymmetry, the ideal situation for point/counterpoint discourses, which intrigued the author in the lives of her real acquaintances and recurs throughout her novels.[9] Mrs.

Allen, for instance, "was one of that numerous class of females, whose society can raise no other emotion than surprise at there being any men in the world who could like them well enough to marry them" (*NA*, 20). The Allen marriage, we have seen, is a schizoidal partnership; and a similar defensive withdrawal afflicts other couples, like the Palmers, the Collinses, the John Knightleys, and the Bertrams. Mrs. Palmer's disposition, "strongly endowed by nature with a turn for being uniformly civil and happy" (*SS*, 106–07), is the elixir that enables two disparate individuals to interact harmoniously, "'Mr. Palmer is so droll! . . . He is always out of humour'" (*SS*, 112). The usual rhetorical pattern of these asymmetrical couples sets in opposition a malcontent who refuses either to talk amiably or to talk at all and a gregarious character who talks uncontrollably; and in all of this comic exchange we see the persistent loneliness of selfhood. Although not really a conversation, nevertheless if it proves to be a euphoric experience, talk can be another play activity for escaping self-consciousness.

In the brilliant first chapter of *Pride and Prejudice*, Mrs. Bennet's imperviousness to her husband's wit initiates the underlying antagonism between male and female, between parents and children, and between courter and courted, which the story develops in the protagonists. While Mr. Bennet has the upper hand throughout this conversation and the narrator dismisses his spouse summarily as a fool, in retrospect we see that neither husband nor wife really disagrees over the "truth universally acknowledged," but that the issue between them is what appropriate verbal strategy to adopt in coping with the urgent need of marrying off their five daughters within the allotted time.

Whereas Mrs. Bennet loudly testifies to the "truth" and echoes the literal terms of the proposition about "A single man of large fortune," Mr. Bennet pretends to a serene detachment from which to bait his wife in a cat-and-mouse game. A cynical recluse who had married a woman for her looks and now must endure her vulgarity, Mr. Bennet functions as yet another interloper in Austen's comic world, one who delights in mocking the predictable language that situations call forth. In this he resembles Henry Tilney when he parodys a young woman's diary at Bath or her thrill at visiting a Gothic mansion, and also Frank Churchill when he teases Mr. Woodhouse about drafts or Jane Fairfax about their secret engagement. If such meddlers may not escape reproach, they still represent the writer's privilege toward the text.

In all this discourse usually one speaker needs to tamper with the frame to gain control over the situation. By a strange twist of reflexivity, Mr. Bennet's self-deprecation is a means of ruling others in a situation where the imminence of his own death—the ultimate detachment—can arouse a sardonic laugh rather than fear and trembling. Like Don Quixote and Mr. Yorick, this character is quite aware of his textual mortality and has no real choice but to submit to his all-seeing author:

> "My dear, do not give way to such gloomy thoughts. Let us hope for better things. Let us flatter ourselves that *I* may be the survivor."
>
> This was not very consoling to Mrs. Bennet, and, therefore, instead of making any answer, she went on as before. (*PP*, 130)

If Mrs. Bennet may be counted upon to articulate what polite conversation rules out, it is Mr. Bennet's prerogative to reflect sardonically on his textual fate, leaving his interlocutor speechless within the scene. At the story level he may be a disgruntled husband and father, but from the perspective of the author and reader he is often the "dramatized narrator" and consequently seems like a lonely prankster among fools, listening to Mr. Collins "with the keenest enjoyment, maintaining at the same time the most resolute composure of countenance, and except in an occasional glance at Elizabeth, requiring no partner in his pleasure" (*PP*, 68).

A less satisfactory role than as butt for her husband's ridicule is Mrs. Bennet's inclusion in the satire on false politeness illustrated at length by Mr. Collins's speeches and stereotyped by Mrs. Philips, who was "quite awed by such an excess of good breeding" (*PP*, 73). Sincerity of feeling and expression is the norm in this novel, and Elizabeth's and Darcy's candor—even rudeness—sets them apart from most of the other speakers. No less a flatterer than Mr. Collins recognizes the value of sincerity and admits that, while "suggesting and arranging such little elegant compliments as may be adapted to ordinary occasions, I always wish to give them as unstudied an air as possible" (*PP*, 68). Though usually remembered for her bluff form of address, Mrs. Bennet occasionally falls in with Mr. Collins's mode of speech whenever something is to be gained by it; and her design inevitably fails.

During the "ceremony of leave-taking," for example, she invites Mr. Collins "with great politeness and cordiality" to return to Longbourn soon only to learn a moment later of his engagement to Charlotte Lucas. Similarly, while aping his obsequiousness toward Lady Catherine, "Mrs. Bennet, all amazement, though flattered by having a guest of such high importance, received her with the utmost politeness" (*PP*, 351) but in turn is spurned "very resolutely and not very politely." Her susceptibility to flattery, however, is more convincing than her attempt to conjure an effect in others; and she responds automatically to her husband's compliment on her alleged beauty and to Mr. Collins's report of her sister's graciousness. Of course, the mere hint of a marriage proposal changes her completely: "the man whom she could not bear to speak of the day before, was now high in her good graces" (*PP*, 71). Since mainly functional as the voice of unmentionable ideas, Mrs. Bennet's role in the satire on false politeness is neither consistent nor important, possibly yet another example of remnant cloth from the cutting room.

In the eighteenth-century moral psychology incorporated in Austen's narrative, repressed emotion is a means of some personal autonomy under circumstances that are finally beyond the individual's control. Consequently, moments of greatest tension translate into incomplete messages, like Darcy's abrupt proposal (*PP*, 189), which requires a long letter of explanation afterward, like Georgiana's "short sentence" (*PP*, 267), painfully produced during a hostile conversation, or like the total silence at certain points in the text, whether remarked briefly by the narrator or simply left as a gap. Difficulty in speaking, in any case, is one proof of sincerity; however, an eruption of words may be proof of a different kind.[10] Against this ideal of self-discipline in emotion and speech, Mrs. Bennet voices frustrations that motivate Elizabeth's own rebelliousness toward male hegemony in general and economic motives to marrying in particular; yet the rationalistic narrator categorizes her simply as a hypochondriac: "When she was discontented she fancied herself nervous" (*PP*, 5). But Mrs. Bennet's view of the world, far from being illusory, bears out the opening sentence of this novel; and "poor nerves" are her best weapon against an economic and social caste system that trivializes the woman as pawn.

Like any other form of play, polite conversation is regulated, framed activity. Mrs. Bennet's emotional abandon, however, renders her ineligible for any disinterested game: "The sight of Miss Lucas was odious to her. As her successor in that house, she regarded her with jealous abhorrence. Whenever Charlotte came to see them she concluded her to be anticipating the hour of possession" (*PP*, 130). Her joy as well as despair is too visceral to meet the narrator's rational standards; for instance, upon hearing that Lydia is to be married: "She was now in an irritation as violent from delight, as she had ever been fidgetty from alarm and vexation. To know that her daughter would be married was enough. She was disturbed by no fear for her felicity, nor humbled by any remembrance of her misconduct" (*PP*, 306). Later, the prospect of Lydia's departure for the north brings a renewal of depression until "her mind opened again to the agitation of hope" (*PP*, 331) at the news of Mr. Bingley's return to Netherfield. Turning mechanically like a weather vane to every change of mood, Mrs. Bennet's humor registers the emotional currents in the story at any moment. Under the impact of Elizabeth's announcement of her engagement, she fleshes out all the responses that her daughter could never own to on the occasion, or even permit others to overhear: "Three daughters married! Ten thousand a year! Oh, Lord! What will become of me. I shall go distracted" (*PP*, 378).

Finally, the most revealing aspect of Mrs. Bennet's talk is that, except for infrequent moments of tactical maneuvering and polite design, it is compulsive and unpremeditated—sometimes in the form of quasi-argument and at other times in the associational form of thinking out loud. The simplest example of her "talking for victory" is her attack on the young Lucas boy, who vowed that if he had Darcy's money he would "keep a pack of foxhounds, and drink a bottle of wine every day" (*PP*, 20). Although her scruples against alcoholism may be well-founded, her threat of seizing the bottle from him, if necessary, collapses ethical doctrine into a see-saw for dominance: "The boy protested that she should not [take the bottle away from him]; she continued to declare that she would, and the argument ended only with the visit" (*PP*, 20).

Without any hope that Mr. Darcy would ever be a candidate for husband to one of her daughters, Mrs. Bennet luxuriates in hostility toward him and thus provides a context for reading Elizabeth's own deep-seated prejudice. The mother's argument with him at Netherfield over the relative complexity of city as opposed to country people astonishes everyone by its audacious support of her daughter's assertion about human nature in general. Instantly, after having "fancied she had gained a complete victory over him," however, she "continued her triumph" by distorting his original point and forcing Elizabeth to his defense (*PP*, 43).

Mrs. Bennet's comical determination to win a case by any verbal expedient backfires when she attempts to explain away Elizabeth's rejection of Mr. Collins's proposal:

> "She is a very headstrong foolish girl, and does not know her own interest; but I will *make* her know it."
>
> "Pardon me for interrupting you, Madam," cried Mr. Collins; "but if she is really headstrong and foolish, I know not whether she would altogether be a very desirable wife to a man in my situation, who naturally looks for happiness in the marriage state. If therefore she actually persists in rejecting my suit, perhaps it were better not to force her into accepting me, because if liable to such defects of temper, she could not contribute much to my felicity." (*PP*, 110)

By denigrating her own daughter before the suitor as a way of gaining more time for persuasion, Mrs. Bennet inadvertently appeals to his self-interest and bungles everything.

Performative speech may become almost hallucinogenic when the agent surrenders to the current of words. A small but significant part of Mrs. Bennet's talk has the same vatic quality demonstrated at length in Miss Bates's monologues—a freely associational outpouring of words without self-consciousness and without communicating anything specific to the listener; it is language, furthermore, that the narrator as well as other characters in the story tend to ignore. Mrs. Bennet's "rapidity" (*PP*, 99) of words and her "rapacity" (*PP*, 342) toward others indicate an aggressive release that is her only means of presence; and, as she candidly admits to Elizabeth, she is indifferent to her audience. Apparently it is the feeling of momentary power that is therapeutic for her "poor nerves." Performative speech abounds in this novel, and some of the best scenes show the protagonists engaged in brilliant verbal dueling in sharp contrast to characters encoded in clichés (Mr. Collins, Mary Bennet, Miss Bingley, Lady Catherine).

Talk has the power of presence, and the threat of its cessation is always ominous. A glimpse into Mrs. Bennet's existential vacuum comes with the information that she "was not in the habit of walking" (*PP*, 365), a marked difference from her vigorous daughter, who jumps over stiles and leaps puddles in defiance of woman's conventional fixity; to counteract her restrictive physical role, talk is manifest destiny. No matter how vexing to Elizabeth and to others in the story, Mrs. Bennet's oral freedom belongs indispensably to this novel's wordscape; and the loss to the text caused by her absence is abruptly clear after the Netherfield ball when Mrs. Hurst and Miss Bingley snub her:

> They repulsed every attempt of Mrs. Bennet at conversation, and by so doing, threw a languor over the whole party, which was very little relieved by the long speeches of Mr. Collins, who was complimenting Mr. Bingley and his sisters on the elegance of their entertainment, and the hospitality and politeness which had marked their behaviour to their guests. Darcy said nothing at all. Mr. Bennet, in equal silence, was enjoying the scene. (*PP*, 102–03)

Something is strangely out of line. Without this woman's discourse, which, as the narrator implies, contains a needed stimulus to move people in a way the wholly predictable "long speeches" of Mr. Collins do not, only the fictional rejector of the feast, Mr. Bennet, can enjoy the ensuing languor.[11]

4. Miss Bates's Secrets

A crux of interpretation in *Emma* has always been the heroine's relentless hostility toward Miss Bates, a jovial talker who, unlike Mrs. Allen, Mrs. Jennings, and Mrs. Bennet, barely survives at the fringe of the privileged society. No other woman character in Austen is so obdurate against a vulnerable, older person except for Elizabeth Bennet, who readily deplores her mother's indiscretion without ever seeing the family likeness in her own behavior. Perhaps the mirror of diffidence is Catherine Morland, who never raises an objection either to her real or to her surrogate mother's failings; even Fanny Price dares to criticize her parents. Mrs. Jennings, we saw, has Miss Bates's liability in exuding good humor to mostly negative recipients; but despite her widowhood, her place in the family and in society is secure. Emma's hatred of Miss Bates is all the more curious because of the latter's circumstances, and it invites attention to problems of competitiveness and ego defense by way of filling in character.[12]

But a more general approach to the I-thou relationships in Austen's novels should probably begin with Jean-Paul Sartre, whose succinct analysis of positional strategies in discourse helps to account for the latent motives in a given encounter: "The occasion which arouses hate is simply an act by the Other which puts me in the state of *being subject to* his freedom. This act is in itself humiliating."[13] Sartre's analysis of intentionality goes more deeply into the hidden, and mostly self-defensive, motivations than Goffman's relatively hedonistic model of the encounter, which is morally neutral. Although not all "open spaces" in a literary text imply "existential" vacuums, Austen's parodic art deliberately focuses on character as an artifact of language and on the potentially sinister motives of rival discourses. Until the crisis at Box Hill revealed how her transgression provided Miss Bates's talk, for once, with an attentive audience, Emma had pretended to be free from this woman's discourse; but then Mr. Knightley bursts upon her in a frenzy ("I must, I will,—I will tell you truths while I can" [*E*, 375]):

> "She felt your full meaning. She has talked of it since. I wish you could have heard how she talked of it— with what candour and generosity. I wish you could have heard her honouring your forbearance, in being able to pay her such attentions, as she was for ever receiving from yourself and your father, when her society must be so irksome." (*E*, 375)

Whatever the justice, according to the external reader's desires, of Mr. Knightley's reprimand, the awful truth, which his brother would quickly acknowledge, is that anyone's society can be irksome outside the "small band of true friends" (*E*, 484) who matter.

Sartre carries the priniciple to its existential limit: "The Other whom I hate actually represents all Others. My project of suppressing him is a project of suppressing others in general; that is, of recapturing my non-substantial freedom as for-itself."[14] While engrossed in the game, Austen's participants concentrate mainly on strategies of meeting the opponent while ignoring the reasons for competing with the other inherited from the "real" world—and text. What no one inside the story addresses is the possibility that Miss Bates's "dreadful gratitude" may conceal a reciprocal hostility toward Emma herself: "to be grateful for a kindness is to recognise that the Other was entirely free in acting as he has done."[15] Of course, on this particular occasion, Emma knows perfectly well that she does not deserve this woman's gratitude and hence feels under attack by the very word; but it never enters her mind (that is, it is missing in the printed representation of her consciousness) that Miss Bates may resent her as an object who denies *her* freedom of being.[16]

In a novel profoundly structured on the problems of discourse and reading, *Emma* needs a humorous character who can focus on the subversiveness of language; and as a speaker whose power of words is her sole means of presence in the Highbury world, Miss Bates augments the dilemma, shown elsewhere in the story, of being "open" in communication and likewise repressing what it is forbidden to say. Consequently, her humor is a blend of Mrs. Allen's schizoidal talk, Mrs. Jennings's compassionate utterance, and Mrs. Bennet's gregarious energy; but, unlike those more securely fixed identities, she is too vulnerable to afford enemies and thus is under constant stress to say that which is not as well as that which is true. At least three functions appear in her most significant monologue: (1) her "polite speech" is automatic gesture and premeditated design; (2) her talk is the principal medium not only for interpreting the secret engagement but also for revealing the secretiveness in *any* communication; and (3) though unperceived by others in the story, her verbal exuberance hints at a darker reality which her role as festive spirit is supposed to guard against, and from this ambiguous language the reader may glimpse the ontological void underlying the text. Once Miss Bates performs these valuable services, however, the author casts her off, leaving her in the end with Mrs. Elton's unproductive speech habits.

Because of her subordinate status and familiar chatter, most of the characters misread Miss Bates as a simpleton who may be relied upon to say whatever is ingratiating. The scene at the Crown in the second volume shows how each regards her condescendingly. To Churchill's suggestion of inviting her to their council, Mrs. Weston hesitatingly assents, "if you think she will be of any use"; but Emma flatly objects: "She will be all delight and gratitude, but she will tell you nothing. She will not even listen to your questions" (*E*, 255). Earlier, at the Coles's party, Emma had mimicked the poor woman's reiterative expression of gratitude and her indiscriminate blending of moral and material things in one breath (*E*, 225), an idiosyncrasy in the other humorous talkers already discussed. Emma's contempt for Miss Bates's obsequious speech arises partly from feeling it to be insincere, but perhaps mostly from taking it for granted and not really listening to it. By contrast, while Frank Churchill has his private reasons for finding Miss Bates "so amusing, so extremely amusing," Mr. Weston as master of revels deems her a "proper person for shewing us how to do away difficulties" and asserts categorically: "she is a standing lesson of how to be happy" (*E*, 255). No one in the scene reads this character sympathetically. If Mr. Weston believes that Miss Bates is a "standing lesson" of the "sublime and refined Point of Felicity, called *the Possession of being well deceived*,"[17] he is, as usual, imperceptive about manners. Whenever called upon by her society to perform, Miss Bates stands rather like Watteau's *Gilles*—momentarily isolated and awkward, pathetically aware of the clown costume she is expected to wear for her part in the Highbury world; and her eventual banishment to Mrs. Elton's company is hardly less satisfactory than her niece's dubious marriage at the end. Again, the play/"serious" dichotomy comes into question; and though required to perform as the happy and harmless simpleton of the village, she cannot entirely disguise a self-consciousness bound to disturb the other.

On many occasions an ideal performer, in "flow" and oblivious momentarily to her personal misery, nevertheless at times Miss Bates can be quite deliberate about what to communicate and thus undermines her assigned play roles. Faced with Emma's same domestic arrangement of coddling an invalid parent, for instance, Miss Bates keeps secret from her mother anything alarming, like Jane's not eating properly, and when necessary uses talk to divert her attention from any painful subject: "so I say one thing and then I say another, and it passes off" (*E*, 237). But on reading of Jane's illness she spontaneously blurts out the news and alarms the old woman, who then requires a yet more abundant dose of words to soothe her nerves. At the height of Jane's crisis, however, when Miss Bates herself is too distressed to conceal the truth, her mother immediately begins to regain her sight and hearing: "'I am afraid Jane is not very well,' said she, 'but I do not know; they *tell* me she is well'" (*E*, 378). Far from the Panglossian optimist that Mr. Weston imagines, Miss Bates is rather a "standing lesson" of how best to *appear* happy in a world that denies her the right to be otherwise.[18]

Double-bind situations cause unavoidable difficulties in speech. An important secret revealed at moments in Miss Bates's discourse is that, contrary to Emma's interpretation of her insincerity (she hides the truth even from herself in Sartre's concept of "bad faith"), her deepest plight is in attempting to be both "open" and "reserved" simultaneously, to be free in releasing her expressive impulse, on the one hand, and in guarding her socially predicted obeisance, on the other; and what is most remarkable for a person on the outskirts of society, she arrives, however inconsistently, at the same truth the principals consciously uphold. Just as Emma comes to value Mr. John Knightley's blunt honesty above Mr. Weston's spineless diplomacy, so Miss Bates, even when caught up in verbiage to the choking point (indicated in the shards of her sentences), shows insight into the evil of polite conversation while desperately sputtering out the words needed to meet its standards and is implicitly aware of Mr. Knightley's attack on Frank Churchill's role-playing: "the practised politician, who is to read every body's character, and make every body's talents conduce to the display of his own superiority; to be dispensing his flatteries around, that he may make all appear like fools compared with himself!" (*E*, 150). Unlike Churchill, who even surpasses his own expectations of performance (his erroneous assumption of Emma's being in on their secret), and also unlike Mr. Woodhouse, who always escapes behind Emma's verbal shield, Miss Bates can never be sure of herself in social confrontations unless she is absurdly submissive in every word to her superior auditors. Only once does she yield to temptation and try to exploit her situation as a dependent by flaunting her benefactor, Mr. Knightley, in front of company gathered in her apartment (*E*, 244–45).

As elsewhere in Austen's text, bad performances communicate by the rules of "irrelevance." Hardly the "practised politician," Miss Bates seems to be haunted by the necessity for false relationships and insincere language in response to the least gesture of beneficence. While trying to find words for Frank Churchill's special solicitude in repairing her mother's spectacles, she intuitively distrusts both his "excessive" praise of the baked apples (his mockery of her exhibitionistic display of Mr. Knightley's gift) and perhaps his alleged reason for being there at all, and her language short-circuits under the stress: "That, you know, was so very. . . . And I am sure, by his manner, it was no compliment" (*E*, 238). Though instinctively "open" in Mr. Knightley's sense, nevertheless Miss Bates feels compelled to flattery or "stroking" as her only means of being in society; and sometimes natural inclination and political tact hopelessly conflict.

Compliment is the code word for "bad faith" messages. On her arrival for the ball at the Crown, for instance, an inner voice reminds Miss Bates, "Must not compliment, I know" (*E*, 323); but she goes ahead and admires Emma's hair anyway and then solicits a compliment in return on behalf of Jane's hair, insinuating pointedly that her niece had done it herself and could match any London hairdresser in skill. In the same breath that she worries about Jane's feet getting wet, though admitting the rain "was but a drop or two," she praises Frank Churchill for being "so extremely—and there was a mat to step upon—I shall never forget his extreme politeness" (*E*, 323). Miss Bates remains without anything of her own to offer except the outright ridicule, intentional or not, of the situation, an effect shown most devastatingly after Box Hill, when Emma comes as a penitent and hears the old words with a new force:

> "So very kind!" replied Miss Bates. "But you are always kind."
>
> There was no bearing such an 'always;' and to

4

break through her dreadful gratitude, Emma made
the direct inquiry of—
 "Where—may I ask?—is Miss Fairfax going?"
(*E*, 380)

In a moment when the heroine believes herself to be fulfilling
at least the letter of the hero's moral law, Miss Bates's "dreadful gratitude" mocks her long habit of acting in bad faith; and
thus the topic of Jane is preferable to any further agony of self-consciousness. Psychoanalytical interpretation of Emma's hostility as a "discharging onto Miss Bates feelings which she has,
but cannot admit, toward her father" accords plausibly with
Freud's family romance; but in metaphysical terms, it is
enough to recognize the heroine's language as a defense
against the dreadful truth of her being-in-the-world, with
which this woman's rampant talk threatens her.[19]

Interpretations of *Emma* that stress knowledge as goal
have emphasized Miss Bates's capacity for giving away secrets.
To the external reader, if not to the characters within the story,
her discourse indirectly reveals the clandestine lovers, whom
Mr. Knightley begins to suspect well before the truth is disclosed; and as Marilyn Butler and others have observed, her
failure to communicate the actually valuable information contained in her speech betrays the fundamental solipsism dividing members of the community at large.[20] When listened to,
however, Miss Bates's words, because of their proximity to the
daily life of Highbury as opposed to the snobbish detachment
at Hartfield, suddenly gain power at critical moments to expose Frank Churchill's blunder and Emma's insult.

Her role as town crier is particularly disturbing to
the elitist heroine; again, Sartre's existential I-thou formula
is apposite: "The Other whom I hate actually represents all
Others."[21] For someone who has "no intellectual superiority to
make atonement to herself, or frighten those who might hate
her, into outward respect," Miss Bates holds an astonishing
grip on Emma's mind; and the violence at Box Hill erupts as
an involuntary discharge from that bondage. Until her crime
subjects her all the more to this woman's freedom, Emma has
enjoyed the illusion of being in full control over her; but Mr.
Knightley steps in to pronounce the nightmarish truth of public humiliation: "She felt your full meaning. She has talked of
it since. I wish you could have heard how she talked of it."
Never before or after does Miss Bates stand so triumphantly

for the voice of the community, with her "candour and gener-osity" displayed against the heroine's private joking; and rather than "reforming" her, Mr. Knightley's chastisement is mostly valuable in leading Emma to face the deep hostility that her behavior toward this poor victim has exposed and to turn to him in order to regain her social standing, which all the thrill of her new submissiveness to him entails. Her contempt for Miss Bates, however, remains to the end of the novel.

Description, no matter how "objective," usually bears some traces of a particular perspective and thus only pretends to leave out the narrator completely. Thanks to subtle intona-tion with free indirect discourse, a rare moment shows Emma having a consciousness of the community that rivals the con-crete imagery of her enemy's speech and also voices an impor-tant difference in their perceptions:

> —Much could not be hoped from the traffic of even the busiest part of Highbury;—Mr. Perry walking hastily by, Mr. William Cox letting himself in at the office door, Mr. Cole's carriage horses returning from exercise, or a stray letter-boy on an obstinate mule, were the liveliest objects she could presume to ex-pect; and when her eyes fell only on the butcher with his tray, a tidy old woman travelling homewards from shop with her full basket, two curs quarrelling over a dirty bone, and a string of dawdling children round the baker's little bow-window eyeing the gingerbread, she knew she had no reason to complain, and was amused enough; quite enough still to stand at the door. A mind lively and at ease, can do with seeing nothing, and can see nothing that does not answer. (*E*, 233)

In contrast to Miss Bates's effusive, unorganized recording of the villagers, this view from Ford's begins and ends under Emma's critical eye, objective to the extent of Keats's "nega-tive capability" and yet intentional in selecting the subject matter for contemplation. Bored with Harriet, who "was still hanging over muslins and changing her mind," she escapes the immediate situation by losing herself in the vision of the street; instead of seeing the few people she had expected and knew by name, "her eyes fell only on" some lowly creatures, including the dogs and carriage horses, usually beneath her notice. Her aesthetic powers "with seeing nothing," however, create all that is needed to satisfy her will; her mind is "at ease" because it is free from the objects seen passively as opposed to the many occasions when the other intrudes upon her private space.

Since her description is usually held subordinate to narration within the storytelling economy, unlike her contemporary Walter Scott, Austen deliberately chose not to give fine brush strokes to her scenes, as if anything other than dramatic function would be superfluous matter. But a compulsive talker can readily furnish details omitted by a restrained narrator, just as Emma's daydreaming at Ford's provides the reader with a glimpse of town life excluded from the story. Miss Bates's speech incorporates other characters' discourse voraciously but nevertheless mentions only the positive:

> "Then the baked apples came home, Mrs. Wallis sent them by her boy; they are extremely civil and obliging to us, the Wallises, always—I have heard some people say that Mrs. Wallis can be uncivil and give a very rude answer, but we have never known any thing but the greatest attention from them. And it cannot be for the value of our custom now, for what is our consumption of bread, you know?" (*E*, 236–37)

Rather than Emma's detached pleasure in visual objects themselves, Miss Bates's circuitous narrative digresses from the main story but serves as a description of pertinent moral relations—unraveling all the interactions and obligations created by the gift of the apples as they proceed from Mr. Knightley's orchard, which in itself has become a social institution ("My mother says the orchard was always famous in her younger days"), and thence to her table by way of demonstrating Mrs. Wallis's true benevolence. As if to reflect the strain of always being judged by superiors, Miss Bates, in direct contrast to Emma's ironic tendency, makes a special point of improving someone else's reputation.

Encounters are always risky, but in *Emma* the threat of annihilation is unusually strong even for Austen's text. Though Miss Bates offends Emma by her mere presence, by her freedom of words as an expression of her subjective being, their antithetical relationship is also a blatant form of the general conflict between self and other unresolved in the novel.

Like Austen's ironic narrator, the nontheistic Sartre uses religious associations for his theory of positional perception: "It is before the Other that I am *guilty*. I am guilty first when beneath the Other's look I experience my alienation and my nakedness as a fall from grace which I must assume."[22] Just as the self experiences guilt in the other's gaze, so the assertion of one's own subjective freedom is a denial of the other's existence. From the freedom to transcend her instrumentally limited world and to look at the other as mere object, Emma "falls from grace" at Box Hill and is punished by being "looked at" as an alien and subject to Miss Bates's generosity, exacerbated, of course, by Mr. Knightley's attestation. While the moralizing narrator posits her "anger against herself, mortification, and deep concern," her heartfelt guilt springs from her ontological nakedness in front of all the witnesses Miss Bates's verbal discharge calls to account; after an initial effort at an apology to this woman, not only does Emma never look back with regret, but the author herself seems constrained to rid the novel of this humorous character.

Memory, we have said, is short-lived in Austen's text; but occasionally the past intrudes in conversation with an unanswerable force. Besides her power to conjure up the whole community's threatening presence in her flow of speech, Miss Bates's age endows her with the authority of the collective past and makes available an awesome range of language against Emma's narrow intent on living in the present. Except for readily admitting her permissive upbringing, the heroine is notably silent about her childhood, which Mr. Knightley suddenly calls forth in his reprimand:

> "—You, whom she had known from an infant, whom she had seen grow up from a period when her notice was an honour, to have you now, in thoughtless spirits, and the pride of the moment, laugh at her, humble her—and before her niece, too—and before others, many of whom (certainly *some*,) would be entirely guided by *your* treatment of her." (*E*, 375)

Hegel's aphorism, "Wesen ist was gewesen ist," according to Sartre, means that the past is in-itself and intrinsically separate from the present, which is for-itself: "everything which can be a For-itself must be it back there behind itself, out of reach."[23] Emma's apparent avoidance of the past doubtless bears on the mother whom she has replaced at Hartfield; and the spectacle of Miss Bates's nurturing role toward her mother and niece uncannily arouses a hostility in the heroine's consciousness that is far more pronounced than in those other characters, discussed previously, who also spurned the maternal ties.

This rivalry between the past (in-itself) and present (for-itself) calls forth conflicting voices in the text that seriously undermine the hero's explicit ideal of sincerity, an ideal some readers have attributed to the author as well.[24] But Miss Bates's "open" discourse exposes a problem in lingual communication that Mr. Knightley's romantic standard misses altogether. At the simplest level of truthfulness, the secret engagement has been a deliberate imposition on all concerned; and after the discovery of this "most dangerous game," only Frank Churchill's words of sympathy for Jane have any credence with his severest reader (*E*, 445). But the narrator recognizes a more general difficulty of communication than the hero's pristine judgment will allow: "Seldom, very seldom, does complete truth belong to any human disclosure; seldom can it happen that something is not a little disguised, or a little mistaken" (*E*, 431).

In Sartre's phenomenology, that "something" lies in the past, "out of reach," not consciously withheld but simply absent to the for-itself. By repressing the past, Emma accommodates the present by living in *bad faith*, "a perpetual game of escape from the for-itself to the for-others and from the for-others to the for-itself."[25] The moralist may denounce Frank Churchill's "game" (not really a game at all, as we have seen), when once known, as a "'system of hypocrisy and deceit, —espionage, and treachery'" (*E*, 399); Emma's "game," more fully knowable to the reader than it ever is to herself, is at bottom a system of existential defenses through vicarious role-playing (Harriet as princess in disguise, Jane as the "other woman," Mrs. Weston as happy newlywed). Her irresistible attraction to Mr. Knightley, her almost desperate longing to prove worthy of him, is a desire to regain selfhood after the annihilation suffered in previous encounters: "Bad faith is possible only because sincerity is conscious of missing its goal inevitably, due to its very nature."[26] It is this darker truth of being-in-the-world that Miss Bates's torrent of words uncovers, and it remains far from clear whether the heroine will actually escape from bad faith encounters even after winning the hero.

Besides her function in reflecting the insincerity of polite discourse and the inherent fragmentariness of any communication, Miss Bates also embodies, more emphatically than other characters in this novel, the affective responses expressed in speech. Just as both the "clever" talkers—Frank Churchill and Emma—are thrown off guard in the moments of Miss Bates's startling penetration, so elsewhere in the text her words bear comparison with the most authoritative voices heard, including the hero's. Perhaps uneasy about presenting this character so inconsistently, Austen has little use for her once the secret engagement becomes known and in the end consigns her to Mrs. Elton's patronage, which mitigates—even justifies—Emma's rudeness.

Earlier in the novel, however, Miss Bates exerts a mysterious power and sheds light on the other characters' struggles to grasp the hidden truth. Her insight into the difference between perception and illusion, for example, sets her apart from the deceivers and self-deceived: "Very odd! but one never does form a just idea of any body beforehand. One takes up a notion, and runs away with it" (*E*, 176). Despite her notion of there being a resemblance between Mr. Dixon and Mr. Knightley here, she does not have the heroine's quixotic imagination and is, surprisingly, one of the few in the story to detect Mr. Elton's amorous interest in Emma (*E*, 176). Given this quickness of observation at such moments, her seeming obliviousness to Frank Churchill is one of the most unaccountable "empty spaces" in this text; and the more we learn about this woman's speech acts, the more plausible it is that she indeed should have had an inkling of the secret engagement soon after Jane's arrival in Highbury. The simplest answer to this crux, of course, is that Austen had not worried adequately about the loose ends of her characterization to avoid this interpretive problem. Nevertheless, in moments of inspired clarity Miss Bates is a reliable judge of reality and shares Mr. Knightley's fear of solipsism, as expressed in Cowper's lines, "while with poring eye / I gaz'd, myself creating what I saw" (*E*, 344).

However "ridiculous" otherwise, Miss Bates's discourse shows that without the capacity for sympathetic responses, knowledge of the other, hence *reading* itself, is impossible. Emma's standards of objectivity, by contrast, sound hackneyed: "It is very unfair to judge of any body's conduct, without an intimate knoweldge of their situation. Nobody, who has not been in the interior of a family, can say what the difficulties of any individual of that family may be" (*E*, 146). Similarly, her terse remark on poverty echoes Mary Bennet's tautological wisdom: "If we feel for the wretched, enough to do all we can for them, the rest is empty sympathy, only distressing to ourselves" (*E*, 87). Such a concern with the measure of evidence and response, no matter how relevant to the author's moral economy in other contexts, belies the heroine's deficient feelings toward others and her consequent blindness until the revelation at Box Hill. Miss Bates, however, feels too much for her own good, caught as she is in an irreconcilable predicament of having to please others while also having to express herself openly.

Again, the ball at the Crown Inn is a pivotal encounter in the characterization. As if to carry out to the letter Mr. Weston's pronouncement on her as a standing lesson of being happy, Miss Bates arrives at the scene in a torrent of civilities that imbues the occasion with the festive mood. The ironic narrator conjures up the woman's wondrous entry as a virtuoso performance to the extent that even Mrs. Elton's "words, every body's words, were soon lost under the incessant flow of Miss Bates, who came in talking" (*E*, 322). Aside from the valuable information her speech imparts concerning Frank Churchill's peculiar interest in Jane and herself, her spontaneous outbursts of joy help free the occasion from the Eltons' subversive plots: "Well! This is brilliant indeed!—This is admirable!—Excellently contrived, upon my word. Nothing wanting. Could not have imagined it.—So well lighted up.—Jane, Jane, look—did you ever see any thing? Oh! Mr. Weston, you must really have had Aladdin's lamp. Good Mrs. Stokes would not know her own room again" (*E*, 322). *Nothing wanting* except the playful humor, "flow," to transform the drab room into "fairy-land"; Miss Bates enters the ball to dispel the tensions and rivalries of the Highbury world, and to unite it for the moment in a fragile accord.

Comic characters defy the laws of gravity. Her public role as word-maker fulfilled in opening the rites of spring, Miss Bates vanishes magically during the sets of dances and returns only in time for the late supper; nobody appears to have noticed her absence, perhaps further proof of the company's absorption in the rhythm of the event rather than just another "empty space" in the text. Only the outside reader is privileged to eavesdrop on her confiding to Jane an astonishing physical feat: "Yes, my dear, I ran home, as I said I should, to help grandmamma to bed, and got back again, and nobody missed me.—I set off without saying a word [!], just as I told you" (*E*, 329).

In contrast to her noisy entrance to the ball—her expected social role—Miss Bates's wordless exit demonstrates the sincerity of her private behavior, though the action of running off alone on a wet night to Hartfield, escorting her mother home and putting her to bed, and then slipping back into the company at the Crown unnoticed may be a strain even on Aladdin's lamp. Her report to Jane here, the only one in the novel without Emma or some other outsider on hand to interpret, gives us a glimpse into the "interior of a family" that Emma had supposedly demanded before making judgments; and like Wemmick's games with his senile father in *Great Expectations*, her narrative assumes the fundamental split between social and kinship loyalties.[27] While the main Highbury folk are celebrating at the Crown, the valetudinarians have a parallel feast at Hartfield, grandmamma coming alive with "a vast deal of chat, and backgammon" and not letting the "little disappointment" of Mr. Woodhouse's sending back the sweetbread and asparagus, the old woman's favorite dish, spoil the mood for the others. Moreover, this "little disappointment" binds the family members in a pact to uphold the social order: "we agreed we would not speak of it to any body, for fear of its getting around to dear Miss Woodhouse, who would be so very much concerned!" (*E*, 329–30).

Simple affection among kin of an impoverished family, however, holds little interest for those in power who distrust the feelings. Although quietly affectionate toward her father and his small circle of friends, Emma never gives way to lingering emotions; and her hostility toward Miss Bates's public demeanor—her flow of words to express the requisite gratitude (parodied by the narrator herself)—results in a loss of perception that isolates her from the central mystery and its solution, provided by this woman's speeches. From the beginning, Emma's disdain for Miss Bates has distorted her reading of her words about Jane and prompted the romantic fantasy of a triangle with Mr. Dixon; her dread of the actual text sent ("though she had in fact heard the whole substance of Jane Fairfax's letter, she had been able to escape the letter itself"

[*E*, 162]) belongs to a pattern of selective responses to her counterpart, including the refusal to admit any evidence linking her with Frank Churchill.

Emma's imagining Jane to be a victim of a hopeless passion for a married man not only testifies to her shoddy intentionality but also to her predatory instincts as a reader—both implicit motives of the romantic genre; and, not surprisingly, when Miss Bates announces her niece's decision to go into slavery as a governess, the heroine's sympathy is forthcoming: "this picture of her present sufferings acted as a cure of every former ungenerous suspicion, and left her nothing but pity" (*E*, 379–80). But this "picture," of course, stems from Miss Bates, who, as usual, intercedes during Jane's absence and expresses genuine grief in the spaces between the formulaic words of gratitude owed to those in authority:

> "It is a great change; and though she is amazingly fortunate—such a situation, I suppose, as no young woman before ever met with on first going out—do not think us ungrateful, Miss Woodhouse, for such surprising good fortune—(again dispersing her tears)—but, poor dear soul! if you were to see what a headach she has. When one is in great pain, you know one cannot feel any blessing quite as it may deserve. She is as low as possible. To look at her, nobody would think how delighted and happy she is to have secured such a situation." (*E*, 379)

On a visit to Miss Bates's in atonement for her sins at Box Hill and with an awareness of Donwell Abbey, Emma still cannot converse with this woman sympathetically, and not because of a moral deficiency on her part: it takes two to communicate, and Miss Bates is in the habit of protecting herself against hostile superiors behind a camouflage of polite words. Failing to touch base, Emma immerses herself in Jane's apparent downfall in Highbury society, relishing the pathos much as any detached newspaper reader does accounts of fallen celebrities.

Emma's failure to learn anything from Miss Bates's discourse throughout the story is at one with her habitual failure to identify with her tone as narrator of events; and this insurmountable barrier to conversation vitiates the many potential signals in either woman's words and gestures. Ironically, Emma's complete indifference to the storyteller's emotions causes her to ignore the important reference to the ostler who saw Frank Churchill leaving town hastily; and, in contrast, Miss Bates's associational imagination drifts away from the intellectual problem of solving the puzzle of events to the simple fact of human misery: "Poor old John, I have a great regard for him; he was clerk to my poor father twenty-seven years; and now, poor old man, he is bed-ridden, and very poorly with the rheumatic gout in his joints—I must go and see him to-day; and so will Jane, I am sure, if she gets out at all" (*E*, 383). Although Emma's explicit avoidance of "empty sympathy" rules out any concern for the unknown lame father of the witness to Churchill's sudden departure, the author's own complicity in this monologue on human suffering implies that her reticence elsewhere in the text is not callous.

For the purposes of the story, however, the most relevant fact is Emma's unimaginative response to the aunt's account of Jane in the first place; and this failure to listen properly results in yet another misreading of the situation: "There was nothing in all this either to astonish or interest, and it caught Emma's attention only as it united with the subject which already engaged her mind. The contrast between Mrs. Churchill's importance in the world, and Jane Fairfax's, struck her; one was every thing, the other nothing—and she sat musing on the difference of woman's destiny" (*E*, 384). Emma's snobbish predilection to value what is said by the speaker's social standing not only closes her off from the mystery of the plot and from what is *unsaid*, but it also leads her to the banal contrast between Mrs. Churchill, who is "every thing"— though at this very moment, dead, unloved, and unmourned— and Jane Fairfax, young, talented, and admired, who is presumably "nothing." It is possible, of course, to interpret the tone here as showing Emma's heartfelt sympathy with Jane's predicament, and the absolute categories as mimicking the way of the world. But in view of Emma's abhorrence to the end of the second- and third-rate, it is more likely yet another failure on the heroine's part to comprehend the moral life of her community and another opportunity to escape through games of illusion.

Conversation is an art, and thus, like other forms of play, it is a means of representation as well as of expression. Surely what draws many readers to Austen's novels is their apparent simplicity and clarity, a luminescent discourse unparalleled in the genre. Yet, if her clever talkers were to stand alone, their reputation among the author's detractors for not saying very much, at least not very much about their contemporary social and political world, might be partly justified. By also representing speech that is artless, however, Austen does not merely provide a backdrop to polite conversation in the way some Renaissance paintings depict tawny servants to offset their radiant mistresses in the foreground. Rather, by breaking the rules of an encounter, the manic talkers appear to come closer than any of the other characters to revealing the truth that lies concealed in all discourse—the truth that words alone signify nothing. It is this truth, of course, that is instrumental in rendering the illusion of "real feelings" as opposed to the regulated and derivative text.

V. Text (Printed)

Character in writing is a phenomenon of verbal clusters recurring in a text. The mere repetition of a word or phrase ("a lively mind," "ashamed of herself," "nice smooth gruel," "Maple Grove") can mark it off from the rest of the language in use and initiate a temporal/spatial pattern that connotes a relative uniqueness. A variety of discourse and situations, we have seen, goes into processing the ontic effects of self and other in a textual field. Yet as long as things are going well, the reader may come under the author's spell and assume for pages the existence of a fictional being within a story. It is our cooperation with the desire represented, Coleridge understood, that makes this illusion a possible experience at all. Seduction ends in disillusion, however, when the reader's critical instincts rebel and try to explain the aesthetic principles at work in the mimesis.

Although (except for Marianne Dashwood) remarkably safe from sexual intrigue, Austen's main characters usually find themselves taken in by someone at least part of the time and live to reflect on their mistaken perceptions. Three novels stage a whole scene with the heroine (Elinor, Elizabeth, and Emma) directly confronting the deceiver (Willoughby, Wickham, and Churchill) after his game is up; and perhaps the most intimate encounters for Catherine and Henry center on Isabella's betrayal, especially when they are alone together reading her letter that explains the broken engagement. Neither Henry Crawford nor Mr. Elliot appears after his disgrace to speak for himself, but again, each culprit's exposure shocks the victims into a recognition of the ugly truth hidden behind graceful manners.

Apart from these extreme cases, numerous people are duped along the way and live to regret it; in fact, anyone who is not eventually disabused is a complete fool. For this reason, Mr. Collins, as J. B. Priestley remarked,[1] is the most fulfilled soul in all of Austen's novels. In their reflexive roles, the disillusioned characters present themselves as reliable truth-tellers at the expense of other characters shown to be only fictional types, tired and sweaty actors without any serious moral purpose.

Notwithstanding the seducer's arts, Austen's more intelligent people understand that it is one's "voluntary delusion," to quote her revered Johnson,[2] which gives the ignis fatuus its irresistible power. Granted the hermeneutic circle inevitable in perceiving events, however, nothing is really certain but belief. The Crown Inn ball exists as a hope for weeks in the breasts of the young Highburyans. Yet even as it "actually" takes place, nobody knows exactly what is happening; and because of this ecstatic mingling of intentions the ball is pronounced a success before it is over. Almost immediately afterward, when attention turns abruptly to Harriet's encounter with the gipsies, the ball sinks into oblivion, becoming scarcely a recordable moment for the witnesses themselves. Similarly, Mrs. Bennet tries enthusiastically to conjure up the Meryton ball to her husband but is interrupted while about to describe the "Boulanger" (*PP*, 13) performed; and the event is lost—to his relief, forever. Hence, the experience of any event is contingent, and not only of brief duration but always of doubtful ontological status.

This temporality, seen in a continual awareness of changing relationships, is the darker side of the conservative belief in permanent values attributed to Austen. Doubtless it gives her characters a peculiar anxiety about the future and motivates them as readers of their world toward some compensating order defined in economic terms. It also reflects their provenance in the text. Like Swift's Modern in *A Tale of a Tub*, Austen's characters appear to be nervous about the longevity of any book and perpetuate themselves at the expense of discarding other texts. Thus the illusions of romance give way to the illusions of the novel. When Catherine exclaims, "Oh! Mr. Tilney, how frightful.—This is just like a book!—But it cannot really happen to me" (*NA*, 159), she is articulating the fictional character's last resort—professing facticity by denying her own fictional origins.

Parody is a defense against the encroachment of writing, and Austen's art excels in strategies toward this end, undermining not only sentimental and Gothic romances in particular but the educational value of *any* book in general. Charlotte Lennox's model[3] seems most explicit in Catherine Morland's and Marianne Dashwood's quixotism, but the later novels show more complex forms of self-delusion, when characters "come alive" with acting *Lovers' Vows* and even Fanny succumbs during Henry's reading of Shakespeare. Without any particular texts mentioned, Emma nevertheless spins out a soap opera with Jane Fairfax and Mr. Dixon (a man she has never even seen) as well as a Cinderella tale for Harriet; driven by jealousy of Frank Churchill, Mr. Knightley exaggerates Jane's fatigue after singing too long into the same Gothic tortures that the heroine herself imagines later in the story.

At its worst, quixotism for Austen is a diseased sensibility, a "mind-style"[4] acquired by uncritical reading of best-sellers. Women characters are usually susceptible to it; but in *Persuasion* it is Captain Benwick who unites "very strong feelings with quiet, serious, and retiring manners, and a decided taste for reading, and sedentary pursuits" (*P*, 97). Even the critical voice, however, turns against itself: Anne Elliot enjoys a brief gush of egoism while correcting his indulgence in romantic depression and afterwards enjoys still more the thought of her uninvited role as mentor on that occasion. In short, because of the dialogical structure, whether they know it or not, Austen's characters have a virtual library at their beck and call whenever the situation demands a text; and no particular fictional genre is off-limits.

From the strategy of generating character in various play situations, culminating in speech acts, our discussion concludes with the fictional representation of reading/writing itself. To begin with the media, there is a priority of the written over the spoken word in Austen even though the ideal of letter-writing is "to-the-moment," in imitation of speech encounters. Other mimetic devices involve the consistent privileging of the written document over the printed medium, as well as an allusive "battle of the books," with novels winning over romances and sermons.

A key method for rendering a character's mind is to show him or her engaged in both reading and writing. If the ideal reader constitutes the text in accordance with the author's intentions, the ability to write well is proof of the same lively mind. This mimetic activity is not for the craven souls in Austen's world, and, like other bad performances, a character's difficulties with the text reveal problems in facing situations. Earned only by devaluing rival texts and by contextualizing the moment emphatically, the "language of real feeling" emerges as the ultimate illusion perpetrated on both the internal and external reader of the text.

1. The Media

Radically concerned with its own means of deception, the novel subverts the discourse that the romance takes for granted. Aside from debunking sentimental or Gothic "mind-styles," Austen's realistic strategy brings the book as artifact into question; for instance, the opening of *Persuasion* uses the *Baronetage of England* to caricature Sir Walter Elliot's egomania:

> there he found occupation for an idle hour, and consolation in a distressed one; there his faculties were roused into admiration and respect, by contemplating the limited remnant of the earliest patents; there any unwelcome sensations, arising from domestic affairs, changed naturally into pity and contempt, as he turned over the almost endless creations of the last century—and there, if every other leaf were powerless, he could read his own history with an interest which never failed. (*P*, 3)

The only book he ever consulted, we are told, the *Baronetage* nevertheless gratifies Sir Walter's manic desires perfectly; and the passage detailing his own immediate family tree could produce euphoria when any other page failed. Some editorial changes, however, were necessary to improve the text:

> Precisely such had the paragraph originally stood from the printer's hands; but Sir Walter had improved it by adding, for the information of himself and his family, these words, after the date of Mary's birth— "married, Dec. 16, 1810, Charles, son and heir of Charles Musgrove, Esq. of Uppercross, in the county of Somerset,"—and by inserting most accurately the day of the month on which he had lost his wife. (*P*, 3)

No matter how limited the character's time and place in memory, as the adverbs "precisely" and "most accurately" imply, the printed record, updated by hand, satisfies a craving for order and permanence in a world of flux. Both print and manuscript, it can be seen, are the media for giving individual identity.

Besides satirizing aristocratic vanity by describing Sir Walter's grotesque absorption with the one book that corresponds to a mirror, Austen also implies that this is the only form of autobiography possible for such a hollow character. For a person lacking a tincture of inner life no other text would do, and it is the complete absence of texts that denies him any "inner life" in the first place. Other fools, by contrast, have at least some redeeming literary resources. John Thorpe is not an exemplary reader, but he can educe the titles of *Tom Jones* and *The Monk* as well as name Mrs. Radcliffe and, by default, Fanny Burney. Mr. Collins's oratorical manner reveals some study of books, and his reading of Fordyce's sermons gives his antifeminist stance a referentiality. Likewise, as if to suggest that hereditary obtuseness can be improved upon, Austen shows Mr. Rushworth mouthing the ideas of Humphry Repton. What is problematic about Sir Walter, however, is not simply his utter dearth of textuality but his assigned role as father of the heroine; and here the author's art of reifying consciousness is at odds with her art of parodying character types. That she could entertain these contradictory purposes from the beginning to the end of her writing career testifies to her Sternean reflexivity.

Once cited and brought within the text, books have no independent status but are a function of the character's "mind-style"; and usually in Austen they are suspect, ersatz objects used for ego gratification rather than real sources of knowledge. Perhaps there is something of Wordsworth in this bias:

> Enough of Science and of Art;
> Close up those barren leaves;
> Come forth, and bring with you a heart
> That watches and receives.[5]

Discrediting books, however, belongs to the whole anti-intellectual fiction of satire; and bookish characters like Mary Bennet, Mr. Collins, Mrs. Morland, and even Mr. Knightley, who summon moral texts to instruct other characters, are in a tradition as old as literacy.[6] A more specific strategy contrasts "writing-to-the-moment" (Richardson's term), objectified in the manuscript, to the printed book, a mass-produced commodity of the marketplace; as a consequence of this antithesis, characters stand or fall according to their power of writing and

(almost synonymously) of reading letters, momentary performances essential to reproducing a unique experience. In Austen's world, quixotism at its best is no less than an ecstatic response to a (hand)written text as opposed to the presumably
debased encounter with the printed book.

A major advancement of the Gutenberg revolution,
according to Elizabeth Eisenstein,[7] was a demystification of
the written word through a mechanical and impersonal technology. It is a commonplace of literary history that the literature of the ancient and medieval worlds survived largely by
means of memorization and repeated transcriptions on parch-
ment. Under these conditions the medium as well as the message appeared to have an inspired origin. But with the invention of the printing press, literacy underwent qualitative as
well as quantitative changes: the printed word became a commodity subject to laws of supply and demand.[8] The economic
cost of producing the printed page, now much more calculable
than under the monastic system of scribes, gives the fictional
character a fresh concern with human mortality. In more ways
than one, there is a real price on his head! Perhaps aware of
this gloomy fact, after repeated harassments from the elusive
enchanter, Don Quixote experiences one of his worst moments when he discovers the printing press at Barcelona to be
the fountain of his being.[9]

In light of the novelistic character's birth in the
marketplace, it was almost predictable that a shrewd, middle-
aged London printer would step in to meet an economic demand with "a new species of writing," something distinctly different from the aristocratic romance long associated with a
pre-Gutenberg, oral culture.[10] Without knowing that he is already part of a new genre, Mr. B. predicts his future by refer-
ring to an old-fashioned one when he tells Pamela, "we shall
make out between us, before we have done, a pretty story in
romance I warrant ye."[11] But eventually, after reading her
journal in Lincolnshire, his romantic fantasy gives way to the
spell of her writing, which, however, is supposedly not the
printed text that the actual reader has been engaged with from
the start. Mr. B., we are to understand, has been treated to
something much more authentic as a reading encounter—the
heroine's manuscripts.[12]

As part of the deeper illusion of reality in the novel
and a reflexive subterfuge for a printer to adopt, the major

characters tend to disparage books, not just "romances," as counterfeits for direct experience in the everyday world. It is for the effete Mr. Williams to enjoy such French texts as Fénelon's *Télémaque* and Boileau's *Le Lutrin,* and in one scene he is startled when the presumably more virile Mr. B. chances upon him while engrossed in reading.[13] "Writing-to-the-moment," by contrast, evinces heartfelt energy; and Mrs. Jewkes has reason to seize Pamela's pen, paper, and ink, as well as her shoes. Despite her vulgarity, moreover, Mrs. Jewkes gives utterance to a truth that Pamela and Mr. B. both share about book learning: "these scholars . . . have not the hearts of mice."[14] The difference between mice and men is the difference between print and script, an idea brought out when Mr. B. threatens to strip Pamela to get at the letters hidden in her underwear and thus to penetrate the secret of her "inner-most" self. It is this power of divining the origin of one's textual selfhood, whether as writer or reader (the two roles are interdependent), that sets these characters apart from the merely literate ones.

Reading in a writerly manner is the most valued attainment of Austen's characters, and thus Catherine Morland's choice of fiction is not in itself at issue:

> Yes, novels;—for I will not adopt that ungenerous and impolitic custom so common with novel writers, of degrading by their contemptuous censure the very performances, to the number of which they are them-selves adding—joining with their greatest enemies in bestowing the harshest epithets on such works, and scarcely ever permitting them to be read by their own heroine, who, if she accidentally take up a novel, is sure to turn over its insipid pages with disgust. (*NA,* 37)

This story distinguishes between those who either misread or only pretend to read novels and those who read them imaginatively, even to a visionary extreme. Henry's disinterested encounter with Gothic romances is a corrective to Catherine's hallucinatory indulgence; but her penchant for this fiction also stems from the ennui of everyday life, which the newspaper and other pulp media try unsuccessfully to record.

The ironic anti-book theme in *Northanger Abbey* pits even useless written artifacts against the pragmatic tomes that men of business need to consult. Catherine's desire to light upon a "precious manuscript" is clearly mediated by Radcliffe's mysterious texts, but it may also evidence her boredom with the humdrum duodecimos of the circulating library. A parallel to her sexual awakening with Henry, her motive in reading is toward an encounter with the real thing rather than its printed surrogate: "Her greedy eye glanced rapidly over a page. She started at its import. Could it be possible, or did not her senses play her false?—An inventory of linen, in coarse and modern characters, seemed all that was before her!" (*NA*, 172).

Notwithstanding this setback, however, Catherine later refuses to believe that General Tilney could actually "be poring over the affairs of the nation for hours" instead of doing something darkly mysterious at night: "To be kept up for hours, after the family were in bed, by stupid pamphlets, was not very likely" (*NA*, 187). Like the newspaper, which indifferent household heads (Mr. Palmer, General Tilney, Mr. Price) employ to escape domestic conversation, the "stupid pamphlets" do not represent reality as opposed to the illusions of romance: they represent forms of public discourse, of journalistic rhetoric associated with the printing medium, vis-à-vis the private letter. It is a testimony to the barrier between mother and daughter that Mrs. Morland must resort to "'a very clever Essay in one of the books up stairs upon much such a subject, about young girls that have been spoilt for home by great acquaintance—"The Mirror," I think'" (*NA*, 241). Such materials are "stupid" because they are inanimate, articles mass-produced for consumption, and thus alien objects for the heroine's real soul hunger, we are to believe.

Whole scenes in Austen show characters struggling with competing forms of discourse; but the personal letter always takes precedence, even over speech, as the most direct expression of the self. The reading/writing experiences sometimes go on simultaneously. As soon as the "anxieties of common life" replace the "alarms of romance," Catherine is finally undeceived about her novel-reading companion after receiving James's account of her breaking their engagement. While the general is safely out of the way "between his cocoa and his newspaper," Catherine reads her brother's letter in Henry's presence; and the triangular situation has the effect of drawing hero and heroine together: "Catherine had not read three lines before her sudden change of countenance, and short exclamations of sorrowing wonder, declared her to be receiving unpleasant news; and Henry, earnestly watching her through the whole letter, saw plainly that it ended no better than it began" (*NA*, 202–03). Presumably a record of the moment, undiluted by copyeditor and printer, and secure from the distractions of a face-to-face meeting with the writer, the letter demands the concentrated attention that the sounds of actual speech could never receive. Once produced and sent off, moreover, the letter becomes appropriated by the receiver's discourse. In this scene what matters is not James's feelings or Isabella's callousness, since this information would add nothing to the story; rather, it is the heroine's experience, shared sympathetically with her beloved, of comprehending at last the treachery of a woman she had trusted. Possible interference from the *senex iratus* with his newspaper adds stimulus to their intimacy in the reading performance. At this stage in the plot Isabella's letter of explanation arrives as an anticlimax; Catherine is already fortified enough to read the "strain of shallow artifice" without the assistance of her mentor: "She must think me an idiot, or she could not have written so; but perhaps this has served to make her character better known to me than mine is to her" (*NA*, 218). Her judgmental response, furthermore, no matter how just, is full of the I-thou awareness and is thus an experience best kept to herself.

In *Sense and Sensibility* the popular print media bring the lovers together ("The same books, the same passages were idolized by each" [*SS*, 47]) just as they initiated the friendship between Isabella and Catherine, and again it is the personal letter that occasions a shock of recognition. Bearing earmarks of the epistolary novel form, the scene (*SS*, II, 7) comprises a triad of voices (Marianne, Elinor, and Mrs. Jennings), but with Elinor's experience of reading Willoughby's letter in the foreground. Delaying tactics, especially Mrs. Jennings's inadvertent chatter about young girls in love, build up suspense; and the sight of "Marianne stretched on the bed, almost choked by grief, one letter in her hand, and two or three others lying by her" (*SS*, 182) is itself a tableau from the sentimental novel. Since the letter appears in full, Elinor's moral indignation is almost superfluous; but of relevance here is the power of the medium to activate consciousness:

> In her earnest meditations on the contents of the letter, on the depravity of that mind which could dictate it, and, probably, on the very different mind of a

very different person, who had no other connection whatever with the affair than what her heart gave him with every thing that passed, Elinor forgot the immediate distress of her sister, forgot that she had three letters on her lap yet unread, and so entirely forgot how long she had been in the room, that when on hearing a carriage drive up to the door, she went to the window to see who could be coming so unreasonably early. (*SS*, 184)

Perhaps intuition tells Elinor that this letter was dictated by Miss Grey; in any case, despite the trauma caused to Marianne, it is to Willoughby's credit as a judge of style, if not as a gentleman, that he refrained from writing on this occasion.

One of the mitigating circumstances of Willoughby's confession near the end of the story is his rapport with Elinor while recalling his wife's "depravity" as author; and his remarkable excuse for not answering Marianne's letters beforehand was his supposed inability to avoid clichés to describe their past relationship:

> "—Every line, every word was—in the hackneyed metaphor which their dear writer, were she here, would forbid—a dagger to my heart. To know that Marianne was in town was—in the same language—a thunderbolt.—Thunderbolts and daggers!—what a reproof would she have given me!—her taste, her opinions—I believe they are better known to me than my own,—and I am sure they are dearer." (*SS*, 325)

Willoughby has the sense to know that thunderbolts and daggers, the stuff of potboilers, do not belong in a letter expressing sincere feeling; and so, lacking his own words, he preferred to give rein to the voice of a jealous woman in this triangle. His honest assessment of his role in this dilemma echoes the author's realpolitik: "And after all, what did it signify to my character in the opinion of Marianne and her friends, in what language my answer was couched?—It must have been only to one end. My business was to declare myself a scoundrel, and whether I did it with a bow or a bluster was of little importance" (*SS*, 328). Despite his failure as a writer, Willoughby disarms Elinor in this scene with his penetration as a reader of his story; and his performance as a speaker eclipses anything done by his counterparts.

The letter not only reveals character but, as with Miss Grey, may be his or her most convincing presence in the narrative. Although such letters as Darcy's and Frank Churchill's written to explain themselves after a bad performance, or Collins's to denounce Lydia after her elopement, all lack tension, others, like Collins's offer of the "olive branch" or Wentworth's proposal, are closely integrated with the dialogical language of the text, symbolized by the script/print antithesis. Just as Mr. Bennet retreats to his library to avoid the "anxieties of common life," so Mr. Collins, lacking the imagination to read or write from the heart, pompously rejects all novels on principle and chooses Fordyce's sermons for drawing-room entertainment. Given his intention to wield a sexist authority over the Bennet girls, he deserves, of course, to be interrupted; but his words nevertheless have dramatic irony for Lydia: "I have often observed how little young ladies are interested by books of a serious stamp, though written solely for their benefit. It amazes me, I confess;—for certainly, there can be nothing so advantageous to them as instruction" (*PP*, 69). Collins's offer to play backgammon with Mr. Bennet immediately after this lecture and his refusal to renew the sermon despite the women's entreaties suggest that "books of a serious stamp" hold little real interest for him either. Books for both men are instruments of power, not the means of what Johnson called "exchanging minds."[15]

2. *The Writerly Reader*

Austen's characters, men as well as women, have notoriously little to do but think and talk about each other. They sometimes engage in outdoor activities like walking and riding, but most of the time characters exist primarily as discourse. No wonder, then, that the act of reading has special importance for hero and heroine alike. To write well, one must also read well—read, as Pope advised, "With the same Spirit that its Author *writ*." In terms of the daily drama of Austen's novels, then, reading the text of the other character is an act requiring not only intelligence, perspicacity, and disinterestedness: ideally it involves "exchanging minds," a creative immersion of self in the other.

Among the other kinds of performances, some impor-

Text

tant scenes depict the central character engaged with a text, whether as a reader or as a letter-writer, and for good measure sometimes both. In *Pride and Prejudice* two successive scenes at Netherfield, which divide groups into card-players (non-readers), on the one hand, and readers/writers, on the other, show the hero's personal integrity in conversation with al-azons. In the first (I, 10), Mr. Hurst and Mr. Bingley play piquet, with Mrs. Hurst as observer, while Mr. Darcy writes a letter to his sister, indubitable proof of his finer tone, and Elizabeth does needlework and derives quiet amusement from Miss Bingley's attempts to ingratiate herself by offering to mend his pen and flattering him: "The perpetual commendations of the lady either on his hand-writing, or on the evenness of his lines, or on the length of his letter, with the perfect unconcern with which her praises were received, formed a curious dialogue" (*PP*, 47). Miss Bingley is quite literally without penetration, unable to invade the hero's privacy to meet the inner self engaged in his correspondence with Georgiana; hence, in her hopeless isolation, she can only talk idly about the mechanics of penmanship. Mr. Bingley, however, addresses the provenance of writing and makes an unlucky comparison of his friend's careful style to his own spontaneous letters, which elicits a sharp attack on the pretense of humility and the hidden claim of inspiration:

> "—for you are really proud of your defects in writing, because you consider them as proceeding from a rapidity of thought and carelessness of execution, which if not estimable, you think at least highly interesting. The power of doing any thing with quickness is always much prized by the possessor, and often without any attention to the imperfection of the performance." (*PP*, 48–49)

Writing should reveal emotion, we are to understand, but it also requires a measured choice of words to communicate ideas forcefully—the plain style used in Darcy's letter of explanation to Elizabeth, and in Mrs. Gardiner's as well. Miss Bingley's "raptures" and Mr. Bingley's "rapidity of thought" are the clichés of romantic authorship and egotism that Willoughby himself deplored.

In the second scene (I, 11), after the failure of his request to play cards ("Mr. Darcy did not wish for cards"), "Mr.

156

Hurst had therefore nothing to do, but to stretch himself on one of the sophas and go to sleep" (*PP*, 54); and his wife occupied herself "in playing with her bracelets and rings" as well as in joining intermittently the dialogue between Jane and her brother. As before, Mr. Darcy is absorbed in reading instead of writing; and again Miss Bingley exposes her illiteracy in her stabs at conversation:

> At length, quite exhausted by the attempt to be amused with her own book, which she had only chosen because it was the second volume of his, she gave a great yawn and said, "How pleasant it is to spend an evening in this way! I declare after all there is no enjoyment like reading! How much sooner one tires of any thing than of a book!—When I have a house of my own, I shall be miserable if I have not an excellent library."
>
> No one made any reply. (*PP*, 55)

Besides the broad hint about the library at Pemberley, her effusion over the pleasure of reading is a transparent ruse to interrupt the hero's silent focus on a text; as in the faux pas committed by the Thorpes in rivalry with Catherine's genuine knowledge of books, so this braggadocio's empty words are enough to condemn her and do not merit comment from the others.

Later, while dancing with Elizabeth at the Lucases', Mr. Darcy proposes a subject for conversation that Miss Bingley no doubt would have seized upon greedily, to her detriment:

> "What think you of books?" said he, smiling.
>
> "Books—Oh! no.—I am sure we never read the same, or not with the same feelings."
>
> "I am sorry you think so; but if that be the case, there can at least be no want of subject.—We may compare our different opinions."
>
> "No—I cannot talk of books in a ball-room; my head is always full of something else."
>
> "The *present* always occupies you in such scenes—does it?" said he, with a look of doubt.
>
> "Yes, always," she replied, without knowing what she said, for her thoughts had wandered far from the subject. (*PP*, 93)

Without knowing what she said. In contrast to Miss Bingley, who had talked designedly to no avail, Elizabeth gains in Darcy's esteem by her spontaneous expressiveness and utter lack of affectation. Above all, with the earlier scene in mind, Mr. Darcy can deduce her genuine seriousness as a reader from her refusal to make small talk about books. Thanks to the previous negative stimulus from Miss Bingley, in other words, the protagonists are nudged as well as drawn together in a textual enterprise.

At best, reading is the word made flesh, a reification of ciphers on the written or printed page. Characters too enervated to make this mental effort grope blindly at the text and as a last refuge make a fetish of the writer's tools. For instance, Harriet's mementoes of Mr. Elton's "courtship" are suspicious on various counts. These "relicks" contrast the heroine's critical detachment from her protégée's sentimentalizing of trivia; but this exaggerated homage to writing implements reveals more than Harriet's dull wits, already well recognized at this stage: the objects reveal a secret about Mr. Elton—his accident while trying to write:

> "—Do not you remember his cutting his finger with your new penknife, and your recommending court plaister?—But as you had none about you, and knew I had, you desired me to supply him; and so I took mine out and cut him a piece; but it was a great deal too large, and he cut it smaller, and kept playing some time with what was left, before he gave it back to me. And so then, in my nonsense, I could not help making a treasure of it—so I put it by never to be used, and looked at it now and then as a great treat." (*E*, 338)

As Emma admits in this scene that she had had some court plaster at the time but wanted Harriet to use hers instead to enhance her intimacy with Mr. Elton, the erotic significance of the material is explicit. When linked to Harriet's "superior treasure," that is, the "end of an old pencil,—the part without any lead" (*E*, 339), a pattern emerges: both mementoes derive from Mr. Elton's problems when cutting a writing instrument (pen and pencil) and needing the women's help; in the first instance, Emma's "new penknife" proves dangerous; in the second, the pencil runs out of lead.

The pen, Anne Elliot reminds us (*P*, 234), has traditionally been the man's prerogative; and Mr. Darcy knows better than to allow Miss Bingley to mend his: "Thank you—but I always mend my own" (*PP*, 47). Likewise, it is the bestowing of this power to write that forms the earliest bond between Fanny and Edmund:

> they went together into the breakfast-room, where Edmund prepared her paper, and ruled her lines with all the good will that her brother could himself have felt, and probably with somewhat more exactness. He continued with her the whole time of her writing, to assist her with his penknife or his orthography, as either were wanted; and added to these attentions, which she felt very much, a kindness to her brother, which delighted her beyond all the rest. (*MP*, 16)

Harriet's mementoes are not just a reiteration of her nonsensical attitude; in the context of Mr. Elton's uxorious role in marriage, these artifacts, in retrospect, suggest that he was never man enough to be Emma's husband, if only because he could not handle her (appropriately) sharp penknife! Moreover, as Harriet is no more successful than Miss Bingley in entering a man's heart through his writing instrument, the first-aid remnant and broken pencil should tell that her loss is not to be mourned. Notwithstanding Mr. Elton's facility at charades, Emma proves to be right about his shallow expressions of gallantry and in suspecting his mercenary motives while proposing to her in the carriage. Possessing so little writer's promise, therefore, it is not unexpected that Mr. Elton is an indifferent reader, capable of winning only Harriet as an audience during her portrait sessions: "Harriet listened, and Emma drew in peace" (*E*, 47).

Despite the reputation attributed to her by the ironic narrator in the first chapter, Emma Woodhouse from the very beginning is an alert, circumspect reader, equal to Mr. Knightley in critical judgment and more daring in imagination. In fact, one character, Robert Martin, who is denied any actual conversation, presents himself largely through the response that his letter involuntarily creates in Emma's mind. At first, outward signs reinforce the heroine's prejudice against his class: "I had no idea that he could be so very clownish, so totally without air" (*E*, 32). Yet upon reading his letter to Harriet, she changes her mind:

> There were not merely no grammatical errors, but as
> a composition it would not have disgraced a gentle-
> man; the language, though plain, was strong and un-
> affected, and the sentiments it conveyed very much to
> the credit of the writer. It was short, but expressed
> good sense, warm attachment, liberality, propriety,
> even delicacy of feeling. (*E*, 50–51)

Against the possibility that someone had dictated the letter,
Emma asserts, with authorial license, that "it is not the style of
a woman; no, certainly, it is too strong and concise; not diffuse
enough for a woman"(*E*, 51). In this act of reading, she enters
Mr. Knightley's discourse exactly: "It is so with some men.
Yes, I understand the sort of mind." [16]

Good writing is of a piece with good reading; and, as
expected, Robert Martin's taste in books is not frivolous. To
Emma's question concerning his background beyond farming,
Harriet replies falteringly:

> "but I believe he has read a good deal—but not what
> you would think any thing of. He reads the Agricul-
> tural Reports and some other books, that lay in one of
> the window seats—but he reads all *them* to himself.
> But sometimes of an evening, before we went to
> cards, he would read something aloud out of the Ele-
> gant Extracts—very entertaining. And I know he has
> read the Vicar of Wakefield. He never read the Ro-
> mance of the Forest, nor the Children of the Abbey.
> He had never heard of such books before I mentioned
> them, but he is determined to get them now as soon
> as ever he can." (*E*, 29)

Martin's effort to accommodate his reading to Harriet's supposed interests in books is good-natured, but his failure to do
so implies the same masculine activism that Mr. Knightley and
his brother represent in the story: "'He has not been able to
get the Romance of the Forest yet. He was so busy the last
time he was at Kingston that he quite forgot it, but he goes
again to-morrow'" (*E*, 32). If the evidence of his reading that
same potpourri used at Hartfield, *Elegant Extracts*, passes
without comment, it may also be significant that the heroine is
silent on his ignorance of Gothic romances. Martin's choice of
Goldsmith, however, probably reveals a Johnsonian seriousness about fiction.

In view of Martin's proven qualities as reader and writer, Emma's premature judgment of his education resounds with dramatic irony:

> "How much his business engrosses him already, is very plain from the circumstances of his forgetting to inquire for the book you recommended. He was a great deal too full of the market to think of any thing else—which is just as it should be, for a thriving man. What has he to do with books? And I have no doubt that he *will* thrive and be a very rich man in time—and his being illiterate and coarse need not disturb *us.*" (*E*, 33–34)

As Emma discovers shortly after this scene, Martin's letter reveals a natural gentility rather than a bookish head; and if business prevents his spending much time at the circulating library, his reading of the agricultural reports, the kind of professional habit the Knightleys also exercise, probably contributes to the "English verdure, English culture, English comfort" (*E*, 360) that she herself so admires.

Emma's talk about education is really for Harriet's benefit and is intended to denigrate Martin; her own capacity to read imaginatively owes little to the medium of print, as Mr. Knightley attests:

> "Emma has been meaning to read more ever since she was twelve years old. I have seen a great many lists of her drawing up at various times of books that she meant to read regularly through—and very good lists they were—very well chosen, and very neatly arranged—sometimes alphabetically, and sometimes by some other rule. The list she drew up when only fourteen—I remember thinking it did her judgment so much credit, that I preserved it some time; and I dare say she may have made out a very good list now. But I have done with expecting any course of steady reading from Emma. She will never submit to any thing requiring industry and patience, and a subjection of the fancy to the understanding." (*E*, 37)

Mr. Knightley's indictment here may be tongue-in-cheek; in any case, his emphasis upon quantity and encyclopedic method, the heritage of the printing revolution and the intellectual achievement of the Enlightenment, is unlikely to improve a lively mind. In the end he recants self-mockingly: "It was very natural for you to say, what right has he to lecture me?—and I am afraid very natural for you to feel that it was done in a disagreeable manner. I do not believe I did you any good. The good was all to myself, by making you an object of the tenderest affection to me" (*E*, 462). In thus renouncing his educational program Mr. Knightley may be only speaking out of love; and Austen's text lacks the tendentiousness of Wordsworth: "Sweet is the lore which Nature brings."[17] Yet, without sending her characters off to a vernal wood to gain wisdom, Austen does imply a norm that undermines the importance of books to stress the intuition of the individual mind: "Nature gave you understanding" (*E*, 462). Neither books nor mentor can do much to improve a reader who lacks this natural gift.

3.   *The Violence of the Word*

Only a few characters are capable of reading in a writerly manner, and sometimes even they lack the will to cope with the text. Authentic experience, not the standardization of that experience in book form, is the aim of the encounter, as the contrast between a line of poetry and the published interpretation suggests: " 'The course of true love never did run smooth—A Hartfield edition of Shakespeare would have a long note on that passage'" (*E*, 75). Given her sureness in penetrating the written text, therefore, Emma's quixotism derives not from books or letters but from narratives related by others, which are, in turn, sometimes a character's account of a letter. Because of Emma's lexical acuity, in fact, the written word can be a threatening presence, not to be glossed over but physically shunned if at all possible. In her triangular confrontations with others, however, the relative freedom of the speech act stimulates her imagination to "read" self-serving arrangements of motives and actions. Thus, from hatred of the speaker and jealousy of the subject, Emma deliberately avoids the possibility of having the romance she has just spun proven illusory by confronting the actual document: "though much had been forced on her against her will, though she had in fact heard the whole substance of Jane Fairfax's letter, she had been able to escape the letter itself" (*E*, 162). Like Emma, Mr. Knightley appears to gain access to Frank Churchill's letters at times; but he cannot be trusted to read a rival's narrative disinterestedly: "His letters disgust me" (*E*, 149). Although perceiving Churchill in the guise of a Lovelace or Montoni throughout the earlier intrigues, the hero at last reads the erstwhile villain's "very thick letter" (*E*, 436) and concedes: "Well, there *is* feeling here.—He does seem to have suffered in finding her ill.— Certainly, I can have no doubt of his being fond of her" (*E*, 447). Secure in possession of his beloved, the hero can afford to respond to the text in the spirit expressed by the author.

As in any performance, an element of danger enters into the act of reading to stimulate the faculties into the requisite "flow." Characters who lack this energy and courage retreat into illiteracy to blinker themselves from the informing word. Mrs. Bates, we know, requires special handling whenever a letter from Jane arrives; and the fear of reading or hearing any bad news about the girl implies the essential violence of writing per se. This old woman's blindness finds a parallel in Mr. Woodhouse's susceptibility to drafts (invasion of privacy) and his cowering behind the shrubbery. Not only is he unable to read, but on one occasion he suffers a significant loss of memory.

Mr. Woodhouse's repeated efforts to recall the popular riddle "Kitty, a fair but frozen maid" (*E*, I, 9) are symptomatic of his neurotic withdrawal from life and dependence on his daughter's protection. The occasion unites him with another illiterate, Harriet, who is "collecting and transcribing all the riddles of every sort that she could meet with, into a thin quarto of hot-pressed paper, made up by her friend, and ornamented with cyphers and trophies" (*E*, 69). Although Harriet's attention, like Miss Bingley's, is typically drawn to the mechanics of writing—the hot-pressed paper and careful penmanship—rather than to the interpretation of the word games, throughout the chapter inspiration, memory, and arcane language are the subjects of conversation; and for the only time in the novel Mr. Elton attains a certain eloquence.

Prompted by his misplaced feelings for Emma, Elton's memory is quick all the while Mr. Woodhouse is fumbling for more than the first line of the elusive riddle:

> [Mr. Elton] was invited to contribute any really good
> enigmas, charades, or conundrums that he might rec-

ollect; and she had the pleasure of seeing him most
intently at work with his recollections; and at the
same time, as she could perceive, most earnestly
careful that nothing ungallant, nothing that did not
breathe a compliment to the sex should pass his lips.
They owed to him their two or three politest puzzles;
and the joy and exultation with which at last he recalled, and rather sentimentally recited, that well-
known charade,

My first doth affliction denote,
　Which my second is destin'd to feel
And my whole is the best antidote
　That affliction to soften and heal. —

made her quite sorry to acknowledge that they had
transcribed it some pages ago already. (*E*, 70)

An interpretative problem quietly injected in all this activity
concerns authorship and intention. The "well-known charade"
derives from the oral tradition of folklore and as such belongs
to the generations of people who passed it down through
memory. Like other forms in this tradition, notably the ballad,
folk song, and country dance, it is being removed from a local
speech-oriented culture and recorded in book collections for
enjoyment by a general reading public.[18] Perhaps a major reason that characters in this scene are having difficulty with their
memories is their greater reliance on books as an ersatz mind,
in imitation of Swift's Modern. Because it is a radically closed
text, the charade offers a number of dramatic ironies within
the action: characters are divided according to their ability to
recall the exact words of the poem, to solve its verbal puzzle,
and even to compose an original one. Mr. Elton has the energy to do all three but nevertheless fails to communicate his
intention adequately to his readers. Emma is expert at solving
the riddles but not at interpreting the writer's intention. Harriet and Mr. Woodhouse, of course, are utterly incompetent to
read any text and also lack the memory requisite to oral, illiterate culture.

　　Without narrative interference, characters struggle
alone against the resistant language and find meanings to fit
their individual needs. When Mr. Elton returns the "very
next day" with a conundrum of his own making, only Emma

solves it but attributes its object as Harriet. Mr. Woodhouse, without comprehending a word of it, nevertheless feels sure of its author: "—Nobody could have written so prettily, but you, Emma" (*E*, 78). Her reading of it, moreover, momentarily evokes his past life: "Your dear mother was so clever at all those things! If I had but her memory! But I can remember nothing;—not even that particular riddle which you have heard me mention; I can only recollect the first stanza; and there are several." Mr. Woodhouse's problem, of course, involves more than mere forgetfulness: for one reason or another he lacks the energy to read and instead relies on the voice for verbal communication. When told that it is one of David Garrick's charades in *Elegant Extracts* [19] and that it is already copied out in Harriet's album, Mr. Woodhouse is mysteriously addled:

> "Aye, very true—I wish I could recollect more of it.
>> Kitty, a fair but frozen maid.
> The name makes me think of poor Isabella; for she was very near being christened Catherine after her grandmama." (*E*, 79)

The fact that the riddle has been found in a book is not much comfort to this illiterate; and unless he can recall the text by memory it will remain forever out of reach. The cause of his amnesia, however, needs interpretation.

Presumably the reader himself is expected to remember the poem attributed to Garrick, which sometimes substitutes the word *forward* for *frozen:*

> Kitty, a fair, but frozen maid,
>> Kindled a flame I still deplore;
> The hood-wink'd boy I call'd in aid,
> Much of his near approach afraid,
>> So fatal to my suit before.
>
> At length, propitious to my pray'r,
>> The little urchin came;
> At once he fought the midway air,
> And soon he clear'd, with dextrous care,
>> The bitter relicks of my flame.
>
> To Kitty, Fanny now succeeds,
>> She kindles slow, but lasting fires:

With care my appetite she feeds;
Each day some willing victim bleeds,
    To satisfy my strange desires.

Say, by what title, or what name,
    Must I this youth address?
Cupid and he are not the same,
Tho' both can raise, or quench a flame—
    I'll kiss you, if you guess.

The name of the youth, we know, is chimney sweeper; and the speaker in the poem is the chimney, who was nearly set afire by Kitty's careless kindling technique; the emended "forward maid" refers to her haste in building the fire, while "frozen maid" tells us her motive in being "forward." Although Cupid and the chimney sweeper are not the same, the persona of the poem is clearly male and is nervous about being in the hands, if not in the arms, of women. In the epoch of the prince regent, to whom this novel is dedicated, the lines "Each day some willing victim bleeds, / To satisfy my strange desires" would invite an erotic interpretation unsuspected by Mr. Woodhouse, who, we may assume, has repressed the violence of desire to the extent of numbing all sensations of the living body. As Alice Chandler has suggested, the "flame I still deplore" may allude to venereal disease, of which the persona is cured by the urchin of the second stanza.[20] Fanny, in the third stanza, is apparently a virginal partner; and the image of the chimney sweeper connotes in general the idea of sexual intercourse. However we read this scene, it is at least clear that while Mr. Elton's wordplay is tamely decorous, the riddle Mr. Woodhouse is attempting to recall is remarkably erotic; and indeed the subject matter may be responsible for his amnesia.

In a novel where much of the action concerns reading and reflexively imitates the actual reader's confrontation with the text, Austen's strategy of alluding to a popular riddle which, as is often the case, hints darkly of a sexual relationship frees her of the onus of authorial intentionality and posits the anonymous conditions of folklore by placing the burden on her audience.[21] Unlike Mrs. Bates's dependence on her daughter to read Jane's letters, Mr. Woodhouse's incapacity toward the written text is not caused by laziness or fear of bad news; instead, it appears to conceal a sexual problem of some kind, perhaps analogous to the one revealed in the riddle. Almost as if someday she anticipated volumes of hermeneutics to explain the mystery, the puckish author seems to be teasing the reader here. In contrast to another fictional widower, Squire Allworthy, who continues to love his wife beyond the grave, Mr. Woodhouse seems to have compensated for the loss of his spouse by forming an emotional attachment to his daughter that waives all male libido under the incest taboo. The role of psychosomatic invalid, perhaps unconsciously assumed, at times surfaces as a deliberate means of shirking responsibilities, as in his refusal to attend the Coles's party and the ball at the Crown Inn. But the cost of denying the body is seen not only in his mental block toward anything erotic but more generally in a failure of desire: hence, his energy level is inferior even to Harriet's feeble wit in trying to probe Mr. Elton's charade. One reads with the body, and the strength of the word is commensurate with the imaginative responsiveness of the perceiver.

Granted this freedom—and challenge—we may see such behaviors as the restrictive diet of "nice smooth gruel, thin, but not too thin," the phobia about drafts, dampness, and almost any meteorological condition, and the hysteria over venturing beyond the shrubbery or the fireplace, as regressive "feminine" denials of energy that the heroine must surmount in her quest for deliverance from male hegemony. Beneath the mantle of sensibility, Mr. Woodhouse unwittingly gives utterance to all the dire fears about sexual union as death. His mournful compassion toward women who marry, and also toward the children who result from parturition, which like death is a mysterious and violent fact of human life, is thus ambivalent: "Ah! poor Miss Taylor! 'tis a sad business"; "poor Isabella"; and her "poor little dears." The Westons' wedding cake was poison to Mr. Woodhouse for reasons other than its enzymes. His premonitions of death at the idea of marriage—and, implicitly, sexual intercourse—underlie his stubborn insistence on the rules of politeness due a bride, when he suddenly assumes patriarchal authority in insisting on Emma's duty to Mrs. Elton (*E*, 280).

Ironically, though again no one in the scene appears to notice, it takes Mrs. Elton's vulgar airs to pronounce the unthinkable about Mr. Woodhouse:

"Here comes this dear old beau of mine, I protest!—
Only think of his gallantry in coming away before the
other men!—what a dear creature he is;—I assure
you I like him excessively. I admire all that quaint,
old-fashioned politeness; it is much more to my taste
than modern ease; modern ease often disgusts me.
But this good old Mr. Woodhouse, I wish you had
heard his gallant speeches to me at dinner. Oh! I assure you I began to think my caro sposa would be absolutely jealous." (*E*, 302)

His "gallant speeches" were probably no more than a gratuitous compliment on her gown and other polite gestures; yet
Mrs. Elton's typically gross interpretation raises at least the
possibility of some libido in Emma's father and thus accounts
for his interest in bawdy charades. In sum, unlike Sir Walter
Elliot, Mr. Woodhouse has a prodigious "inner life" encoded
in his text; and though not a talker to compete with Miss
Bates, he too possesses secrets worth probing.

4. The "Language of Real Feeling"

Austen's carnivalesque prose mimics layer upon layer
of texts, rendering characters within a spectrum ranging from
parodic types, with a minimum of signifiers, to complex modes
of discourse; and as we have seen, both extremes may appear
in the same character at different points in the story. Although
numerous "empty spaces" usual to narrative appear in her presentation,[22] where some indeterminacies like the allusion to
"Kitty" may be functional to the characterization, as if aware of
the need for control, Austen seems deliberately to thematize
the hermeneutic play required of her readers. Without going
so far as Richardson's creation of "spare parts kits" like the
elaborate footnotes and other intrusive commentary appended
to the text of *Clarissa*,[23] Austen is nevertheless at pains to offer
specimens of ideal discourse to assist us in our interpretative
efforts. Thus, in her fiction negative performances that break
the rules of an encounter are always instructive; and a perceptive reader like Fanny Price musters the heroism to reduce
Babel itself to harmony for the moment. During her exile in

Portsmouth, for example, Fanny can be grateful even for Mary Crawford's flippant writing: "There was great food for meditation in this letter, and chiefly for unpleasant meditation; and yet, with all the uneasiness it supplied, it connected her with the absent, it told her of people and things about whom she had never felt so much curiosity as now, and she would have been glad to have been sure of such a letter every week" (*MP*, 394). Apart from the practical interest of correspondence, *to be connected with the absent* is a motive of writing itself; and almost any shred of text suffices to initiate the reading process. But, of course, the absent varies in intensity to the present in accordance with the "mind-style" established in the language.

Reading/writing is a process, a performance; and in a moment of emotional stress even normally inert minds can suddenly become expressive. One of the most powerful letters in *Mansfield Park* appears only fragmentarily in the text, but its import is mediated through Fanny's consciousness. During Tom's illness, Lady Bertram has been keeping her niece at Portsmouth informed with reports

> regularly transmitted to Fanny, in the same diffuse style, and the same medley of trusts, hopes, and fears, all following and producing each other at hap-hazard. It was a sort of playing at being frightened. The sufferings which Lady Bertram did not see, had little power over her fancy; and she wrote very comfortably about agitation and anxiety, and poor invalids, till Tom was actually conveyed to Mansfield, and her own eyes had beheld his altered appearance. (*MP*, 427)

Without being directly on the scene, this emblem of moral sloth has used the word as a means of distancing herself from the crisis; but the visual encounter strikes a nerve that arouses her at last: "Then, a letter which she had been previously preparing for Fanny, was finished in a different style, in the language of real feeling and alarm; then, she wrote as she might have spoken."

Besides the continual privileging of the manuscript over printed matter, Austen's text insinuates still another code to register sincere character—a written language that seems equivalent to speech. To show the metamorphosis (temporary) of a character from insincere to sincere writer a "different style" is required, one that can somehow overcome the polarity between the ciphers on the page and the actual heat of emotion. The attempt is vain, finally, because the sincere ideal rising above discredited discourse is also found to be a role, bound to a rhetorical style in a vicious circle. Without subscribing to his pastoral ideology, Austen resembles Wordsworth in her goal of arranging "a selection of the real language of men in a state of vivid sensation"; but contrary to this poet's belief that feelings create the situation, her narratives, as we have seen, give priority to situation as the cause of feelings.[24] In her mimetic scale advancing from the published book to the "precious manuscript" toward authentic experience, the ultimate trick is altogether to disclaim writing, under certain circumstances, in favor of speech—or rather, of "speech"—the final illusion to be conjured up from the printed page.

Previously, we have seen Austen's extensive use of direct discourse and free indirect discourse to project character immediately in the text, unadulterated by the narrator's judgments. Since her alazons are usually bundles of uncontrollable speech-making, it is not enough simply to renounce writing within a context as a means of promoting the "language of real feeling." On the contrary, a speech encounter like Darcy's ill-fated proposal at Hunsford (*PP*, 189–93) or Wentworth's stilted conversation at the White Hart ("Whether he would have proceeded farther was left to Anne's imagination to ponder over in a calmer hour" [*P*, 225]) fails to communicate the "inner self" to the other and needs a subsequent letter of explanation to reveal the character's sincere motives.

To write as one "might have spoken," then, is no guarantee of "real feeling" when a character is only a tinkling cymbal. Relatively few scenes, in fact, ever privilege speech over writing; and the most notable examples are in *Persuasion*, where the heroine's interior monologue foregrounds the action and her "actual" voice goes almost unheard throughout the story. Anne Elliot's unusually assertive conversation with Captain Benwick about Byron and Scott, celebrated writers whose influence she criticizes, gives speech rather than script precedence over books; and upon recall the event amuses even the normally restrained performer (*P*, 101).

That scene prepares us, moreover, for the finale at the White Hart, when she speaks eloquently to Captain Harville about the sexes while her lover is writing a letter. This is a tour de force of competing discourses—written, printed, and oral

simultaneously; and at least during the moment of the encounter it appears as if the tongue is mightier than pen, print, or sword! What activates the harangue on a woman's constancy are conversations about *real* events (Mrs. Musgrove and Mrs. Croft on Henrietta's engagement, Captain Harville on Louisa's), and Anne gains her voice from a "nervous thrill" that is communicated automatically to Wentworth and causes his pen to stop writing; at a later moment, it even falls from his hand and alters her sense of audience, thus implying her complete loss of self-consciousness in the performance: "Anne was startled at finding him nearer than she had supposed, and half inclined to suspect that the pen had only fallen, because he had been occupied by them, striving to catch sounds, which yet she did not think he could have caught" (*P*, 233–34). Then, as if by association with this accident, Anne rises to the occasion when Harville makes the mistake of appealing to printed texts as evidence against her feminist dissent:

> "But let me observe that all histories are against you, all stories, prose and verse. If I had such a memory as Benwick, I could bring you fifty quotations in a moment on my side the argument, and I do not think I ever opened a book in my life which had not something to say upon woman's inconstancy. Songs and proverbs, all talk of woman's fickleness. But perhaps you will say, these were all written by men."
>
> "Perhaps I shall.—Yes, yes, if you please, no reference to examples in books. Men have had every advantage of us in telling their own story. Education has been theirs in so much higher a degree; the pen has been in their hands. I will not allow books to prove any thing." (*P*, 234)

After several centuries of the Gutenberg press, Anne is aware of man's enhanced power through the mass media and, quite understandably, dismisses the manufactured opinion that has standardized woman's inferior character in the long campaign for male supremacy.[25]

Though politically "correct," Anne's eloquent speech in this context seems a trifle forced, like one of Mr. Knightley's or even Mr. Collins's "lectures." The triangular situation here offsets her words ironically, as Captain Wentworth has just lost his pen and Captain Harville probably never uses one. In fact, the real target of this attack is not the pen but the male press, and of the various captains in this story Benwick is the only one subject to the influence of books. Harville, who tries lamely to argue from printed authority, "was no reader; but he had contrived excellent accommodations, and fashioned very pretty shelves, for a tolerable collection of well-bound volumes, the property of Captain Benwick" (*P*, 99). Instead of a pen, Harville wields a brush or an awl to keep his mind employed according to a Johnsonian standard: "He drew, he varnished, he carpentered, he glued; he made toys for the children, he fashioned new netting-needles and pins with improvements; and if every thing else was done, sat down to his large fishing-net at one corner of the room" (*P*, 99). Like Austen's positive characters in general, male or female, Harville is anything but bookish and presents himself effortlessly toward others: "Captain Harville, though not equalling Captain Wentworth in manners, was a perfect gentleman, unaffected, warm, and obliging" (*P*, 97). Arising from a spontaneous impulse to vent her repressed feelings vis-à-vis Wentworth, therefore, this feminist speech addressed to Harville is really beside the point; but indirectly, of course, Anne's message of undying love reaches the right person with great force.

No matter how climactic, this scene is too deliberately staged with podium and props to render the quintessential "language of real feeling." It is after the feminist oratory, however, that the narrator describes a necessary condition of this privileged language: "Captain Wentworth was folding up a letter in great haste, and either could not or would not answer fully" (*P*, 236). To write as one would have spoken from immediate emotion requires an unfinished form to convey "—the work of an instant!" (*P*, 236). Mr. Bingley's principle of writing-to-the-moment was not itself at fault, but rather his pretense of using it as an excuse for careless expression. Otherwise, since spontaneity is of the highest value in an encounter, writing that approaches the circumstances of excited speech will suppress the past and focus on the incomplete moment of composition. The lovers in this scene never talk directly to each other about their feelings; instead, the one delivers an irrelevant speech to a third person while the other hastily responds to her in writing.

Not speech heard, but speech *read*, we are to understand, is the ultimate context of heartfelt exchange. Two discrete moments are involved in the reunion of minds here: his written response to her speech and her reading of that response. To be connected with the absent is the universal desire of the writer; and thus, paradoxically, it is not fulfillment, the real thing—motion—but the incomplete text, the quasi transcript of speech—symbolic action—that reveals the "innermost" self.

In the grip of the tension of his own shyness about speaking directly to Anne, as well as his consciousness of the others present, Wentworth has no tongue here, only a pen: "I can listen no longer in silence. I must speak to you by such means as are within my reach" (*P*, 237). Even when the two lovers are in the same room, they are absent from each other and can only meet through the written text; and the lover's discourse repeats the familiar questions about interpreting signs of his desire simultaneously with her outpouring about constancy:

> "For you alone I think and plan. — Have you not seen this? Can you fail to have understood my wishes?—I had not waited even these ten days, could I have read your feelings, as I think you must have penetrated mine. I can hardly write. I am every instant hearing something which overpowers me. You sink your voice, but I can distinguish the tones of that voice, when they would be lost on others." (*P*, 237)

If writing the letter releases tension in the performance while building it up in the spectator, reading it afterward is cathartic to a dangerous extent: "The revolution which one instant had made in Anne, was almost beyond expression" (*P*, 237). But as if to prevent fulfillment of desire too early, others arrive to interrupt her euphoric privacy:

> The absolute necessity of seeming like herself produced then an immediate struggle; but after a while she could do no more. She began not to understand a word they said, and was obliged to plead indisposition and excuse herself. They could then see that she looked very ill—*were shocked and concerned—and would not stir without her for the world. This was dreadful! Would they only have gone away,* and left her in the quiet possession of that room, it would have

> been her cure; but to have them all standing or wait-
> ing around her was distracting, and, in desperation,
> she said she would go home. (*P*, 238; my emphasis)

The encounter with the letter, as the free indirect discourse
shades in (my italics), eclipses all social ties for the moment
and increases desire in inverse proportion to the interference
from the others in the scene. Although she longs for the "possibility of speaking two words to Captain Wentworth," Anne's
first impulse is toward "the quiet possession of that room," the
reader's solitary space.

Within the Austen story, then, the "language of real
feeling" derives from a situation of competing discourses—
printed versus written versus spoken versus "spoken" (written)—that is represented as being read, as well as written,
utterly without any regard to audience. It is a style perceived
by the character as unquestionably sincere, hence, not a *style*
at all but a momentary expression of self possible even for an
egregious nonwriter and nonreader like Lady Bertram or for
such interlopers as Willoughby and Frank Churchill. Given
the intensive privileging of texts and media, the illusion of
words "spoken" from the heart usually requires battering the
character beforehand with a total loss of self-esteem and possibly even of any future at all.

Writing purposes to be connected with the absent.
Fanny's wisdom brings this study to full circle with the phenomenological theory of representation that opened our inquiry. The "language of real feeling" is the ace the author
holds in her hand for the right moment in the action; and
when played against the cacophony of hackneyed utterance, it
carries conviction. Those spontaneous moments when Darcy,
Knightley, and Wentworth suddenly articulate their desire to
marry the heroine endow a romantic convention with unusual
power; but there are many lesser performances in Austen's
novels that convey the sense of feelings deeper than the written text can bear. As Jonathan Richardson urged, the artist
"must not say all he can on his Subject, and so seem to distrust
his *Reader*."[26] Writing is the dialogical means to the absent,
and like the busy talkers in Austen's stories, the insistence of
the word is a function of the unsaid. Silence, in narrative as in
music, is crucial to expression; and it is this power of arrested
speech that strengthens a character's presence and arouses our
curiosity about her.

Conclusion

Writing, to recall Fanny Price's thoughts during her exile in Portsmouth, connects one with the absent (*MP*, 394). In Fanny's predicament the idea is a truism of epistolarity; but we have seen that in moments of greatest tension, even when Austen's characters occupy the same room or garden, they may resort to writing letters rather than speaking face-to-face. Thus under *any* circumstances the act of writing is a surrogate medium, an abstract of intentionality to connect the self with the Sartrean other; at best it is a form of role-playing, and usually suspicious. To help overcome the implied distance from the reader, writing, in Austen's fiction, needs to imitate the situation of actual speech; to communicate "real feelings," moreover, it needs to contextualize speech so that occasional moments of sincerity can be made credible amidst the usual babble of everyday situations. As in Richardson, Fielding, and Sterne, whose "new species of writing" explicitly turned theory into practice, Austen appears to be quite deliberate in thematizing her reflexive strategy toward the dialogical text and sometimes calling into question the mirage of reading as well as the subterfuge of writing.

Like the eighteenth-century masters of English fiction, Austen was defensive about the literary merit of novel-writing and pursued rigorous narrative economies toward verisimilitude; as a result, by means of parody she discovered a language for rendering consciousness. Parody is commonly regarded as a specific form of literary satire; and in her early spoofs Austen, we know, ridiculed the bathos and pretentiousness of sentimentalism, Gothic horror, epistolary style, and history writing. But already in her first novels she turned parody into an intertextual art that carries out two related purposes: it undermines mimetic conventions by asserting a "deeper" reality supposedly free from convention, and it also discloses the rules of an encounter by showing when they are broken in faulty communication. Above all, by ostensibly circumventing narrative omniscience, through free indirect discourse Austen's parody achieves the remarkable power of reporting not only a character's speech but also his or her apparent consciousness.

Although eighteenth-century novelists experimented

with individualizing characters through idiomatic dialogue, Austen appears to have been the first major English writer to grasp fully the technique of using free indirect discourse to represent the *lived* self in the moment. The discovery of this narrative method, ubiquitous in modern fiction, may have been an accident of changing conventions for indicating various kinds of discourse on the printed page. At any rate, like other means of production in a historical culture, the provenance of literary texts is not wholly conscious but part of what Raymond Williams calls a "structure of feeling"; and in his illuminating Foucauldian study of "transparency" in later eighteenth-century prison designs, John Bender likens free indirect discourse to the surveillance system instituted in the Panopticon: "Both the realist novel and the penitentiary pretend that character is autonomous, but in both cases invisible authority is organizing a mode of representation whose way of proceeding includes the premise, and fosters the illusion, that the consciousness they present is as free to shape circumstance as to be shaped by it."[1] Despite the extent of transparency in rendering her characters through free indirect discourse, however, Austen hardly reveals them completely to the reader; and their strength as individuals, we have seen, may depend on keeping something concealed from the other characters, even from those most admired and trusted.

While exposing the character to the reader without narrative interference, free indirect discourse supposedly uncovers "real feelings" rather than yet another convention of storytelling. This valorizing of sincerity in novelistic discourse can be compared to similar privileged stances in the eighteenth-century semiotics of landscape architecture, stage acting, dancing, public speaking, and other cultural encoding. Austen's well-known interest in the picturesque helps to explain her own devices in addressing the irrational basis of her characters' (and presumably the reader's) responses in an encounter. From William Gilpin she could have learned that the quest for knowledge is hardly the whole of a story:

> But it is not from this *scientifical* employment, that we derive our chief pleasure. We are most delighted, when some grand scene, tho perhaps of incorrect composition, rising before the eye, strikes us beyond the power of thought—when the *vox faucibus haeret*; and

every mental operation is suspended. In this pause of intellect; this *deliquium* of the soul, an enthusiastic sensation of pleasure overspreads it, previous to any examination by the rules of art. The general idea of the scene makes an impression, before any appeal is made to the judgment. We rather *feel*, than *survey* it.[2]

Austen recognized that challenging the reader with the riddle of the plot—Fanny Price's dilemma in refusing Henry Crawford or the mystery concerning Frank Churchill and Jane Fairfax—gives a strong incentive to cope with the text; but, like Gilpin, she attributed the reader's highest pleasure to those encounters that involve ecstatic emotion. When characters do not know what they are saying in the moment but consequently find themselves engaged to marry, their "*deliquium* of the soul" eludes description and can only be referred to fragmentarily. It is when the "voice sticks in the throat" (*vox faucibus haeret*), Austen's speech-oriented narrative would persuade us, that the character reveals the "language of real feeling."

Besides the irrational principle of aesthetic pleasure, Gilpin's stressing the reader's complicity in creating the illusion required in any painting, drama, and literary text seems akin to Austen's practice: "How absurdly would the spectator act, if instead of assisting the illusion of the stage, he should insist on being deceived, without being a party in the deception?—if he refused to believe, that the light he saw, was the sun; or the scene before him, the Roman capital, because he knew the one was a candle-light, and the other, a painted cloth?"[3] Austen would have met a similar emphasis in Edmund Burke: "A true artist should put a generous deceit on the spectators, and effect the noblest designs by easy methods. . . . No work of art can be great, but as it deceives."[4] Again, the reader enters into a contract with the artistic work and surrenders to the illusion for the sake of pleasure. Rather than simply ridiculing popular fiction, then, Austen's parodic intertextuality serves the critical purpose of sharpening the reader's awareness of which illusions are worth submitting to.

Although later eighteenth-century theorists stressed the subjective apprehension of the object, of course there was always something more than the reader's willful hallucination involved in constituting the text. Sincere expression implies an objective norm: no matter how much a fine wine depends on one's taste to determine its value, the fermented juice is nevertheless a product of chemical activity as well. The ideal of sincerity, like the related ideal of grace in art criticism since the Renaissance, may be understood as a by-product of rationalistic, and parodic, textuality.

Grace as something to be snatched from beyond the reach of art (that is, the "rules") had intrigued the French neoclassical formalists decades before Pope's "Essay on Criticism." When applied to the body in movement, it became the *je ne sçai quoi* of the aristocratic mystique, the defining characteristic of a gentleman's and lady's "walk" and "air," a refined essence hopelessly beyond the *bourgeois gentilhomme* and, needless to say, the lower classes. Briefly stated, during the eighteenth century the elusive quality of grace was a kinetic phenomenon that belonged to the general nurture/nature debate in educational discourse. With the ascendency of primitivistic doctrines on the Continent during the middle of the century, the human machine increasingly became the psychosomatic wonder of creation.[5] Although in 1753 Hogarth roundly attacked Dürer and Lomazzo for their geometrical models and stressed the importance of the empirical eye in perceiving beauty, he himself advanced the Line of Beauty, the serpentine form, as the ideal. Moreover, he understood elegance to be a quality acquired by one's being subjected to "a variety of constant regular movements . . . and fashioned by a genteel education." According to Hogarth, far from being instinctive in the body, grace was a trait usually limited to the upper-class person: "contrary to most other copyings or imitations, people of rank and fortune generally excel their originals, the dancing-masters, in easy behaviour and unaffected grace; as a sense of superiority makes them act without constraint; especially when their persons [bodies] are well turn'd."[6]

Only a year later, however, Louis de Cahusac's *La Danse ancienne et moderne* anticipated modern theorists in kinesics who connect linguistic communication with bodily motion; and, as in Rousseau, the child is the model of self-expression: "Observe . . . the tender children, from their entry into the world, to the moment in which their reason unfolds itself, and you will see that it is primitive nature herself, that manifests herself in the sound of their voice, in the features of their face, in their looks, in all their motions."[7] Similarly, Claude-Henri Watelet argues that grace is natural to the young body and vanishes with age altogether: "l'enfance & la jeunesse sont l'âge des graces. La souplesse & la docilité des membres sont tallement nécessaires aux graces, que l'âge mûr s'y refuse, & que la vieillesse en est privée."[8] In contrast, Hogarth observed that children "have movements in the muscles of their faces peculiar to their age, as an uninformed and unmeaning stare, an open mouth, and simple grin: all which expressions are chiefly formed of plain curves, and these movements and expressions idiots are apt to retain."[9]

In attributing the "language of real feeling" and grace of movement to Nature, Austen, together with late-eighteenth-century theorists, recognized a fundamental principle explored in modern behavioral studies. The pioneer of kinesics, Ray Birdwhistell, for instance, points out the mysterious phenomenon in all societies of a child's acquiring the essentials of communication by the age of six, which cannot be explained by rationalistic criteria: "Communication control is not achieved through a simple additive process which involves the accumulation of parcels of sounds or body motion which carry encapsulated chunks of meaning." Birdwhistell goes on to say how little is yet known about the "patterned way" we learn as human beings. In contrast to neoclassical theorists, who could enumerate more than a score of bodily gestures corresponding to definable passions (they amounted to as many as thirty-two different kinds by the end of the eighteenth century), present studies recognize as many as 250,000 different facial expressions alone.[10] In describing this awesome variability of behavior we have to make do with the handful of emotive words available in our language. It is an important insight of writers in the later eighteenth century that the old moral psychology, with its finite categories of emotion, was no more than a working model for describing a very complex phenomenon.

Despite the emphasis in romantic aesthetics on the fragmented and subjective basis of the picturesque, however, rationalistic theorists like Gilbert Austin were aspiring to describe ever more precisely the semiotics of the bodily expression. With learned citations from classical rhetoric, Austin attacks the cult of primitivism and outdoes any of the seventeenth-century French theorists by devising a geometric system to track every expressive movement of the body within a spherical space. A "strange prejudice," he complains, "has seemed to prevail against every effort to improve delivery."[11]

Because of a mistaken idea about wishing to appear natural and spontaneous, although they studied intonations of voice, public speakers entirely ignored the value of countenance and gesture to expression. In Austin's view, this "strange prejudice" arose from inappropriate use of gestures and from the inherent difficulty in determining their decorum in the first place.

Although admitting that theatricality should be avoided in church situations, Gilbert Austin nevertheless rejects Addison's contention that gesture per se is out of keeping with the English character: "Our preachers stand stock still in the pulpit, and will not so much as move a finger, to set off the best sermons in the world."[12] Sincere communication need not be boring, and Austin endorses Thomas Sheridan's view that the Evangelical movement owed as much to rhetorical principles as it did to religious doctrine:

> There is no emotion of the mind, which nature does not make an effort to manifest by some of those signs (tones, looks, and gestures), and therefore a total suppression of those signs is of all other states apparently the most unnatural. And this, it is to be feared, is too much the state of the pulpit elocution in general in the church of England. On which account, there never was perhaps a religious sect upon earth, whose hearts were so little engaged in the act of public worship, as the members of that church. To be pleased, we must feel, and we are pleased with feeling.[13]

No matter how fanatical the Presbyterians, Methodists, and Quakers, at least they find their worship stimulating in contrast to the perfunctory Church of England congregation. To prove that body language is "natural," Austin quotes Erasmus Darwin at length on the associationism between gesture and emotional response, and then attempts to work out an exact science of rhetorical encoding.

Despite the lack of direct evidence, it is not unlikely that the Austen family knew about *Chironomia*, especially considering the coincidence of the author's name with their own. In any case, James Fordyce, whose pulpit eloquence Gilbert Austin highly praises, was of course cited by Mr. Collins for the edification of such spirited young women as Lydia and Kitty Bennet. Although Mary Wollstonecraft deplored Fordyce's "*mellifluous* precepts" toward subjugating women, in the comically disastrous reading scene in *Pride and Prejudice* Austen shows that Mr. Collins's pompous delivery itself is enough to alienate his captive audience, notwithstanding the antifeminist he educes as an authority; and the context also suggests that he actually welcomes Lydia's interruption of his reading as an excuse to play backgammon with Mr. Bennet (*PP*, 69).

In a much more elaborate reading scene in *Mansfield Park*, which contrasts religious to dramatic discourse, Austen may be alluding to Gilbert Austin and James Fordyce as examples of pulpit eloquence and spiritual poverty. After his momentous reading of Shakespeare to Fanny (*MP*, 337–38), Henry Crawford raises with Edmund the topoi of histrionic art, pulpit eloquence, and audience response that interested Gilbert Austin. Despite his success as a reader of dramatic poetry, Henry quickly loses ground with Fanny when he emulates Austin's harangue on pulpit delivery: "It is more difficult to speak well than to compose well; that is, the rules and trick of composition are oftener an object of study" (*MP*, 341). The implied norm here is clearly something ineffable, not to be communicated either by a mellifluous voice or by "the rules and trick of composition." When Crawford affectedly demands a selective congregation for his eloquence ("I must have a London audience, I could not preach, but to the educated; to those who are capable of estimating my composition"), Fanny "involuntarily shook her head," a sincere gesture that cuts through the premeditated delivery of the speaker and reduces him to guilty bewilderment, "instantly by her side again, intreating to know her meaning" (*MP*, 341). A minute previously she had already responded to his irreverent attitude to hearing sermons by moving her lips (*MP*, 340). Now again she is "vexed with herself for not having been as motionless as she was speechless" (*MP*, 342). The scene culminates in Crawford's becoming intoxicated by his own verbal monopoly; but when he adopts the lover's hackneyed discourse of "angel talk" toward the heroine ("it is 'Fanny' that I think of all day, and dream of all night.—You have given the name such reality of sweetness, that nothing else can now be descriptive of you" [*MP*, 344]), he loses everything that he had gained by reading Shakespeare so well and ends up being a hammy Lovelace.

Presumably influenced by Crawford, Edmund also

appears to be an advocate of the *Chironomia* in finding a pulpit delivery that can compete with the Evangelicals for emotional effect:

> "Even in my profession"—said Edmund with a smile— "how little the art of reading has been studied! how little a clear manner, and good delivery, have been attended to! I speak rather of the past, however, than the present.—There is now a spirit of improvement abroad; but among those who were ordained twenty, thirty, forty years ago, the larger number, to judge by their performance, must have thought reading was reading, and preaching was preaching. It is different now. The subject is more justly considered. It is felt that distinctness and energy may have weight in recommending the most solid truths; and, besides, there is more general observation and taste, a more critical knowledge diffused, than formerly; in every congregation, there is a larger proportion who know a little of the matter, and who can judge and criticize." (*MP*, 339–40)

Although Edmund does read "very well," according to Fanny, his progressivism in this scene seems no less vainglorious than Henry's parade of his talents before an apparently passive listener. But Edmund, we know, is "so inconsistent" at the time because he is so "full" of the Crawfords; his uncharacteristic manner here betrays a misplaced emulation of Henry's zeal for an urbane, rhetorically conditioned audience rather than for one responsive to the Word.

As in Austen's ironic allusions to modernist architects like Humphry Repton, Nature is the norm in this conversation; and Edmund's phrase "a spirit of improvement" is as suspect as his abetting Henry's attempts to overcome Fanny's resistance to seduction. Just as insensitive landscape architects were raping the land to display wealth ostentatiously, so high-powered media experts like Gilbert Austen were trying out scientific methods of persuasion without attending to the substance of the message. The fact, reported from someone's point of view, that the wedding service for Maria and Mr. Rushworth "was impressively read by Dr. Grant" (*MP*, 203) should suffice to make us wary of the "spirit of improvement" abroad. It is Dr. Grant who eventually leaves Mansfield for the "London audience" that Henry required and, true to Tom Bertram's prediction, subsequently dies of an apoplexy brought on "by three institutionary dinners in one week" (*MP*, 469).

Behind all the competing discourses in the reading scene at Mansfield, then, is a barely discernible revered silence of which Fanny alone is aware. Contrary to a familiar reading of Fanny as a latter-day saint, however, her physicality is no less remarkable than her finely tuned receptiveness to spiritual messages in an increasingly secular world. Within the discourses of *Mansfield Park*, only she can feel the coarseness of Henry's and even Edmund's attempts to manipulate an audience through methods resembling Pavlov's experiments in a later age. Yet she does nonetheless attest to the efficacy of rhetoric: "To *good* reading, however, she had been long used; her uncle read well—her cousins all—Edmund very well; but in Mr. Crawford's reading there was a variety of excellence beyond what she had ever met with. . . . —It was truly dramatic.—His acting had first taught Fanny what pleasure a play might give, and his reading brought all his acting before her again" (*MP*, 337).

As *Chironomia* proudly proclaimed, the whole geometrical system of gesture was based not only on the best classical authorities but, most importantly, on the principles of Nature—that is, on the way human beings communicate with one another. Jane Austen did not pretend to deny that narrative art means artfulness, deceit, regulated stimulus/response, voluntary delusion, and the whole game of filling in the charade's "empty spaces"; on the contrary, while demonstrating the heroine's model receptivity to mimetic performances of one kind or another throughout *Mansfield Park*, the author sneaks in the most privileged discourse—the unspoken and unheard religious presence that depends on the onion-peeling of false discourses on elocution like Gilbert Austin's, Henry Crawford's, and Edmund Bertram's. From the strategy of novelistic structure, what matters is our temporary belief in the unspoken and unheard language referred to in Fanny's musings.

Notwithstanding Park Honan's scrupulous analysis of Austen's holograph letter concerning her intentions in *Mansfield Park*,[14] the ideal of ordination (investing with priestly authority) valorizes the heroine's discourse in her struggle to save Edmund from the Babylonians who have invaded the temple; and what is most remarkable about this apparently religious novel is its secular method of depicting the poor in spirit. By a process of elimination, all the worldly contenders are found to speak in a defunct language; and at last it is the heroine's silence that is triumphant.

By contrast to this literary quietism, in *Sense and Sensibility* and *Persuasion* wisdom is perhaps too closely identified with the discourse of conduct books about filial duty; and in the end we are asked to accept Marianne Dashwood's renunciation of passionate love and Anne Elliot's unwavering deference to Lady Russell's original advice against marrying Wentworth. When the ludic spirit is most light and bright and sparkling, as in *Pride and Prejudice* and *Emma*, the rival discourses still need the ballast of at least some "serious" talk, as both heroines must undergo a degree of humiliation before winning "happiness." Of all Austen's novels, however, it is mainly in *Emma*, as we have seen, that the reflexive text brackets even the most privileged discourse and calls attention to the essential deceitfulness of any narrative art.

Notes

Introduction

1. Here the term is taken to mean any face-to-face social arrangement that enables the participants to monitor each other in some formalized activity, whether a card game, a dance, a recital, a "theatrical," or simply a polite conversation. For an extended discussion of the concept, see Erving Goffman, *Encounters* (Indianapolis and New York: Bobbs-Merrill, 1961). A common meaning of the word as an unexpected or troubling occurrence is not primarily at issue here. In later discussions I introduce the Sartrean self/other as a specific narrative principle of the encounter.

2. See Elizabeth L. Eisenstein's monumental *The Printing Press as an Agent of Change*, 2 vols. (Cambridge: Cambridge University Press, 1979). Her *The Printing Revolution in Early Modern Europe* (Cambridge: Cambridge University Press, 1983) is an abridgment. Walter J. Ong, *Orality and Literacy: The Technologizing of the Word* (London and New York: Methuen, 1982). Alvin Kernan, *Printing Technology, Letters and Samuel Johnson* (Princeton, N.J.: Princeton University Press, 1987).

3. Paul Alkon, *Defoe and Fictional Time* (Athens: University of Georgia Press, 1979), p. 185.

4. Ibid., p. 195.

5. The first three editions of *Clarissa*, for example, provide a startling typographical record of the author's revisions and additions. After the first edition (1747–48), Richardson added more than a hundred pages to the second (1749) and third editions (1751). Not only did he publish in 1751 *Letters and Passages Restored to Clarissa* so that owners of the first edition could benefit by the additions, but he also used printer's bullets and dots in the third edition to show the reader exactly where the revisions occurred in the text. This procedure demonstrates the degree of responsibility that Richardson consigned to his reader in constituting the story. See Florian Stuber, "On Original and Final Intentions, or Can There Be an Authoritative *Clarissa*?" TEXT: *Transactions of the Society for Textual Scholarship* 2 (1985): 229–44.

6. Janet Altman, *Epistolarity: Approaches to a Form* (Columbus: Ohio State University Press, 1982), pp. 95–96.

7. See Mikhail Bakhtin, *Rabelais and His World*, trans. Helene Iswolsky (Bloomington: Indiana University Press, 1984) and *The Dialogic Imagination*, ed. Michael Holquist, trans. Caryl Emerson and Michael Holquist (Austin: University of Texas Press,

1981). Besides the books by Alkon and Altman referred to above, see Walter L. Reed, *An Exemplary History of the Novel: The Quixotic versus the Picaresque* (Chicago: University of Chicago Press, 1981), and Michael McKeon, *The Origins of the English Novel, 1600–1740* (Baltimore: Johns Hopkins University Press, 1987).

8. McKeon, *Origins of the English Novel*, p. 14. Northrop Frye, *Anatomy of Criticism* (New York: Atheneum, 1968), pp. 39–40, 226–28.

9. Robert Alter, *Fielding and the Nature of the Novel* (Cambridge, Mass.: Harvard University Press, 1968), pp. 90–94.

10. Tobias Smollett, *The Expedition of Humphry Clinker*, ed. Lewis M. Knapp (London: Oxford University Press, 1966), p. 81.

11. T. C. Duncan Eaves and Ben D. Kimpel, *Samuel Richardson: A Biography* (Oxford: Clarendon, 1971), pp. 108–09.

12. Samuel Richardson, *Clarissa*, Everyman's Library, 4 vols. (London: Dent; New York: Dutton, 1962), 3:159.

13. In *Factual Fictions: The Origins of the English Novel* (New York: Columbia University Press, 1983), pp. 42–70, Lennard J. Davis argues that the news/novel discourse was inherently reflexive and that the reader would have no way of knowing whether the account was true or fictional. The mere fact that something is printed, however, carries weight with the reader.

14. McKeon, *Origins of the English Novel*, pp. 50–52.

15. Daniel Defoe, *The Fortunes and Misfortunes of the Famous Moll Flanders, Etc.*, ed. G. A. Starr (London: Oxford University Press, 1971), p. 255.

16. Linda Hutcheon, *A Theory of Parody: The Teachings of Twentieth-Century Art Forms* (New York and London: Methuen, 1985), p. 37. For some important earlier studies of parody as a prototype of fictionality, see Bertel Pedersen, *Parodiens teori: (Teoriens parodi)* (Copenhagen: Berlingske Forlag, 1976); Margaret Rose, *Parody/Metafiction* (London: Croom Helm, 1979); and Gerard Genette, *Palimpsestes* (Paris: Seuil, 1982).

17. Quoted from Hutcheon, *Theory of Parody*, p. 29.

18. Park Honan, *Jane Austen: Her Life* (New York: St. Martin's Press, 1987), p. 142.

19. Ibid., p. 140.

20. Ibid., p. 144.

21. A recent Austen biographer, for instance, singles out her reflexive endings: "If she has one overriding fault as a writer, it is her obvious and overhasty desire, near the ends of her novels, to wrap up loose ends and get the thing over with, once the *dénouement* has been reached, as quickly as possible. It is as if she has had enough of her people by the end of the book and cannot wait to get rid of them once they have reached their happy ending" (John Halperin, *The Life of Jane Austen* [Baltimore: Johns Hopkins University Press,

1984], p. 78). In contrast to such blanket dismissals, see the cogent defense of Austen's mixed narrative forms by Frank J. Kearful, "Satire and the Form of the Novel: The Problem of Aesthetic Unity in *Northanger Abbey*," *ELH* 32 (1965): 511–27. My own emphasis in this study, of course, should obviate Halperin's notion that Austen was tired of her characters in the end; on the contrary, she never had any doubts about their artificiality (artfulness/artifice) in the first place.

22. Nearly all of Austen's characters are round, as E. M. Forster observed (*Aspects of the Novel* [New York: Harcourt, Brace and World, 1927], p. 74); in other words, the most transparent stereotype exhibits some temporal dimension. In the comical proposal scenes, for instance, Mr. Collins and Mr. Elton both show a stock male presumption while reciting commonplaces of courtship; yet they are very different suitors of the moment, the former exhibiting no more than the empty gesture of passion, the latter at least individualized by the brief history of his misplaced feelings for the heroine. Despite his more burlesque role as foolish suitor, nevertheless Mr. Collins does have a past (as the narrator informs us in chapter fifteen of the first volume), which helps to account for his behavior and gives him the verisimilitude of a creature living in time. An interpretation that overlooks this important temporality in even some relatively minor characters is John Lauber's "Jane Austen's Fools," *SEL* 15 (1975): 511–24.

23. Austen was perfectly aware of the narrative slippage created by printing conventions and tried to avoid the obvious signposts for the reader except when absolutely necessary. Consider her remark on *Pride and Prejudice*: "There are a few typical errors; and a 'said he,' or a 'said she,' would sometimes make the dialogue more immediately clear; but 'I do not write for such dull elves / As have not a great deal of ingenuity themselves'" (*Letters*, pp. 297–98). Claude Rawson traces this speech-orientation of character in Fielding. See "Dialogue and Authorial Presence in Fielding's Novels and Plays," *Order from Confusion Sprung* (London: George Allen and Unwin, 1985), pp. 261–310.

24. I do not pretend, of course, to be the first to make this claim for Austen's art. Irvin Ehrenpreis, for instance, has written eloquently on this same tendency in her fiction. See "Austen: The Heroism of the Quotidian," *Acts of Implication* (Berkeley and Los Angeles: University of California Press, 1978), pp. 112–45. Other books have appeared since I began this inquiry more than ten years ago while teaching seminars for dedicated Austenites; among the more mentionable are the following: Julia Prewitt Brown, *Jane Austen's Novels: Social Change and Literary Form* (Cambridge, Mass.: Harvard University Press, 1979); Daniel Cottom, *The Civilized Imagination: A Study of Ann Radcliffe, Jane Austen, and Sir Walter Scott* (Cambridge: Cambridge University Press, 1985), pp. 88–105; Susan

Morgan, *In the Meantime: Character and Perception in Jane Austen's Fiction* (Chicago: University of Chicago Press, 1980); Mary Poovey, *The Proper Lady and the Woman Writer: Ideology as Style in the Works of Mary Wollstonecraft, Mary Shelley, and Jane Austen* (Chicago: University of Chicago Press, 1984), pp. 172–240; Tony Tanner, *Jane Austen* (London: Macmillan, 1986); and Judith Wilt, *Ghosts of the Gothic: Austen, Eliot, and Lawrence* (Princeton, N.J.: Princeton University Press, 1980), pp. 121–72.

Among the most original theoretical approaches, D. A. Miller's chapter "The Danger of Narrative in Jane Austen," in *Narrative and Its Discontents: Problems of Closure in the Traditional Novel* (Princeton, N.J.: Princeton University Press, 1981), pp. 3–106, and Joseph Litvak's "Reading Characters: Self, Society, and Text in *Emma*," *PMLA* 100 (October 1985): 763–72, confirm my own earlier hunches about Austen's artfulness. Gerald Bruns's insightful essay "Interpretation of Character in Jane Austen," in his *Inventions, Writing, Textuality, and Understanding in Literary History* (New Haven and London: Yale University Press, 1982), pp. 111–24, also anticipated the emphasis of this study.

Chapter I

1. John Dewey, *Art as Experience* (New York: Putnam, 1934), p. 35. Quoted by Mihalyi Csikszentmihalyi, *Beyond Boredom and Anxiety: The Experience of Play in Work and Games* (San Francisco, Calif.: Jossey-Bass, 1975), p. 36.

2. Alistair M. Duckworth, *The Improvement of the Estate: A Study of Jane Austen's Novels* (Baltimore: Johns Hopkins University Press, 1971), p. 165 n. There is, of course, abundant evidence, as Duckworth convincingly shows, of Austen's love of games as well as dancing and the drama. See his very informative essay "'Spillikins, Paper Ships, Riddles, Conundrums, and Cards': Games in Jane Austen's Life and Fiction," *Jane Austen: Bicentenary Essays*, ed. John Halperin (Cambridge: Cambridge University Press, 1975), pp. 279–97.

3. In a remarkably original chapter on *Pride and Prejudice*, Howard Babb stresses the central importance of the word *performance* in the dialogue and shows how much of the action concerns reading character by means of gesture. See *Jane Austen's Novels: The Fabric of Dialogue* (Columbus: Ohio State University Press, 1962), pp. 113–44. Two very different studies of music in Austen's novels further develop the idea of performance: Patrick Piggott, *The Innocent Diversion: Music in the Life and Writings of Jane Austen* (London: Douglas Cleverdon, 1979); and Robert K. Wallace, *Jane Austen*

and Mozart (Athens: University of Georgia Press, 1983). A book that came to my attention too late to influence this chapter is Peter Hutchinson's *Games Authors Play* (London and New York: Methuen, 1983). Although he does not mention Austen, Hutchinson sketches the various functions of play in literature and the other arts, and emphasizes the way in which authors tease their readers.

4. I am following Northrop Frye's terminology here. The *alazon* and *eiron*, Greek words for an imposter and a self-deprecating person, respectively, are among the most common stereotypes in fictional modes. See his *Anatomy of Criticism*, pp. 39–41.

5. See Erving Goffman, "Fun in Games," in his *Encounters*, pp. 17–81. The main narrative purpose of regulated activities in Austen's text is to frame characters within an *encounter*. The concept of a "frame" for the events of a game derives from Gregory Bateson. See "A Theory of Play and Fantasy," *Psychiatric Research Reports 2*, American Psychiatric Association, 1955, p. 44.

6. Goffman, "Fun in Games," p. 18.

7. Ibid., p. 19. See n. 1 to the Introduction, p. 185.

8. Throughout this chapter, at the risk of offending some readers who are allergic to the nomenclature of the social sciences, I use the concept of "flow" from Mihalyi Csikszentmihalyi: "In the flow state, action follows upon action according to an internal logic that seems to need no conscious intervention by the actor. He experiences it as a unified flowing from one moment to the next, in which there is little distinction between self and environment, between stimulus and response, or between past, present, and future." *Beyond Boredom and Anxiety*, p. 36.

9. Goffman, "Fun in Games," pp. 51–54.

10. Another self-critical performer takes the opportunity to be alone when playing before an indifferent audience: "These were some of the thoughts which occupied Anne, while her fingers were mechanically at work, proceeding for half an hour together, equally without error, and without consciousness" (*P*, 72). The Musgroves, however, deserve nothing better after having instigated the performance: "Well done, Miss Anne! very well done indeed! Lord bless me! how those little fingers of yours fly about!" (*P*, 47). After such rude inattentiveness, their compliments only exacerbate the individual's sense of isolation from the group.

11. Lionel Trilling, *Sincerity and Authenticity* (Cambridge, Mass.: Harvard University Press, 1972), p. 75. For the revolutionary implications of the theatricals, see especially Avrom Fleishman, *A Reading of "Mansfield Park"* (Minneapolis: University of Minnesota Press, 1967), pp. 24–29; and Marilyn Butler, *Jane Austen and the War of Ideas* (Oxford: Clarendon, 1975), pp. 231–36.

12. Denis Diderot, *"Rameau's Nephew" and "D'Alembert's*

Dream," trans. L. W. Tancock (Harmondsworth, Middlesex, Eng.: Penguin, 1966), p. 121.

13. For an early nineteenth-century formulation of classical oratory, complete with detailed facial expressions and hand gestures, see Gilbert Austin, *Chironomia: or, A Treatise on Rhetorical Delivery,* ed. Mary Margaret Robb and Lester Thonssen (Carbondale and Edwardsville: Southern Illinois University Press, 1966), pp. 187–206.

14. The modern reader may exaggerate the extent of this particular dance's significance for the encounter. As Patrick Piggott observes (*The Innocent Diversion,* pp. 92–93), this "waltz" was not the new dance that had arrived in England by 1812 and was shocking because of its indecent requirement of holding the partner by the waist. Instead, it was probably no more than another country dance, but with a 3/4 tune. Thomas Wilson's *An Analysis of Country Dancing* (1811), for instance, invented a "new & elegant system of dancing called Country dance Waltzing or Waltz Country dancing." The "irresistible waltz" tune that joined Frank and Jane at Weymouth may have been no more erotic than the popular German import of the time, "Ach du lieber Augustine." See R. W. Chapman's appendix, "The Manners of the Age," *Emma,* pp. 503 and 511, respectively.

15. Piggott, *The Innocent Diversion,* pp. 91 and 92, respectively.

16. Roger Caillois gives a more systematic analysis of play than Huizinga and stresses the freedom from any pursuit in the real world as one of its defining characteristics. See "Unity of Play: Diversity of Games," *Diogenes* 19 (Fall 1957): 105, 120, especially.

17. Duckworth, *The Improvement of the Estate,* p. 163.

18. For an argument that this narrative is imbued with a sense of the heroine's past, see K. R. Ireland, "Future Recollections of Immortality: Temporal Articulation in Jane Austen's *Persuasion,*" *Novel* 13 (Winter 1980): 204–20.

19. An implicit norm for the encounter of the Crown Inn is the English country dance, which was performed according to certain figures and in step with traditional folk tunes. In contrast to the minuet and other highly formalized dances, this ritual activity held a deep nationalistic significance and was ever an anomaly to the eighteenth-century dancing-master, who was usually a product of French court tastes. Raoul Auger Feuillet, for example, set out condescendingly to teach the French improvements on the original, "demonstrated in an easie method adapted to the meanest capacity" (*For the Further Improvement of Dancing,* trans. John Essex [1710], title page). A certain xenophobia against the French hegemony over the English body persisted throughout the period and is still evident in Dickens's caricature of old Mr. Turveydrop's Deportment, associated

with the Regency. Bob Acres's complaint in Sheridan's *The Rivals* reflects an age weary of the pressure to move strictly to foreign rule:

> "Sink, slide, coupée. Confound the first inventors of cotillons! say I—they are as bad as algebra to us country gentlemen. I can walk a minuet easy enough when I am forced!—and I have been accounted a good stick in a country dance. Odds jigs and tabours!—I never valued your cross-over to couple—figure in—right and left—and I'd foot it with e'er a captain in the country!—but these outlandish heathen allemandes [probably the German dances P. Rameau had recommended in place of the English country dance] and cotillons are quite beyond me! I shall never prosper at 'em, that's sure—mine are true-born English legs—they don't understand their curst French lingo!
>
> . . . —damn me! my feet don't like to be called Paws! No, 'tis certain I have most Antigallican toes!" (III, iv)

On this hegemony, see Claude J. Rawson, "Gentlemen and Dancing-Masters," *Henry Fielding and the Augustan Ideal under Stress* (London: Routledge and Kegan Paul, 1972), pp. 3–29.

20. See Frances Rust, *Dance in Society: An Analysis of the Relationship between the Social Dance and Society in England from the Middle Ages to the Present Day* (London: Routledge and Kegan Paul, 1969), p. 67. Rust also cites Reginald St. Johnston's belief that Miss Berry introduced the fad in England and that the duke of Devonshire made it fashionable in 1813.

21. Edmund Burke, *Reflections on the Revolution in France*, ed. Connor Cruise O'Brien (Harmondsworth, Middlesex, Eng.: Penguin, 1968), p. 171.

22. Austen's characters usually talk during *any* performance for obvious reasons, but it is the very simplicity of the country dance figures that helped make it popular among the sociable but musically indifferent English gentry. In the aftermath of the Revolution and the radical Jacobin spirit on both sides of the Channel, to judge by Thomas Wilson's 1809 indictment of public dancing, English motion was losing some of its traditional class hierarchy:

> In our modern assemblies, a Dance composed of more than two parts, or what is called a single figure, generally gains the reception of a bad play, or rather worse, it is damned at its announcement; and the Lady who has the temerity to call it, is instantly pronounced the wife or daughter of a cheesemonger or oil-man. . . . It indeed appears now, in fashionable life, a crime to attempt any thing that requires a

capacity beyond what the more sagacious brutes are endowed with; for bad Dancing is now considered as strong a proof of good breeding as bad writing, good driving, or boxing.

The Treasures of Terpsichore; Or, A Companion for the Ball-Room (London, 1809), pp. iii–iv. A dance that does not require finesse and exhibitionism in its performance is just the thing for a Darcy or a Knightley.

Chapter II

1. Quotations from Samuel Johnson, "The History of Rasselas, Prince of Abissinia," chaps. 3 and 8, respectively, in *Rasselas, Poems, and Selected Prose*, ed. Bertrand H. Bronson (New York: Rinehart, 1952), pp. 511 and 522.

2. Cf. Roland Barthes: "What is proposed, then, is a portrait—but not a psychological portrait; instead, a structural one which offers the reader a discursive site: the site of someone speaking within himself, *amorously,* confronting the other (the loved object), who does not speak," *A Lover's Discourse: Fragments*, trans. Richard Howard (New York: Hill and Wang, 1978), p. 3.

3. Marc Eli Blanchard, *Description: Sign, Self, Desire: Critical Theory in the Wake of Semiotics* (The Hague: Mouton, 1980), p. 2.

4. Miguel de Cervantes, *Don Quixote*, ed. Joseph R. Jones and Kenneth Douglas (New York: Norton, 1981), pt. 2, chap. 32, p. 601.

5. Thackeray describes listening to a French singer of a sentimental ballad who not only made his audience weep but reduced himself to tears by his own performance. See *The English Humourists*, Everyman's Library (London: Dent, 1912), pp. 233–34.

6. Barthes, *A Lover's Discourse*, pp. 22–24. I discuss free indirect discourse at length in the next chapter. See especially chap. 3, n. 14, below.

7. Alexander Pope, *The Rape of the Lock*, ed. Geoffrey Tillotson, *The Twickenham Edition of the Poems of Alexander Pope*, 3d ed. (London: Methuen; New Haven and London: Yale University Press, 1962), 2:206 (canto 5, ll. 67–70).

8. Henry Fielding, *The History of Tom Jones, A Foundling*, ed. Fredson Bowers, *The Wesleyan Edition of the Works of Henry Fielding* (Middletown, Conn.: Wesleyan University Press, 1975), p. 34 (I, i).

9. Northrop Frye, *Anatomy of Criticism*, p. 41.

10. Bernard Paris, *Character and Conflict in Jane Austen's Novels* (Detroit: Wayne State University Press, 1978), p. 85.

11. At the center of Johnson's essay is a norm hopelessly beyond the reach of the poor: although the action of giving and receiving is reciprocal among the privileged classes, "by what means can the man please . . . who has no power to confer benefits; whose temper is perhaps vitiated by misery . . . ?" *The Rambler*, ed. W. J. Bate and Albrecht B. Strauss, *The Yale Edition of the Works of Samuel Johnson* (New Haven and London: Yale University Press, 1969), 5:118.

12. René Girard, *Deceit, Desire, and the Novel*, trans. Yvonne Freccero (Baltimore: Johns Hopkins University Press, 1965), p. 66.

13. Ibid., pp. 58–59.

14. Brummell invoked models from ancient Greece and Rome to justify his taste in fashions. See Beau Brummell, *Male and Female Costume*, ed. Eleanor Parker (New York: Arno, 1978).

15. Girard, *Deceit, Desire, and the Novel*, p. 73.

16. Some modern readers welcome this diminution of the gentleman's prerogative. Julia Prewitt Brown, for instance, remarks about Mr. Knightley's move to Hartfield: "Since he has no really important relationship to give up in leaving his estate, the sacrifice is proper." *Jane Austen's Novels: Social Change and Literary Form*, p. 124.

17. M. C. D'Arcy, *The Mind and Heart of Love* (Cleveland, Ohio: World Publishing, 1967), p. 100.

18. La Rochefoucauld, *Maxims*, trans. L. W. Tancock (Baltimore: Penguin Books, 1959; reprint 1967), no. 68.

19. Ibid., no. 28.

20. Denis de Rougemont, *Love in the Western World* (New York: Harper and Row, 1974), pp. 75–82.

21. A. O. J. Cockshut, *Man and Woman: A Study of Love and the Novel, 1740–1940* (New York: Oxford University Press, 1978), p. 27.

22. Frye, *Anatomy of Criticism*, p. 235.

23. Gottfried von Strassburg, *Tristan*, trans. A. T. Hatto (Harmondsworth, Middlesex, Eng.: Penguin, 1978), p. 262.

24. Quoted by Gordon Rattray Taylor, *The Angel Makers: A Study in the Psychological Origins of Historical Change, 1750–1850* (New York: Dutton, 1974), p. xii. See *Letters* for repeated mention of food and eating (pp. 5–6, 28, 287, 363, and 424–25).

25. *Letters*, p. 175.

26. Ibid., p. 61.

27. T. S. Eliot, "The Wasteland," *Collected Poems, 1909–1935* (London: Faber & Faber, 1957), p. 200 (III, l. 223). Lionel

Trilling, *"Mansfield Park," Jane Austen: A Collection of Critical Essays*, ed. Ian Watt, Twentieth Century Views (Englewood Cliffs, N.J.: Prentice-Hall, 1963), p. 129.

28. Mary Wollstonecraft, *A Vindication of the Rights of Woman* (New York: Norton, 1967), p. 207.

29. See Martin Battestin, *The Moral Basis of Fielding's Art: A Study of "Joseph Andrews"* (Middletown, Conn.: Wesleyan University Press, 1959), pp. 130–49.

30. Austen's theme regarding the clergy has a long history:

> For if a preest be foul, on whom we truste,
> No wonder is a lewed man to ruste;
> And shame it is, if a prest take keep,
> A shiten shepherde and a clene sheep.

"General Prologue," *Canterbury Tales*, ll. 501–04. *The Works of Geoffrey Chaucer*, ed. F. N. Robinson, 2d ed. (Cambridge, Mass.: Riverside, 1957), p. 22.

31. As a foil to the enthusiasts of fresh air and exercise in Sanditon, Arthur Parker exploits the role of invalid in order to indulge in rich cocoa and buttered toast: "He could not get command of the Butter however, without a struggle; His Sisters accusing him of eating a great deal too much, & declaring he was not to be trusted;— and he maintaining that he only eat enough to secure the Coats of his Stomach" (*MW*, 417).

32. The OED gives a meaning as follows: "To handle roughly or indelicately; to touse, tousle; to upset the arrangement of (anything neat or orderly); to disorder, rumple; to disarrange by tossing: e.g. to tumble bedclothes, a bed, or dress." Two quotations suggest possibilities for Austen's text: "Quoth she before you tumbled me, you promis'd me to Wed," *Hamlet*, IV, v, 62; "To deliver up her fair body to be tumbled and mumbled by Heartfree," Vanbrugh, *Provoked Wife*, V, iii.

33. See my article "Philanthropy and the Selfish Reader in Goldsmith's *Life of Nash*," in *Studies in Burke and His Time* 19 (1978): 197–207; and my chapter "*The Vicar of Wakefield*: A 'Sickly Sensibility' and the Rewards of Fortune," in *The Discourse of the Mind in Eighteenth-Century Fiction* (The Hague: Mouton, 1974), pp. 148–72.

34. See Gustave Flaubert, *Madame Bovary*, ed. Paul de Man (New York: Norton, 1965), p. 149.

35. *Letters*, p. 118.

36. Taken out of context, Austen's quip sounds remarkably Blakean: "Energy is the only life, and is from the Body; and Reason is the bound or outward circumference of Energy" ("The Marriage of Heaven and Hell," plate 4, *Complete Writings*, ed. Geoffrey Keynes

[London: Oxford University Press, 1972], p. 149). In the era of Napoleon, Goethe, and Beethoven, the concept of energy as a global force emerges in almost any discourse; but its early application to understanding the phenomenon of electricity seems especially relevant to Austen's novels, where characters find themselves moving about like charged particles. Analogous with magnetism, electricity, according to one late-eighteenth-century writer, is a condition of "excitement" caused by the activity of ether and phlogiston on each other; and its distinctive feature is the power over movement:

> A body is in an electric state, when it is capable of attracting, and then repelling light bodies, within a certain distance of it; and, as that state is communicable, or destructible, at pleasure, 'tis evident, that it must depend upon some kind of *subtile fluid,* surrounding the surface of the body electrified like an *atmosphere*; and all the phenomena of electricity are produced by the active properties of this electric atmosphere.

M. D. Peart, *On Electricity; With Occasional Observations on Magnetism* (Gainsborough, Eng., 1791), p. 1. Since her brother Edward was induced to take electric "bath" therapy for his gout, Austen probably knew about Francis Lowndes, the "medical electrician," who touted a cure-all from static electrical vibrations. In short, the idea that all motion is not only mechanical but also electrical in nature underlies the commonplace term *energy* in Austen's period.

37. *Letters*, p. 292. As Warren Roberts argues, despite her silence, Austen had a personal awareness of the war. While visiting Edward's family at Godmersham, she also visited Francis, who was stationed at Ramsgate and was organizing fishing fleets to help guard against an invasion. In May 1804, Francis was assigned to the *Leopard*, the flagship of a squadron blockading Napoleon's forces at Boulogne (see *Jane Austen and the French Revolution* [New York: St. Martin's, 1979], p. 95). Pasley's fervid imperialism doubtless gave meaning to the war effort, but it was his vigorous style that Austen specifically admired. Along with his thoroughgoing research into British naval history as well as into the precise details of Frank and Charles Austen's careers during this period, Park Honan stresses the author's unusual interest in military events of the day: "As a student of Pasley's work on military policy Jane Austen was to read demonstrations showing how numbers favoured a Napoleonic victory—and she would discuss foreign affairs, though women of the gentry were not meant to read *public news*." See *Jane Austen*, p. 199.

38. Charles William Pasley, *Essay on the Military Policy and Institutions of the British Empire* (London, 1810), p. 11. The italics are mine.

Chapter III

1. Thomas Docherty, *Reading (Absent) Character: Towards a Theory of Characterization in Fiction* (Oxford: Clarendon, 1983), p. 28.

2. See ibid., chap. 1, "From Description to 'Position.'"

3. Cf. Scott, *Quarterly Review* (1816): "The narrative of all her novels is composed of such common occurrences as may have fallen under the observation of most folks." Reprinted in *Jane Austen: "Emma," A Casebook*, ed. David Lodge (London and Basingstoke: Macmillan, 1968), p. 40.

4. *Anton Chekhov's Short Stories*, ed. Ralph E. Matlaw, Norton Critical Edition (New York: Norton, 1979), p. 269.

5. Quoted phrase and summary from Joel Weinsheimer, "Theory of Character: *Emma*," *Poetics Today* 1 (1979–80): 195.

6. For an attempt to distinguish between two basic kinds of characterization in Austen, see D. W. Harding, "Character and Caricature in Jane Austen," *Critical Essays on Jane Austen*, ed. B. C. Southam (London: Routledge and Kegan Paul, 1968), pp. 83–105. Cf. Frank J. Kearful, "Satire and the Form of the Novel: The Problem of Aesthetic Unity in *Northanger Abbey*," 511–27.

7. Ian Watt, *The Rise of the Novel: Studies in Defoe, Richardson and Fielding* (London: Chatto and Windus, 1960), p. 92. My interpretation of the self/other discourse in Austen has been influenced by previous interpretations of eighteenth-century novelists, especially Defoe. See Homer O. Brown, "The Displaced Self in the Novels of Daniel Defoe," *ELH* 38 (1971): 562–90; and John J. Richetti, *Defoe's Narratives: Situations and Structures* (Oxford: Clarendon, 1975).

8. Wayne C. Booth, *The Rhetoric of Fiction* (Chicago: University of Chicago Press, 1961), p. 265.

9. Marilyn Butler, *Jane Austen and the War of Ideas*, p. 260.

10. Barbara Hardy, *A Reading of Jane Austen* (N.Y.: New York University Press, 1976), p. 105.

11. Gilbert Ryle, "Jane Austen and the Moralists," *Critical Essays on Jane Austen*, ed. Southam, p. 106.

12. Martin Price, "The Other Self: Thoughts about Character in the Novel," *Imagined Worlds*, ed. Maynard Mack and Ian Gregor (London: Methuen, 1968), p. 294. This essay is incorporated in his *Forms of Life: Character and Moral Imagination* (New Haven and London: Yale University Press, 1983), pp. 65–89.

13. R. W. Chapman, "Notes" to *Emma*, 3d ed. (London: Oxford University Press, 1933), pp. 491–92.

14. Identified late in the nineteenth century by German and French philologists as *die erlebte Rede* or *le style indirect libre*, respectively, free indirect discourse is the narrative technique that largely accounts for Austen's "psychological realism." Just as it eluded the classical rhetoricians, so its practice has a remarkably short history in Western literature and seems to be connected with changes in printing conventions of represented speech during the seventeenth and eighteenth centuries. Although traces of this style occur almost at random in pages of Richardson, Fielding, Fanny Burney, and other early novelists, Austen seems by all accounts to have been the first major English writer to have seized upon its potential for characterization. To my knowledge the earliest study of free indirect discourse in Austen is Willi Bühler, *Die "Erlebte Rede" im Englischen Roman: Ihre Vorstufen und ihre Ausbildung im Werke Jane Austens, Schweizer anglistiche Arbeiten*, vol. 4 (n.d., but 1936). More recently: Norman Page, *Speech in the English Novel*, English Language Series no. 8 (London: Longman, 1973), esp. pp. 24–50; Roy Pascal, *The Dual Voice* (Manchester, Eng.: Manchester University Press, 1977), esp. pp. 45–60; and Graham Hough, "Narrative and Dialogue in Jane Austen," *Critical Quarterly* 12 (1970): 201–29. Alfred McDowell, "Fielding's Rendering of Speech in *Joseph Andrews* and *Tom Jones*," *Language and Style* 6 (1973): 83–96, stresses earlier instances. For a comprehensive survey of the scholarship on this technique, see Brian McHale, "Free Indirect Discourse: A Survey of Recent Accounts," *PTL: A Journal for Descriptive Poetics and Theory of Literature* 3 (1978): 249–87.

A blend of features from direct and indirect discourse, this new style, if the latter is taken as the starting point, involves five grammatical transformations: (1) removing the construction of reporting verb (saying/thinking) and conjunction *that* (also *whether* and *if* in cases of questions and exclamations); (2) retaining the third person and past tense of indirect discourse; (3) using the auxiliary and subject word-order of direct questions; (4) reviving to such direct discourse features as interjections that were barred from indirect discourse; and (5) returning to the deictic elements of direct discourse, which may have been converted by indirect discourse. McHale points out that grammatically free indirect discourse may be indistinguishable from nonreportive narration; thus, despite the philological criteria, the objective approach inevitably falls short of the real complexity in recognizing free indirect discourse in context (p. 252).

15. See Vivienne Mylne, "The Punctuation of Dialogue in Eighteenth-Century French and English Fiction," *Library*, ser. 6, 1 (1979): 43–61.

16. These two extremes of responses to *Mansfield Park* may be represented by Lionel Trilling's and Douglas Bush's admiration,

on the one hand, and by Joel C. Weinsheimer's and Marilyn Butler's condemnation, on the other. See Trilling's essay, *"Mansfield Park,"* reprinted in *Jane Austen: A Collection of Critical Essays*, ed. Ian Watt, pp. 124–40; also, *Sincerity and Authenticity*, pp. 75–80. Bush, *Jane Austen* (New York: Macmillan, 1975). Weinsheimer, *"Mansfield Park:* Three Problems," *Nineteenth-Century Fiction (NCF)* 29 (1974): 185–205. Butler, *Jane Austen and the War of Ideas*, pp. 219–49. For a recent attempt to interpret the ironic allusiveness in *Mansfield Park* and thus situate this novel in Austen's parodic art, see Margaret Kirkham, *Jane Austen, Feminism and Fiction* (Brighton, Sussex, Eng.: Harvester; Totowa, N.J.: Barnes and Noble, 1983), pp. 101–20.

17. V. N. Volosinov [M. M. Bakhtin], *Marxism and the Philosophy of Language*, trans. Ladislav Matejka and I. R. Titunik (New York: Seminar Press, 1973), p. 153.

18. See M. M. Bakhtin, "Discourse in the Novel," *The Dialogic Imagination*, pp. 259–422.

19. Graham Hough, "Narrative and Dialogue in Jane Austen," pp. 206–09.

20. See Wolfgang Iser's discussion of Austin, *The Act of Reading: A Theory of Aesthetic Response* (Baltimore: Johns Hopkins University Press, 1978), p. 55.

21. Quoted by W. J. Harvey, *Character and the Novel* (London: Chatto and Windus, 1960), p. 163.

22. Roland Barthes, "The Death of the Author," in *Image— Music—Text*, trans. Stephen Heath (New York: Hill and Wang, 1977), p. 148.

23. "When we say of a novel, 'Yes, this is the world,' our act of recognition and surrender transcends all our critical theories. Most aesthetic systems, after all, are either rationalizations of taste or weapons in a continuing critical debate," Harvey, *Character and the Novel*, p. 183.

24. Jan Mukařovský, "Intentionality and Unintentionality in Art," *The World and Verbal Art: Selected Essays by Jan Mukařovský* trans. and ed. John Burbank and Peter Steiner (New Haven and London: Yale University Press, 1977), p. 99.

25. Docherty quotes Merleau-Ponty on how the baptism of naming is requisite in overcoming this basic indeterminacy of the object: "L'objet le plus familier nous paraît indéterminé tant que nous n'avons pas retrouvé le nom," *Reading (Absent) Character*, p. 46.

26. For succinct commentaries on various aspects of the "rules" controversy, see the full annotations to Pope's *An Essay on Criticism*, ed. E. Audra and Aubrey Williams, *The Twickenham Edition of the Poems of Alexander Pope* (New Haven and London: Yale University Press, 1961), 1:197–326. See also E. B. O. Borgerhoff, *The Freedom of French Classicism* (Princeton, N.J.: Princeton University Press, 1950).

27. Leonardo da Vinci, *The Art of Painting* (New York: Philosophical Library, 1957), p. 214. Quoted by Mukařovský in "Intentionality and Unintentionality in Art," p. 90.

28. Jonathan Richardson, *An Essay on the Theory of Painting* (London, 1715), pp. 67–68.

29. See Denis Diderot's aesthetic theories, in his *Essay on Painting*, written in 1765 and published in 1796; in his essay on the Beautiful in the *Encyclopédie*; and in his *Lettre sur les Sourds et Muets*. Quotation from William Knight, *The Philosophy of the Beautiful, Being Outlines of the History of Aesthetics* (New York: Scribners, 1891), p. 106.

30. For his interest in the elemental forms of objects, Hogarth's *The Analysis of Beauty* (1753) is of fundamental importance. See Ronald Paulson's discussion of this work in *Hogarth: His Life, Art, and Times*, 2 vols. (New Haven and London: Yale University Press, 1971), 2:153–87.

31. Edmund Burke, *A Philosophical Enquiry into the Origin of Our Ideas of the Sublime and Beautiful*, ed. James T. Boulton (London: Routledge and Kegan Paul, 1958), p. 60.

32. Cf. Schiller: "Unconsciousness combined with reflection constitutes the poet-artist." Quoted by Mukařovský, "Intentionality and Unintentionality in Art," p. 91.

33. Uvedale Price, *Essays on the Picturesque, as Compared with the Sublime and the Beautiful; and, on the Use of Studying Pictures, for the Purpose of Improving Real Landscape*, 2 vols. (London, 1810), 1:22.

34. Roland Barthes, *Image—Music—Text*, p. 148.

35. *Letters*, pp. 299–300.

36. Laurence Sterne, *Tristram Shandy*, ed. Ian Watt, Riverside Editions (Boston: Houghton Mifflin, 1965), p. 83 (II, xi).

37. *Letters*, p. 401.

38. Walter Scott's anonymous review of *Emma* in the *Quarterly Review* (1816), quoted by Watt, *Jane Austen*, p. 3.

39. Graham Hough, "Narrative and Dialogue in Jane Austen," p. 208.

40. Samuel Johnson, *The Rambler*, ed. W. J. Bate and Albrecht B. Strauss, 4:86.

41. Reuben A. Brower, "Light and Bright and Sparkling: Irony and Fiction in *Pride and Prejudice*," *Jane Austen*, ed. Watt, p. 62.

42. The phrase "Voice of the Author" is Hough's term. Another supposed Johnsonian trait in Austen's narrative is a stylistic hierarchy of the general over the particular: "It is noticeable," according to Hough, "that material objects, physical details and practical arrangements appear very little in the speech of the most approved characters" (p. 217). But unfortunately he chooses as evidence the

dialogue between Mr. Weston (disapproved) and his wife (approved) about the length of the passage at the Crown Inn, a scene that contradicts his point: it is Mr. Weston, after all, who is telling his wife, always attentive to Mr. Woodhouse's fears, not to worry about narrow passages and drafts. A concern with trivial things may in some situations reflect a small mind (Harriet with the mementoes of Mr. Elton), but at critical moments it may actually reveal a magnanimous sympathy toward others (Emma's provident table for Mrs. Bates and Mrs. Goddard, her supplying the Hartfield porker to Miss Bates, and Mr. Knightley's meticulous preparations for Mr. Woodhouse's visit to Donwell).

43. Daniel Cottom, "The Novels of Jane Austen: Attachments and Supplantments," *Novel: A Forum on Fiction* 14 (Winter 1981): 156. This essay is incorporated in his *The Civilized Imagination,* pp. 88–105.

44. Cf. Coleridge: "it was agreed that my endeavors should be directed to persons and characters supernatural, or at least romantic; yet so as to transfer from our inward nature a human interest and a semblance of truth. . . . Mr. Wordsworth, on the other hand, was to propose to himself as his object to give the charm of novelty to things of every day, and to excite a feeling analogous to the supernatural, by awakening the mind's attention from the lethargy of custom and directing it to the loveliness and the wonders of the world before us." *Biographia Literaria,* chapter 14. *The Norton Anthology,* ed. M. H. Abrams et al., 4th ed. (New York: Norton, 1979), p. 397.

45. Ann Radcliffe, *The Mysteries of Udolpho, A Romance,* ed. Bonamy Dobree (London: Oxford University Press, 1966), p. 151.

46. Mark Schorer, "Fiction and the 'Analogical Matrix,'" *Critique and Essays on Modern Fiction,* ed. John W. Aldridge (New York: Ronald, 1952), pp. 83–98; and Dorothy Van Ghent, *The English Novel: Form and Function* (New York: Harper and Row, 1953), pp. 99–111.

47. Michel Foucault, *The Order of Things: An Archaeology of the Human Sciences* (New York: Pantheon, 1970), esp. chap. 3, "Representing," pp. 46–77.

48. Edmund Burke, *A Philosophical Enquiry,* p. 173.

49. Alan McKillop, *The Early Masters of English Fiction* (Lawrence: University of Kansas Press, 1956), pp. 214–17; and Barbara Hardy, "Objects in Novels," *Genre* 10 (1977): 485–500, quotation on 500.

50. G. H. Alexander, ed., *The Leibniz-Clarke Correspondence* (Manchester, Eng.: Manchester University Press, 1956), p. 398.

51. There is doubtless a residue of the eighteenth-century idiom of sensibility in Austen's affective taxonomy. What inspires Yorick to apostrophize the "great—great SENSORIUM" is his belief

that the slightest feeling within the individual's nervous system testifies to a divine presence in the world. See Laurence Sterne, *A Sentimental Journey Through France and Italy by Mr. Yorick*, ed. Gardner D. Stout, Jr. (Berkeley and Los Angeles: University of California Press, 1967), pp. 278–79. On this matter, see my article, "The Sensorium in the World of *A Sentimental Journey*," *Ariel* 13 (1982): 3–16; and its enlarged version as "Yorick and the 'Eternal Fountain of our Feelings,'" *Psychology and Literature in the Eighteenth Century*, ed. Christopher Fox (New York: AMS Press, 1987), pp. 259–76.

52. My reading here parallels Joseph Litvak's "Reading Characters: Self, Society, and Text in *Emma*," pp. 763–72.

53. Henry Fielding, *The History of Tom Jones, A Foundling*, ed. Fredson Bowers, p. 690 (XIII, ii).

54. On the "naturalness" of Pope's Palladianism, which may be compared to Mr. Darcy's, see Maynard Mack, *The Garden and the City: Retirement and Politics in the Later Poetry of Pope, 1731–1743* (Toronto: University of Toronto Press, 1969), esp. pp. 53–57.

Chapter IV

1. Marilyn Butler, *Jane Austen and the War of Ideas*, p. 271. See Mary Lascelles, *Jane Austen and Her Art* (Oxford: Oxford University Press, 1939), pp. 177–78.

2. Susan Morgan, *In the Meantime*, p. 14.

3. La Rochefoucauld, *Maxims*, no. 113.

4. For a succinct interpretation of the antithetical style of *Sense and Sensibility*, see A. Walton Litz, *Jane Austen: A Study of Her Artistic Development* (New York: Oxford University Press, 1965), pp. 72–82.

5. Shortly after their marriage, Mr. B. admires his wife's body:

> He was pleased to take notice of my dress, and spanning my waist with his hands, said, "What a sweet shape is here! It would make one regret to lose it; and yet, my beloved Pamela, I shall think nothing but that loss wanting to complete my happiness." I put my bold hand before his mouth and said, "Hush, hush! O fie, Sir! The freest thing you have ever yet said, since I have been yours!"

Samuel Richardson, *Pamela*, Everyman's Library, 2 vols. (London: Dent, 1962), 1:336.

6. The motherly old woman who acts as go-between and advises young girls on the problems of love is a stereotype that seems

to originate in Ovid's Dipsas in the *Amores*. Dipsas, in turn, is the model for *la Vieille* in Jean de Meun's *Romance of the Rose* and for Chaucer's Wife of Bath. (See *Chaucer: Sources and Backgrounds*, ed. Robert P. Miller [New York: Oxford University Press, 1977], pp. 407–10, and 467–73.) The Nurse in *Romeo and Juliet* is in this tradition of the old governess as procuress. Mrs. Jennings's sincere compassion and earthy joking may reflect the shift from wit to good nature in eighteenth-century comedy. See Stuart M. Tave, *The Amiable Humorist* (Chicago: University of Chicago Press, 1960), pp. 140–63. Tave's *Some Words of Jane Austen* (Chicago: University of Chicago Press, 1973) emphasizes Mrs. Jennings's "impulse of the utmost good will" (p. 89).

7. See Litz, *Jane Austen*, p. 79.

8. See above, chapter 1, n. 4.

9. Especially in her early letters, Austen showed a continuing interest in reading a woman's character from the evidence of her choice of a husband. An acquaintance living at Portsmouth without any servants in the house causes her to exclaim: "What a prodigious innate love of virtue she must have, to marry under such circumstances" (*Letters*, p. 26). Age difference could also arouse scorn: "Mrs. John Lyford is so much pleased with the state of widowhood as to be going to put in for being a widow again;—she is to marry a Mr. Fendall, a banker in Gloucester, a man of very good fortune, but considerably older than herself & with three little children" (p. 105).

10. In defining the genre of the sentimental novel, G. A. Starr observes the way in which Dickens creates sincerity vis-à-vis the alazons in *Hard Times* (Gradgrind, Bounderby, Harthouse, and Slackbridge): "Those who are 'no clackers'—Stephen Blackpool, Sleary—are barely articulate, and speech impediments, bizarre dialects, and a fundamental diffidence about verbal communication are stigmata attesting the validity of what they do manage to say. Sentimental figures tend to be babes linguistically (as in other ways), out of whose mouths comes much odd-sounding sense"(*Genre* 10 [1977]: 503). Though not so flatly consistent as Dickens's characters, Mr. Woodhouse and Mrs. Bates also exhibit "fundamental diffidence about verbal communication" that suggests the problem of living in good faith that lies at the heart of the story. In contrast to those gregarious talkers Miss Bates and Mrs. Elton, they withdraw to a warm corner and shirk not only society en masse but also the written letter itself as a sign of presence. Like speech impediments, illiteracy is a proof of linguistic innocence.

11. Mudrick overlooks this character's real influence in the story and lumps her together with Lydia, Mr. Collins, Lady Catherine, and other simple characters who are distinguished by their "powerlessness." See *Jane Austen: Irony as Defense and Discovery* (Princeton, N.J.: Princeton University Press, 1952),p. 104.

12. Bernard Paris, *Character and Conflict in Jane Austen's Novels*, pp. 74–91.

13. Jean-Paul Sartre, *Being and Nothingness: A Phenomenological Essay on Ontology*, trans. Hazel E. Barnes (New York: Washington Square, 1956), p. 533.

14. Ibid.

15. Ibid.

16. Halperin approvingly quotes Virginia Woolf's sense of fear toward this author's malicious intent, and this fear supports a reading of Miss Bates's caution toward Emma. See *The Life of Jane Austen*, p. 186.

17. Jonathan Swift, *A Tale of a Tub*, ed. A. C. Guthkelch and D. Nichol Smith (Oxford: Clarendon, 1958), p. 174. Austen herself hardly indulged in any sentimental illusions about poverty: "People get so horridly poor & economical in this part of the World, that I have no patience with them.—Kent is the only place for happiness, Everybody is rich there;—I must do similar justice however to the Windsor neighbourhood" (*Letters*, p. 41).

18. Without the option of marriage, the female déclassé character is usually powerless to repay beneficence. After receiving Jarndyce's proposal, Esther feels ambivalent but is ultimately dutiful in her response: "To devote my life to his happiness was to thank him poorly, and what had I wished for the other night but some new means of thanking him?" *Bleak House* (New York: New American Library, 1964), chap. 44, p. 617.

19. Paris, *Character and Conflict*, p. 86.

20. See n. 1 above.

21. Sartre, *Being and Nothingness*, p. 533.

22. Ibid., p. 531.

23. Ibid., p. 175.

24. Graham Hough, for instance, takes the position that Mr. Knightley is the "personal embodiment of the moral and social norm," "Narrative and Dialogue in Jane Austen," p. 222. For a recent analysis of this position, see Frederick M. Keener, *The Chain of Becoming* (New York: Columbia University Press, 1983), pp. 273–74.

25. Sartre, *Being and Nothingness*, p. 100.

26. Ibid., p. 111.

27. Wemmick tells Pip: "No; the office is one thing, and private life is another. When I go into the office, I leave the Castle behind me, and when I come into the Castle, I leave the office behind me. If it's not in any way disagreeable to you, you'll oblige me by doing the same. I don't wish it professionally spoken about" (*Great Expectations*, Everyman's Library [London: Dent, 1962], chap. 25, p. 195). This inward turn, already clear-cut in *Sir Charles Grandison*, becomes fully expressed in the Victorian division between the private and the public self.

Chapter V

1. J. B. Priestley: "Jane Austen was no friend to romance, and she would certainly be surprised if one of her avowedly satirical figures were pressed into service in defence of the romantic attitude; yet the fact remains that this ridiculous Mr. Collins of hers, with his snobberies soaring sky-high, lost in wonder, innocently and ostentatiously marching under the banner of toadyism until it is no longer the banner of toadyism, this Mr. Collins is at once a child of romance and perhaps the happiest creature in all her pages" ("Mr. Collins," *The English Comic Characters* [London: Bodley Head, 1963], p. 177). Priestley forgets to mention the telltale sign of his happy performance as husband attested by the parting news of Charlotte's pregnancy.

2. Richard Savage, for instance, "willingly turned his Eyes from the Light of Reason, when it would have discovered the Illusion, and shewn him, what he never wished to see" (Samuel Johnson, *Life of Savage,* ed. Clarence Tracy [Oxford: Clarendon, 1971], p. 74). Mimetic illusion, in Austen's aesthetic, appears to depend on a similar participation of the reader's will.

3. Extreme psychic states as opposed to self-imposed delusions were not Austen's real subject. For a recent interpretation of Lennox's particular concern with woman's proclivity to madness, as well as to the reading of romances, see Leland E. Warren, "Of the Conversation of Women: *The Female Quixote* and the Dream of Perfection," *Studies in Eighteenth Century Culture,* vol. 11, ed. Harry C. Payne (Madison: University of Wisconsin Press, 1982), pp. 367–80. In 1807, Austen was rereading *The Female Quixote* and enjoying it as much as before (*Jane Austen's Letters,* p. 173).

4. This term for a linguistic bundle to denote a character's worldview is taken from Roger Fowler, *Linguistics and the Novel* (London and New York: Methuen, 1977; reprint 1979), pp. 76, 103–13.

5. William Wordsworth, "The Tables Turned: An Evening Scene on the Same Subject," ll. 29–32, *The Norton Anthology of English Literature,* 2:154.

6. Chaucer's Wife of Bath and Pardoner, to mention two vivid characters, are infinitely resourceful in quoting chapter and verse to justify their worldviews. Fielding's parsons, both good and bad—from Adams and Harrison to Barnabas, Trulliber, and Thwackum—rely on authoritative texts to promulgate their opinions. For the influence of Rabelais on Swift and Sterne, see D. W. Jefferson, "*Tristram Shandy* and the Tradition of Learned Wit," *Laurence Sterne,* ed. John Traugott, Twentieth Century Views (Englewood Cliffs, N.J.: Prentice-Hall, 1968), pp. 148–67.

7. Elizabeth L. Eisenstein, *The Printing Press as an Agent of Change: Communications and Cultural Transformations in Early-Modern Europe,* 1:122.

8. Walter J. Ong, *Orality and Literacy: The Technologizing of the Word*, pp. 132–35.

9. "'I have heard of this book [*Don Quixote*] already,' said Don Quixote, 'and verily and on my conscience I thought it had been by this time burned to ashes as useless,'" *Don Quixote*, pt. 2, chap. 62, p. 777.

10. Lennard J. Davis, *Factual Fictions: The Origins of the English Novel*, esp. pp. 25–84. Michael McKeon, *The Origins of the English Novel, 1600–1740*, pp. 52–89.

11. Samuel Richardson, *Pamela*, 1:20.

12. Cervantes plays upon this illusion of authenticity by interrupting the narrative with "missing text" and then continuing the story from the supposed manuscripts by Cide Hamete Benengali, an Arab scholar (see *Don Quixote*, pt. 1, chap. 9, pp. 66–68). Mackenzie's fat curate happens upon Harley's story in "a bundle of papers" but keeps it only for gun wadding because of its poor handwriting and lack of syllogisms. The narrator, however, is a true reader and can thus respond to "a bundle of little episodes, put together without art, and of no importance on the whole, with something of nature, and little else in them." See Henry Mackenzie, *The Man of Feeling*, ed. Brian Vickers (London: Oxford University Press, 1967), p. 5.

13. *Pamela*, 1:252 and 272, respectively.

14. Ibid., 1:133.

15. Mr. Collins bears a resemblance to Johnson's character of Goldsmith: "[He] referred every thing to vanity; his virtues, and his vices too, were from that motive. He was not a social man. He never exchanged mind with you" (*Boswell's Life of Johnson*, ed. R. W. Chapman [London: Oxford University Press, 1965], p. 743).

16. With such sound judgment here, it is not easy to decide between Emma and Knightley concerning Frank Churchill's handwriting; against her assertion that he "writes one of the best gentlemen's hands I ever saw," the jealous rival demurs: "It is too small—wants strength. It is like a woman's writing" (*E*, 297). Mr. Knightley, to his credit, had earlier pronounced Emma's hand to be strong. Unless we are to assume that Emma unconsciously admires Churchill's hand to provoke Knightley's reaction, from the evidence of her disinterested reading of Robert Martin's letter there is no unequivocal reason to side with the hero in this scene. What is most revealing here is that, even in the privacy of the act of reading, Emma is not alone but is conscious of Knightley's presence.

In comical contrast to Emma, Harriet is incapable of judging Robert Martin's character by his letter:

> "A woman is not to marry a man merely because she is asked, or because he is attached to her, and can write a tolerable letter."
>
> "Oh! no;—and it is but a short letter too."

> Emma felt the bad taste of her friend, but let it
> pass with a "very true; and it would be a small consolation to
> her, for the clownish manner which might be offending her
> every hour of the day, to know that her husband could write
> a good letter." (*E*, 54–55)

Just as Harriet later treasures the material objects that, ironically, remind us of Mr. Elton's unmanly penmanship, so her only response to
Martin's writing involves some "pencilled marks and memorandums
on the wainscot by the window. *He* had done it" (*E*, 187). Illiterate
("Nobody cares for a letter" [*E*, 55]), Harriet is nevertheless inclined
to make souvenirs of her suitors' writing implements and gratuitous
jottings.

17. Wordsworth, "The Tables Turned," l. 25.

18. An example of an early collection of word games is the
anonymous *Delights for the Ingenious: or A Monthly Entertainment
for the Curious of Both Sexes. Containing a Vast Variety of Pleasant
Enigma's; Delightful Arithmetical Questions; Curious Stories; Witty
Epigrams; Surprising Adventures; and Amazing Paradoxes. Together
with Songs, Anagrams, Emblems, Dialogues, Elegies, Epitaphs; and
other Useful and Diverting Subjects, both in Prose and Verse. To be
continued Monthly. By the author of the Ladies-Diary* (London,
1711). See the charades written by Austen and her family, *Charades
Etc. Written a Hundred Years Ago* (London: Spottiswood, 1895). On
the impact of printing on village culture, see Eisenstein, *The Printing
Press*, 1:130.

19. As R. W. Chapman points out, Austen appears to have
mistaken this anthology for another, *The New Foundling Hospital for
Wit, the Fourth Part* (1771), which first published this riddle. It was
reprinted later in many compilations. See *The Novels of Jane Austen*,
4:489–90, which also reproduces the complete version of the riddle
discussed below.

20. Alice Chandler, "'A Pair of Fine Eyes': Jane Austen's
Treatment of Sex," *Studies in the Novel* 7 (1975): 88–103.

21. For an analysis of what the folktale implies about its audience, see Barbara Herrnstein Smith, "Narrative Versions, Narrative Theories," *Critical Inquiry* 7 (Autumn 1980): esp. 215–23.

22. By "empty spaces," I mean the inevitable interruptions
in a text that give rise to intentional or unintentional meanings. For
this phenomenology of the text, see Roman Ingarden, *The Literary
Work of Art: An Investigation on the Borderlines of Ontology, Logic,
and Theory of Literature*, trans. George G. Grabowicz (Evanston,
Ill.: Northwestern University Press, 1973), pp. 246–54.

23. On Richardson's manic attempts to control the essential
instability of his text, see Terry Eagleton, *The Rape of Clarissa: Writing, Sexuality and Class Struggle in Samuel Richardson*, (Minneapolis: University of Minnesota Press, 1982), esp. pp. 21–23. The

striking idea of Richardson's providing kits of spare parts for reading his novel is Eagleton's.

24. William Wordsworth: "I should mention one other circumstance which distinguishes these poems from the popular poetry of the day; it is this, that the feeling therein developed gives importance to the action and situation, and not the action and situation to the feeling," "Preface to *Lyrical Ballads*," *Norton Anthology*, pp. 160 and 165, respectively.

25. See Margaret Kirkham, *Jane Austen, Feminism and Fiction*, pp. 147–48.

26. Jonathan Richardson, *An Essay on the Theory of Painting*, p. 68.

Conclusion

1. Raymond Williams, *Marxism and Literature* (Oxford: Oxford University Press, 1977), pp. 128–35. John Bender, *Imagining the Penitentiary: Fiction and the Architecture of Mind in Eighteenth-Century England* (Chicago: University of Chicago Press, 1987), p. 212.

2. William Gilpin, *Three Essays: On Picturesque Beauty; On Picturesque Travel; and on Sketching Landscape: With a Poem, On Landscape Painting*, 3d ed. (London, 1808), pp. 49–50.

3. Ibid., p. 140.

4. Edmund Burke, *The Sublime and Beautiful*, p. 76.

5. See, for instance, L. J. Rather, *Mind and Body in Eighteenth Century Medicine: A Study Based on Jerome Gaub's "De regimine mentis"* (Berkeley and Los Angeles: University of California Press, 1965); and Aram Vartanian's introductory monograph to his edition of La Mettrie's *L'Homme Machine* (Princeton, N.J.: Princeton University Press, 1960), esp. pp. 57–94.

6. William Hogarth, *The Analysis of Beauty*, ed. Joseph Burke (Oxford: Clarendon, 1955), pp. 141, 149–50, respectively.

7. Louis de Cahusac, quoted by Giovanni-Andrea Gallini, *A Treatise on the Art of Dancing*, facsimile of the 1762 London edition (New York: Broude Brothers, 1967), p. 52.

8. Claude-Henri Watelet, *L'Art de Peindre* (Amsterdam, 1761), p. 112.

9. Hogarth, *The Analysis of Beauty*, p. 140.

10. Ray L. Birdwhistell, *Kinesics and Context: Essays on Body-Motion Communication* (London: Allen Lane, The Penguin Press, 1970), p. 8.

11. Gilbert Austin, *Chironomia: or, A Treatise on Rhetorical Delivery*, p. 5.

12. Ibid., p. 7.

13. Ibid.

14. Park Honan, *Jane Austen*, pp. 335–36.

Index

Alkon, Paul, 3–4, 5
Alter, Robert, 5
Altman, Janet, 4, 5
Austen, Jane: aim of rendering speech in narrative, 1–4, 13–15, 87, 112, 127; attitudes toward food, 66–67, 73, toward French culture, 50–51, toward Miss Bates, 139, toward the poor, 53, toward sensibility, 147; and Burke, 177; and Coleridge, 121; and country dances as village social ritual, 37, 40–41; defensive about the novel as a serious art form, 10, 175; distrustful of community as a whole, 35; energy as personal and political modus vivendi in writings of, 75; and Flaubert, 73; and Gilpin, 95–96, 176–77; and innuendo in narrative and dialogue, 30, 66; I-thou relationship in narratives of, 129; and Johnson, 58, 98–99; and memory, 137; and moral psychology, 125–26; and narrative strategies of the fragment, 97, 100, 101, 136, 139; and oral interpretation of characters in *PP*, 10–11; and parody as means of creating deeper mimetic illusion, 8–10, 47, 98–99, 146, 168; and play as mimetic ruse, 18, 35, 81, 85, 166–68; and role-playing compared to Diderot, 27; and satire on book learning, 148–49, 151; and teleology in plots, 37, 78, 100–101; and temporality in narrative, 20, 22–23, 44; Tory interpretations of, 84–85, 93, 97, 146; and Wordsworth, 121, 162, 170
Austen, Jane: works
Emma, 13, 58–64, 76, 77–78, 106–7, 111, 138–39, 159–62, 205n. 16; the ball at the Crown Inn, 35–40, 140–41;

Miss Bates as *pharmakos*, 52, 131–34; charades, 162–68; charity, 53–54, 59, 63; daydreaming, 86–87, 109–10, 135–36; discourse on gruel, 89–90; emotive vocabulary, 103–5; heroine's ludic spirit, 11, 34–35, 138; "irresistible waltz," 30–32; Mr. Knightley's dialogical relationship to Emma, 90–92; Mr. Knightley's reprimand at Box Hill, 53, 129–30, 137; "power of eating and drinking," 67–68, 73; punishment and "penitence," 32–33, 59, 61–62, 142–43; seduction motif, 50–51; snobbism, 55–57
Letters, 193nn. 25, 26, 194n. 35, 195n. 37, 199nn. 35, 37, 202n. 9, 203n. 17, 204n. 3; advice to niece on economy of description, 97; reading of Pasley essay, 75; critical remarks on *PP*, 10–11, 97, 187n. 23; ironic references to food, 67, 193n. 24
Mansfield Park, 12, 58, 76, 77, 79, 83, 104, 105, 175; acting theme, 27–30, 181–83; card games, 1–2; Edmund's assistance to Fanny in writing letter, 159; Fanny's reading of Lady Bertram's letter, 169–70; references to food, 70–71, 74; seduction motif, 51
Minor Works: "Love and Freindship," 9; "Sanditon," 194n. 31; "Lady Susan," 49
Northanger Abbey, 50, 76, 78, 102, 123; Mrs. Allen's talking humor, 114–16; Catherine reading brother's letter with Henry Tilney, 152–53; James Austen as source for Henry, 10; parodic textuality, 47, 146, 151; partner-